JOURNAL

OF THE

Proceedings and Debates

IN THE

CONSTITUTIONAL CONVENTION

OF THE

STATE OF MISSISSIPPI,

AUGUST, 1865.

BY ORDER OF THE CONVENTION.

JACKSON, MISS.:
E. M. YERGER, STATE PRINTER.

1865.

JOURNAL.

The Constitutional Convention of the State of Mississippi convened at the Capitol, in the City of Jackson, on Monday, the fourteenth day of August, in the year of our Lord, one thousand eight hundred and sixty-five, and of the independence of the United States of America, the ninetieth, in pursuance of a proclamation of His Excellency, WILLIAM L. SHARKEY, Provisional Governor of the State of Mississippi, bearing date the 1st day of July, 1865, which Proclamation is as follows:

PROCLAMATION:

Fellow-Citizens of the State of Mississippi:

The President of the United States, by virtue of the power vested in him by the Constitution of the United States, has been pleased to appoint the undersigned Provisional Governor of the State of Mississippi, "for the purpose of enabling the loyal people of said State to organize a State Government, whereby justice may be established, domestic tranquility insured, and loyal citizens protected in all their rights of life, liberty and property." And, to accomplish that object, has directed me, "at the earliest practicable period, to prescribe such rules and regulations as may be necessary and proper for convening a Convention of Delegates, to be chosen by that portion of the people of said State who are loyal to the United States, and no others, for the purpose of altering or amending the Constitution thereof," so that the State may be able to resume its place in the Union. And being anxious to carry out the wishes of the President, and to restore the dominion of civil government as speedily as possible, I do hereby ordain and declare as follows, to-wit:

First. To avoid the delay which would necessarily occur from the separate organization of each county by special appointments of the several county officers, the persons who exercised the functions pertaining to the following named officers, on the day when the archives and other public property were taken posssession of by the United States, to-wit. the 22d day of May, 1865, are hereby appointed to fill those offices in each county, to-wit: the office of judge of probate and clerk of the probate court, the office of sheriff and coroner, the office of justice of the peace and constable, the office of board of county police, the office of county treasurer and collector, and assesor and county surveyor, and the several municipal offices of every incorporated city or town, whose organizations have been regularly kept up.

This general appointment of officers is not intended to revoke any special appointment made by me prior to the date of the proclamation. And inasmuch as it is necessary that these several offices should be filled by incumbents who are loyal to the United States Government, I reserve the power to remove any one who may be exceptional in this respect, and I earnestly invoke the loyal citizens of each county to give me timely and the most authentic information that can be procured, in regard to any officer who is obnoxious to this serious objection.

Second. These several officers, before they enter upon the discharge of the duties of their respective offices, shall take and subscribe the amnesty oath prescribed in the President's proclamation of the 29th May, 1865, and must immediately transmit the oath so taken to this office. At the end of the amnesty oath, after the word "slaves," must be added the words "and will faithfully discharge the duties of my office to the best of my ability." And any one who may undertake to act in his official capacity without compliance with this requisition, will subject himself to punishment. This oath may be taken before any commissioned officer, civil, military or naval, in the service of the United States, or before the Judges of Probate hereby appointed, or heretofore appointed by me, after they shall have taken the oath themselves, or before the Judge of the Criminal Court of Warren county. But no one can hold any of these offices who is exempted in the President's proclamation from the benefits of the amnesty unless first specially pardoned by the President.

Third. In counties which have been disorganized, or where there are no persons who can fill the several county offices, either in consequence of death or otherwise, special appointments will be immediately made, when the necessity for such appointments shall be made known to me.

Fourth. The sheriffs hereby appointed, or in case there be

no sheriffs, the judge of probate, or the coroner, or any justice of the peace, in the order in which they are here placed, shall hold an election at the several election precincts in each county, on Monday, the 7th day of August next, for delegates to a Convention for the purposes mentioned in the President's proclamation, Voters for delegates to this Convention must possess the qualifications required by the Constitution and laws as they existed prior to the 9th day of January, 1861, and must also produce a certificate that they have taken, before a competent officer, the amnesty oath prescribed by the proclamation of the 29th May, 1865, which certificate shall be attached to, or accompanied by a copy of the oath, and no one will be eligible as a member of this Convention who has not also taken this oath. The sheriff shall give public notice of the election by posting up this proclamation, or otherwise.

Fifth. Each county and town entitled to separate representation, shall be entitled to be represented in the Convention by the same number of representatives they were entitled to in the lower branch of the Legislature, prior to the 9th day of January, 1861.

Sixth. The returning officers of the election, shall give to the persons having the highest number of votes, a certificate of election, and the delegates so elected shall assemble at the city of Jackson, on Monday, 14th day of August next, and shall organize a Convention by electing proper officers, and adopting necessary rules, and after taking an oath to support the Constitution of the United States, may proceed in the discharge of their duties.

Seventh. The trustees of the University of Mississippi are required to meet at Oxford, on Monday, the 31st day of July, for the purpose of putting the institution in operation.

Eighth. Crime must be suppressed, and guilty persons punished. The commanding general at this post has kindly offered to use the forces under his command for the protection of the people and for the apprehension of offenders against the law, and it is hoped the people will give him timely information, and render such assistance as will enable him to carry out this laudable object. I would advise the people when it may become necessary, in consequence of their remoteness from a military force, to organize themselves into a county patrol, for the apprehension of offenders, who when arrested, if they cannot be safely confined in the county, may be brought to Jackson for confinement in the military prison, until they can be disposed of by civil law.

In taking recognizances, the justices of the peace will make them returnable to the next term of the circuit court as now established by law, or that may hereafter be established by law.

Probably there are some persons who have some conscientious scruples about taking the amnesty oath, because they believe the emancipation proclamation unconstitutional. I allude to this subject only because I have understood there are a few such.

This objection certainly cannot be raised with propriety by such as denied that they were subject to the Constitution of the United States as the supreme law, when the proclamation was issued. Whether it be constitutional or not, is a question which the people have no right to determine. The determination of that question rests with the supreme judicial department of the goverment. Legislative bodies often pass unconstitutional acts, but they must be regarded as valid, and they must be observed as the law until the proper department of the government declares them void. Every presumption is in favor of their validity. And it is precisely the same case with the executive acts. This proclamation therefore must be regarded as valid until the Supreme Court shall decide otherwise. When it does so decide, parties will be absolved from the obligation of the oath.

Perhaps, however, parties who believe the proclamation void, are over-sanguine in the correctness of their opinions. There is a general principle in the law of nations which authorizes one belligerent party to do towards his enemy whatever will strengthen himself and weaken his enemy, limited of course by the laws of humanity. Some writers of high authority hold that legitimate power in war, towards an enemy, is co-extensive with necessity. Even the desolating of a country and the burning of towns and villages are held to be justifiable acts in certain cases. Whether these principles be broad enough to cover the taking of slaves, as they certainly are with regard to other property, is not for me to determine, and I mention them only to show to those who entertain this opinion, that perhaps it does not rest on as solid a foundation as they imagine it does. The people of the Southern States were in rebellion; the President of the United States had a right to prescribe terms of amnesty; he has done so, and it is hoped the people will all cheerfully take his oath with a fixed purpose to observe it in good faith. Why should they now hesitate or doubt since slavery has ceased to be a practical question? It was the ostensible cause of the war, it was staked upon the issue of the war and that issue has been decided against us, It is the part of wisdom and of honor to submit without a murmur. The negroes are free, free by the fortunes of war—free by the proclamation—free by common consent—free practically as well as theoretically, and it is too late to raise technical questions as to the means by which they became so. Besides it would be bad policy now to undertake to change their condition if we could do so. It would be nothing less than an effort to establish slavery where it does not exist.—Therefore let us cordially unite in our efforts to organize our State government, so that we may by wise legislation, prepare ourselves to live in prosperity and happiness in the changed condition of our domestic relations. Fellow-citizens, I accept the office of Provisional Governor in full view of the troubles and responsibities incident to it. I was actuated by no other motive than a desire to aid the people in organizing a civil government preparatory to the restoration of their harmonious relations with the government of the United States. That I shall commit errors I know full well, but I know also that I shall very soon leave the office, and that I shall carry with me the consoling reflection that I endeavored to subserve the best interest of the people in this critical and trying conjunction of public affairs.

The people of the South have just passed through a most terrible and disastrous revolution, in which they have signally failed to accomplish their purpose. Perhaps their success would have proved to be the greatest calamity that could have befallen the country, and the greatest calamity to the cause of civil liberty throughout the world. The true patriot finds his greatest enjoyment in the noble and pleasing reflection that his government is to live with an honored name, to shed its blessings on millions through future centuries. And as good governments are things of growth, improved by the lights of experience and often by revolutions, let us hope—sad and disastrous as this revolution has been—that the lessons it has taught us will not be destitute of value.

The business of improving our government, if it should be found to need it, and of promoting reconciliation between the Northern and Southern people, are now prominent duties before us, so that we may hereafter live in the more secure and perfect enjoyment of the great patrimony left us by our fathers, and so that those who are to come after us may long enjoy in their fullest functions, the inestimable blessing of civil liberty, the best birthright and noblest inheritance of mankind.

Done at the city of Jackson, on the first day of July, A. D., 1865.

[L. S.] W. L. SHARKEY,

By the Governor:

JAS. R. YERGER, Secretary of State.

MONDAY, AUGUST 14TH, 1865.

At 12 o'clock M., his Excellency, Gov. Wm. L. Sharkey, called the Convention to order, when the Hon. Jas. R. Yerger, Secretary of State, called the roll of counties.

The following delegates came forward, and presented the amnesty oath for the inspection of the Governor:

Adams—William T. Martin, S. H. Lambdin.

Amite—David W. Hurst.

Attala—Elijah H. Sanders, Jason Niles.

Bolivar—

Calhoun—Charles A. Lewers, Eli J. Byars.

Carroll—William Hemingway, John A. Binford.

Chickasaw—James M. Wallace, Allen White.

Choctaw—James H. Dorris, Robert C. Johnson, Robert B. Wooley.

Claiborne—James H. Maury.

Clarke—

Coahoma—

Copiah—Ephraim G. Peyton, Wm. A. Stone.

Covington—Alex. H. Hall.

DeSoto—Reuben T. Sanders, Thomas S. Tate, Franklin J. Malone.

Franklin—K. R. Webb.

Greene—

Hancock—Daniel C. Stanley.

Harrison—

Hinds—William Yerger, Amos R. Johnston, George L. Potter.

Holmes—Robert H. Montgomery, J. F. Sessions.

Issaquena—Lawrence T. Wade.

Itawamba—John M. Simonton, Braxton Cason, Wiley W. Gaither.

Jackson—

Jasper—Caleb Lindsey.

Jefferson—Geo. P. Farley.
Jones—T. G. Crawford.
Kemper—James S. Hamm.
Lafayette—Richard W. Phipps, Hugh A. Barr.
Lauderdale—Chas. E. Rushing, Peyton King.
Lawrence—E J. Goode.
Leake—Dempsey Sparkman.
Lowndes—James T. Harrison, T. C. Billups.
Madison—Wm. McBride.
Marion—Hamilton Mayson.
Marshall—W. C. Compton, J. F. Trotter, Wm. Wall, Laurence Johnson.
Monroe—Lock E. Houston, C. Dowd.
Neshoba—Joseph M. Loper.
Noxubee—Hampton L. Jarnagin.
Oktibbeha—David Pressley.
Panola—Samuel Matthews, Lunsford P. Cooper.
Perry—J. Prentiss Carter.
Pike—James B. Quin.
Pontotoc—Charles T- Bond, Joseph L. Morphis, Nicholas Blackwell.
Rankin—Richard Cooper, John B. Lewis.
Scott—J. G. Owen.
Simpson—
Smith—Harvey F. Johnson.
Sunflower—Wm. McD. Martin.
Tallahatchie—James S. Bailey.
Tippah—J. H. Kennedy.
Tishomingo—Wm. L. Duncan, Robert A. Hill, Benj. C. Rives.
Tunica—Francis A. Owens.
Washington—J. Shall Yerger.
Wayne—James A. Horne.
Wilkinson—
Winston—
Warren—Charles Swett.
Yallobusha—James Wier, Robert M. Brown.
Yazoo—J. H. Wilson, R. S. Hudson.

On motion of Mr. Cooper, of Rankin, Mr. Johnston, of Hinds, was appointed President, pro tem.

On motion of Mr. Mayson,

Mr. D. P. Porter, of Rankin, was appointed Secretary pro tem.

Mr. Johnson, of Smith, moved that the Convention proceed to the election of permanent President, by ballot.

Which was adopted.

The President announced Messrs. Stone, Cooper, of Rankin, and Peyton, as tellers.

Mr. Johnson, of Smith, placed in nomination the name of Amos R. Johnston, of Hinds.

Mr. Sanders, of Attala, placed in nomination the name of J. Shall Yerger, of Washington.

No other nominations being made, the Convention proceeded to ballot, resulting as follows;

Mr. Yerger received	64	votes.
Mr. Johnston "	14	"
Mr. Cooper "	2	"
Total votes cast	80	"

Mr. Yerger having received a majority of all the votes cast, was declared duly elected President of the Convention; and on being conducted to his seat, by Messrs. Stone, Peyton and Cooper, thanked the Convention in appropriate and eloquent terms for the honor conferred upon him.

The Convention then proceeded to the election of permanent Secretary.

Mr. Mayson placed in nomination the name of Mr. D. P. Porter, of Rankin.

Mr. Johnson, of Marshall, placed in nomination the name of Mr. J. L. Power, of Hinds.

Mr. Sanders, of Attala, placed in nomination the name of Mr. Sam Young, of Attala.

Mr. Houston placed in nomination the name of Mr. Hillyer, of Natchez.

Mr. Lindsey placed in nomination the name of Mr. D. A. Dozier, of Jasper.

No other nominations being made, the Convention proceeded to the

FIRST BALLOT.

Mr. Porter received	21	votes.
Mr. Power "	26	"
Mr. Young "	17	"
Mr. Hillyer "	16	"
Mr. Dozier "	1	"
Total votes cast	81	"
Necessary to a choice	41	"

Neither candidate having received a constitutional majority, the Convention proceeded to the

SECOND BALLOT.

Power received	....	31 votes.
Porter "	....	23 "
Young "	....	18 "
Hillyer "	....	9 "
Total votes cast	....	81 "
Necessary to a choice	....	41 "

Neither candidate having received a constitutional majority, the Convention proceeded to the

THIRD BALLOT.

Power received	....	39 votes.
Porter "	....	22 "
Young "	....	16 "
Hillyer "	....	4 "
Total votes cast	....	81 "
Necessary to a choice	....	41 "

Neither candidate having received a constitutional majority, the Convention proceeded to the fourth ballot.

Mr. Sanders withdrew the name of Mr. Young.

FOURTH BALLOT.

Power received	....	47 votes.
Porter "	....	32 "
Hillyer "	....	2 "
Total votes cast	....	81 "

Mr. Power having received a majority of all the votes cast, was declared duly elected permanent Secretary of the Convention, took the oath of office, and entered upon the discharge of his duties.

Mr. Johnston, of Hinds, moved that the Convention adjourn until 9 o'clock to-morrow morning.

Mr. Stone moved to amend by striking out the words, "9 o'clock to-morrow morning," and inserting, "4 o'clock, P. M., this day."

Which was adopted.

When the Convention adjourned until 4 o'clock P. M.

FOUR O'CLOCK, P. M.

The Convention met pursuant to adjournment.

Mr. Johnston, of Hinds, offered the following resolution, which was adopted:

Resolved, That the reporters for the press in this State and elsewhere, in attendance at this Convention, be permitted to occupy seats within the bar of the House.

On motion of Mr. Mayson, the Convention proceeded to the election of Sergeant-at-Arms, by ballot.

The President appointed Messrs. Hill, Horne and Compton, as tellers.

Mr. Yerger placed in nomination the name of T. C. McMackin, of Hinds.

Mr. Simonton placed in nomination the name of James J. Denson, of Pike.

The roll of counties being called,

T. C. McMackin received............ 55 votes.
J. J. Denson " .... 21 "

Majority for T. C. McMackin........ 34 "

Mr. McMackin was therefore declared duly elected Sergeant-at-Arms of the Convention, took the oath of office, was instructed in and entered upon the discharge of his duties.

On motion, the Convention proceeded to the election of Doorkeeper.

Mr. Matthews placed in nomination the name of D. R. Corley, of Tishomingo.

Mr. Johnson, of Marshall, placed in nomination the name of W. Tradewell, of Amite.

Mr. Yerger placed in nomination the name of Wm. J. Brown, of Hinds.

Mr. Lewis placed in nomination the name of J. C. Robertson, of Hinds.

Upon a call of the counties,—

FIRST BALLOT.

Corley received..................... 31 votes.
Tradewell " .... 15 votes.
Brown " .... 31 "
Robertson " .... 1 "

Total votes cast..................... 78 "
Necessary to a choice................. 40 "

There being no election, the Convention proceeded to the

SECOND BALLOT.

Corley received.................... 38 votes.
Brown " .... 35 "
Tradewell " .... 5 "

Total votes cast....................... 78
Necessary to a choice................ 40

There being no election, the Convention proceeded to the third ballot—Mr. Johnson, of Marshall, withdrawing the name of Mr. Tradewell.

THIRD BALLOT.

Brown received.................... 42 votes.
Corley " .... 38 "

Majority for Brown.................. 4

Mr. Brown was therefore declared duly elected Door-keeper of the Convention, took the oath of office, and entered upon the discharge of his duties.

Mr. Malone, of DeSoto, offered the following resolution, which was unanimously adopted:

Resolved, That the Clergy of the City be invited to open the proceedings of this Convention each day, by invoking the blessing of an all-wise Being over its deliberations.

Mr. Matthews moved that the President be authorized to appoint four pages for the Convention.

Which was adopted.

The President appointed as said pages: Lewis Fite, Leo Phillips, George Donnell and Charles E. Tolbert.

Mr. Harrison offered the following resolution:

Resolved, That the rules of the House of Representatives of the State of Mississippi, for the year 1860, be adopted, as far as applicable for the Government of this Convention.

Mr. Lewers offered the following amendment, by way of additional resolution:

Resolved, That the Secretary be requested to furnish each member of the Convention with a copy of said rules, as soon as practicable.

Mr. Johnson, of Smith, moved to lay the amendment offered by Mr. Lewers upon the table,

Which was lost.

Upon a division of the question, the resolution offered by Mr. Harrison was adopted.

The question recurring on the adoption of the amendment offered by Mr. Lewers, it was rejected.

Mr. Johnson, of Smith, offered the following resolution:

Resolved, That a Committee of —— be appointed by the President whose duty it shall be, so soon as practicable, to draft and report to this Convention, for its action, such amendments to the State Constitution as it stood on the 9th day of January, 1861, as may be deemed necessary for the future peace and welfare of the State.

Mr. Sanders, of Attala, offered the following as a substitute for the above resolution:

Resolved, That the following Standing Committees be appointed by the President, to-wit:

1. A Committee on Credentials and Citizenship of the members of this Convention.
2. A Committee on State Constitution.
3. A Committee on Federal Relations.
4. A Committee on Finance.
5. A Committee on State Judicatories.

And that the said Committee inquire into matters properly belonging to them, and report by ordinance or otherwise.

Mr. Simonton, of Itawamba, raised the following point of order, to-wit: That it was incompetent for the members to proceed to business after the organization, until they had qualified by taking the oath to support the Constitution of the United States, as indicated in paragraph 6th, of the Governor's proclamation.

The resolution being again read, Mr. Johnson, accepted the substitute offered by Mr. Sanders.

Mr. Potter, of Hinds, moved to strike out so much of the resolution as provided for the appointment of a committee on State Jurisdiction.

Which was adopted.

Mr. Goode, of Lawrence, renewed the point of order raised by Mr. Simonton; when,

On motion of Mr. Matthews, of Panola, the further consideration of the pending resolution was postponed.

Mr. Simonton, of Itawamba, moved that the oath to support the Constitution of the United States be at once administered by the President to the members of the Convention.

Mr. Goode, of Lawrence, moved to amend so as to require each member to present his credentials. Adopted.

The motion of Mr. Simonton, as amended was then adopted, and all the members qualified accordingly.

Mr. James A. Heard, of Clarke, presented his credentials, and was sworn in as a member of the Convention.

Mr. Brown, of Yallobusha, offered the following resolution:

Resolved, That the President of this Convention proceed by Committee, or in such other manner as he may deem appropriate, to communicate to Gov. Sharkey, that this Convention is now duly organized, and ready to proceed to business, and to ascertain if he has any official communication to make to them.

Which was adopted.

On motion of Mr. Jarnigan, of Noxubee, the vote adopting the above resolution, was reconsidered, when he moved to amend the same by striking out the words, "and to ascertain if he has any official communication to make to them."

Mr. Cooper, of Rankin, moved to lay the resolution and amendment upon the table.

Which was adopted.

Mr. Johnson, of Smith, called up the resolution providing for the appointment of committees; when

Mr. Stone, of Copiah, offered the following amendment:

Amend by inserting after the word "committee," the words, "consisting of five delegates each."

On motion of Mr. Jarnagin, the resolution and amendment was laid upon the table.

On motion of Mr. Yerger, the Convention adjourned until to morrow morning, 9 o'clock.

SECOND DAY.

TUESDAY, AUGUST 15TH, 1865.

The Convention met pursuant to adjournment.

Prayer by the Rev. C. Chamberlain.

The journal of yesterday was read and approved.

The following delegates, not present yesterday, appeared in their seats, came forward and presented their credentials, and were duly qualified as members of the Convention:

T. R. Gowan, of Simpson county.

J. M. Wylie, of Pontotoc county.

Henry J. Gulley, of Kemper county.

A. Reid, of Winston county.
G. Y. Woodward, of Winston county.
A. E. Reynolds, of Tishomingo county.
L. L. Davis, of Harrison county.
Wm. Grffin, of Jackson county.

Mr. Cooper, of Rankin, offered the following resolution:

WHEREAS, Messrs. Burnham and Bartlett, short-hand reporters, prcpose to make a full and accurate report of all the proceedings of this Convention, if desired; therefore—

Resolved, That a committee of three be appointed by the President to examine into the qualifications of said reporters; and, if deemed ample, to report the cost of such to this Convention, by resolution or otherwise, as soon as practicable.

Mr. Houston offered the following, as a substitute, which was accepted by Mr. Cooper:

Resolved, That the President appoint a committee of five to take into consideration the propriety of employing Messrs. Burnham and Bartlett as reporters of the proceedings of this Convention, and that said committee report by ordinance or otherw se.

The question being taken on the adoption of the resolution, it was rejected.

Mr. Wier offered the following resolution:

Resolved. That the Secretary of the Convention be required to procure a d furnish the Convention, as early as practicable, one hundred printed copies of the Constitution of the State of Mississippi as in force in 1860.

Mr. Jarnagin moved to lay the resolution on the table, Which motion was adopted.

Mr. Cooper, of Panola, offered the following resolution:

Resolved, That the P esident appoint a committee of ten, whose duty it shall be to report to this Convention what changes in and amendments to our Constitution are necessary to restore our former relations to the Federal Government.

Mr. Yerger, of Hinds, offered the following as a substitute:

Resolved, That a committee of   members be appointed by the President to inquire into and report to this Convention such alterations and amendments of the Constitution as may be proper and expedient to restore the State of Mississippi to its constitutional relations to the Federal Government, and entitle its citizens to protection by the United States against invasion and domestic violence

Resolved, That a committee of   members be appointed

by the President to inquire into and report to this Convention such action as is proper and expedient to be taken relative to an act commonly known as the Ordinance of Secession, adopted and approved on the 9th day of January, 1861, by a Convention of delegates of this State; and also what action should be taken for the purpose of ratifying such legislative, executive and judicial acts not in conflict with the Constitution of the United States, as were passed and adopted by the authorities acting in this State in a legislative, executive and judicial capacity since the 9th day of January, 1861.

On motion of Mr. Yerger, the blanks in the above resolutions were filled with the number fifteen.

Mr. Trotter, of Marshall, offered the following ordinance and resolution, as a substitute:

ORDINANCE.

Be it ordained by the people of the State of Mississippi, That the ordinance of secession which was adopted by a Convention of the people of this State, assembled at the city of Jackson on the 9th day of January, 1861, be and the same is hereby repealed and abrogated, together with all ordinances or acts of the State since adopted to carry the said ordinance into effect.

RESOLUTION.

Resolved, That all rights acquired or obligations incurred by virtue of any act or contract made and entered into since the 9th day of January, 1861, and not inconsistent with the Constitution of the United States, are declared to be valid and binding upon the parties to any such contract; and that all the acts of the several officers and public magistrates of the State, done in performance of the duties required of them, and all decrees and judgments of the several courts of this State, including acts of the Legislature not inconsistent with the Constitution of the United States, be in like manner declared to be valid to all intents and purposes.

After some discussion, Mr. Trotter withdrew the above ordinance and resolution; when—

The question recurring on the resolutions offered by Mr. Yerger, it was decided in the affirmative.

Mr. Stone offered the following resolution:

Resolved, That hereafter all resolutions in relation to an amendment to the Constitution, the Ordinance of Secession, and the validity of legislative, executive and judicial acts since the 9th day of January, 1861, be referred to the appropriate committees without debate.

Mr. Jarnagin moved to lay the resolution on the table; Which motion was lost.

The question recurring on the adoption of the resolution, it was decided in the affirmative.

On motion of Mr. Johnson, of Marshall,

The Convention proceeded to the election of Printer for the Convention.

The President appointed Messrs. Sanders, of Attala, Matthews and Wall, as tellers.

Mr. Duncan, of Tishomingo, placed in nomination the names of Messrs. Cooper & Kimball, publishers of the Mississippian.

Mr. Cooper, of Rankin, placed in nomination the name of A. J. Frantz, of the Brandon Republican.

Mr. White, of Chickasaw, placed in nomination the names of J. J. Shannon & Co., of the Clarion.

Mr. Wilson, of Yazoo, placed in nomination the name of E. M. Yerger, of the Jackson News.

Mr. Barr, of Lafayette, placed in nomination the name of I. M. Patridge, of the Vicksburg Herald.

No other nominations being made, the Convention proceeded to the

FIRST BALLOT.

E. M. Yerger received	26	votes.
J. J. Shannon & Co.	22	"
A. J. Frantz	16	"
Cooper & Kimball	15	"
I. M. Patridge	10	"
Total votes cast,	89	

Necessary to a choice, 45. Neither candidate having received a constitutional majority, the Convention preceeded to the second ballot,

Mr. Barr withdrew the name of Mr. Patridge.

SECOND BALLOT.

J. J. Shannon & Co. received	32	votes.
E. M. Yerger	25	"
Cooper & Kimball	20	"
A. J. Frantz	12	"
Total votes cast,	89	

Necessary to a choice, 45. Neither candidate having received a constitutional majority, the Convention proceeded to the third ballot.

Mr. Cooper, of Rankin, withdrew the name of Mr. Frantz.

THIRD BALLOT.

J. J. Shannon & Co. received............29 votes.
Cooper & Kimball.......................29 "
E. M. Yerger...........................29 "

Total votes cast,......................87

Necessary to a choice, 44. Neither candidate having received a constitutional majority, the Convention proceeded to the

FOURTH BALLOT.

E. M. Yerger received..................33 votes.
J. J. Shannon & Co.....................30 "
Cooper & Kimball.......................24 "

Total votes cast.......................87

Necessary to a choice, 44. Neither candidate having received a constitutional majority, the Convention proceeded to the fifth ballot;

Mr. Cooper, of Rankin, re-nominating Mr. Frantz.

FIFTH BALLOT.

J. J. Shannon & Co. received...........31 votes.
E. M. Yerger...........................28 "
A. J. Frantz...........................16 "
Cooper & Kimball.......................12 "
I. M. Patridge.........................1 "

Total votes cast.......................88

Necessary to a choice, 45—neither candidate receiving a constitutional majority.

Mr. Johnson. cf Smith, offered the following resolution, which was adopted:

Resolved, That on each succeeding ballot, the candidate receiving the lowest number of votes shall be dropped.

The Convention then, by order of the President, proceeded to the

SIXTH BALLOT.

E. M. Yerger received..................32 votes.
J. J. Shannon & Co.....................30 "
Cooper & Kimball.......................18 "
A. J. Frantz...........................9 "

Total votes cast,......................89

Necessary to a choice, 45—neither candidate having received a constitutional majority.

Mr. Cooper, of Panola, moved that the Convention adjourn until 4 o'clock P. M.,

Which was lost.

Mr. Goode moved that the Convention take a recess for half an hour,

Which was lost.

The Convention then, by order of the President, proceeded to the

SEVENTH BALLOT.

E. M. Yerger received	39	votes.
J. J. Shannon & Co	35	"
Cooper & Kimball	14	"
Total votes cast,	88	

Necessary to a choice, 45. Neither candidate having received a constitutional majority, the Convention proceeded to the

EIGHTH BALLOT.

E. M. Yerger received	44	votes.
J. J. Shannon & Co	42	"
I. M. Patridge	1	"
Total votes cast,	87	

Mr. Yerger having received a majority of all the votes cast, was declared duly elected Printer for the Convention.

Mr. Peyton, of Copiah, moved that the Convention adjourn until 4 o'clock, P. M.

Mr. Jarnagin moved to amend by striking out 4 o'clock, P. M., and inserting: to-morrow morning, 9 o'clock.

Which was lost.

The motion of Mr. Peyton was then adopted, when—

The Convention adjourned until 4 o'clock, P. M.

FOUR O'CLOCK, P. M.

The Convention met pursuant to adjournment.

The President announced as the committees under the resolutions introduced in the morning session by Mr. Yerger, of Hinds, as follows:

On State Constitution—Messrs. Harrison, of Lowndes; Hill, of Tishomingo; Simonton, of Itawamba; Houston, of Monroe; Yerger, of Hinds; Hamm, of Kemper; Rushing, of Lauderdale; Niles, of Attala; Lewis, of Rankin; Peyton, of Copiah; McBride, of Madison; Martin, of

Adams; Maury, of Claiborne; Hemingway, of Carroll; Owens, of Tunica.

On Ordinances and Laws.—Messrs. Johnston, of Hinds; Reynolds, of Tishomingo; Johnson, of Choctaw; Potter, of Hinds; Trotter, of Marshall; Bailey, of Tallahatchie; Lindsey, of Jasper; Sanders, of Attala; Sessions, of Holmes; Jarnagin, of Noxubee; Goode, of Lawrence; Wier, of Yalobusha; Hurst, of Amite; Cooper, of Rankin; Billups, of Lowndes.

On motion of Mr. Harrison, of Lowndes,

The Convention adjourned until to morrow morning, 9 o'clock.

THIRD DAY.

WEDNESDAY, AUGUST 16TH, 1865.

The Convention met pursuant to adjournment.

Prayer by the Rev. H. J. Harris.

Journal of yesterday read and approved.

The following delegates, not present at previous sessions, appeared in their seats, came forward, presented their credentials, and were duly qualified as members of the Convention:

T. A. Marshall, of Warren county.

W. L. Stricklin, of Coahoma county.

L. Jones, of Bolivar.

Mr. Johnson, of Smith, offered the following resolution:

Resolved, That the President appoint a standing committee of seven on finance and taxation.

On motion of Mr. Harrison, of Lowndes,

The resolution was laid upon the table.

Mr. Cooper, of Panola, offered the following resolution,

Which was adopted:

Resolved, That the Hon. J. A. Orr and Col. W. D. Holder be invited to seats inside the bar of the Convention during their stay in the city.

Mr. Woodward, of Winston, offered the following resolution, which was referred, under the rule, to the special committee of fifteen on State Constitution:

WHEREAS, The Probate Court law and practice is onerous and burdensome, as the times for said court to hold their sessions are appointed by law, and are most usually monthly, parties interested in cases pending in said court are often at great inconvenience, living at a distance, or in cases where administration is very important at an early day; and if, perchance, the judge should be absent, nothing can be done for another month. Again, the judge often resides at a distance—the business of his office being such as not to require him to keep regular office hours; hence great trouble and inconvenience, with delay of time on the part of parties interested; therefore—

Resolved, That the Constitution be so altered or amended as to require the election of a Judge of Probate for each county, as now provided for; and that said judge be ex-officio clerk of said court, so that said court may be opened at all times for business.

On motion of Mr. Harrison,

The Convention adjourned until to-morrow morning, 9 oclock.

FOURTH DAY.

THURSDAY, AUGUST 17TH, 1865.

The Convention met pursuant to adjournment.

Prayer by the Rev. C. Johnson.

Journal of yesterday read and approved.

The following delegates, not present at previous sessions, presented their credentials, and were duly qualified as members of the Convention:

J. W. C. Watson, of Marshall county.

M. C. Cummings, of Itawamba county.

Wm. L. Brandon, of Wilkinson county.

A. Slover, ot Tippah county.

W. A. Crum, of Tippah county.

Mr. Stone, of Copiah, offered the following resolution which was adopted:

Resolved, That the door-keeper be instructed to furnish each member of the Convention with one copy of the Daily Mississippian and the Daily News.

Mr. Duncan, of Tishomingo, offered the following resolution, which was referred, under the rule, to the committee on State Constitution:

Resolved, That the committee on amendments to the Constitution be instructed to inquire into the expediency of authorizing the Legislature to confer jurisdiction to the court of justices of the peace, in action of debt, where the principal of the amount in controversy does not exceed one hundred dollars upon an open account, and two hundred and fifty dollars upon a promisory note or writing obligatory, and report to this Convention as early as practicable, by ordinance or otherwise.

Mr. Hudson, of Yazoo, offered the following ordnance, which was read the first time and placed on the calendar:

ORDINANCE.

Be it ordained by the loyal people of the State of Mississippi in Convention assembled, That for the offences of grand larceny, robbery, rape, arson and burglary, hereafter committed in this State, the penalty of death by hanging shall be inflicted, as in other cases made capital by the laws of this State; but the Legislature of the State may, at any time, alter, change, or repeal said penalty as to offences of either kind committed after such alteration, change or repeal.

Mr. Rives, of Tishomingo, offered the following ordinance, which was read the first time and placed on the calendar:

Be it ordained by the people of the State of Mississippi in Convention assembled, That all the official acts done and performed by any and all persons whomsoever who have been formally elected or appointed to any office, either of the state or any county therein, or in any incorporated city or town in said state of Mississippi, since the 9th day of January, A. D. 1861, not repugnant to the Constitution of the United States nor of the state of Mississippi, nor the laws of the state of Mississippi, which were in force on the 9th day of January, A. D. 1861, shall be and the same are hereby declared to be legal and valid, as if the said officers had been duly elected and qualified as such according to the constitution and laws of the state in force previous to the 9th day of January, A. D. 1861.

Mr. Jarnagin, of Noxubee, offered the following resolution, which was referred, under the rule, to the committee on State Constitution:

Resolved, That the committee on Constitution be requested to inquire into the expediency and propriety of this Convention memorializing the President of the United States on the subject of garrisoning our towns with negro troops, setting forth the danger to the loyal citizens of this state arising from the presence of black troops, and the demoralizing influence produced upon the recently freed blacks of the State, and the propriety of asking the President, if it shall be necessary to continue the armed garrisons in the state, that said garrisons may consist of white troops, and not of freed blacks; and that said committee report by memorial or otherwise.

Mr. Johnson, of Marshall, offered the following resolution, which was unanimously adopted:

Resolved, That his Excellency, Wm. L. Sharkey, Provisional Governor of the State of Mississippi, be invited to a seat within the bar of the Convention.

Mr. Matthews asked leave of absence for Mr. Stricklin, of Coahoma, on account of illness; which was granted.

Mr. Hudson, of Yazoo, offered the following ordinance, which was read the first time and placed on the calendar:

Be it ordained by this Convention, That all marriage licenses heretofore issued by any probate clerk, and bonds taken in such cases, and marriages had thereunder, in accordance with the laws of this state existing on the 9th January, 1861, and the registration of all marriage licenses, bonds and certificates of marriages, be and the same are hereby declared valid and binding, and in full force and effect.

2d. That all deeds, bonds and mortgages, acknowledgements, wills and other instruments, made, taken, proved, registered, certified and authenticated, by or before any probate clerk of this state, or any other officer, pursuant to and in compliance with the laws of this state, existing on 9th January, 1861, be and the same are hereby ratified and held for valid, binding, and in full force and effect.

3d. That all the proceedings, judgments, orders and decrees made by any probate judge, and all proceedings had and done thereunder, and all bonds and obligations taken by or before him in the premises, and all acts of the probate clerks touching the same, according to the laws of this state in existence and force on the 9th day of January, 1861, be and the same are hereby ratified, and held for valid and binding.

4th. That all acts of any clerks of any court, and all acts of any judge and court, and all acts of every civil officer, grand jurors, petit jurors, judicial proceedings, bonds, recognizances, decrees, judgments, execution, process, service of process, in this state, since the 9th January, 1861, and pursuant to and in accordance with the laws of this state in force on 9th day of January, 1861, be and the same are hereby recognized and ratified, and declared valid and binding, and the said several civil officers entitled to compensation therefor at the rates and in the manner directed by the laws of this State in force on 9th January, 1861, if not already paid.

5th. That the several acts of the Legislature of this state known as the stop or stay laws, suspending the collection of debts, the institution and prosecution of suits, and the suspension of the several statutes of limitations of this state, and all acts authorizing persons of non-age to dispose of their property by will or otherwise, passed since 9th day of January, 1861, be and the same are hereby recognized and ratified, and held to be valid and in full force and operation.

6th. That no civil or military officer of this state shall be held liable for trespass, damages, or suit of any kind, for any act done by any such officer, in good faith and within the scope and authority of the recognized civil or military law of this state, during the late war; and that all their acts in such official capacity and good faith, be and the same are hereby recognized and ratified, and held for valid, so far as to give them the protection aforesaid.

7th. That all crimes heretofore committed during the war, and not yet punished, if crimes against the laws of this state in force on 9th January, 1861, shall remain crimes, and be proceeded with according to the laws of this state in force on 9th January, 1861.

8th. That all acts of the legislative, executive and judicial departments of this state, done and performed during the late rebellion, not in conflict with the Constitution of the United States, and the laws thereof pursuant thereto, nor in conflict with the Constitution of this state, be and the same are hereby recognized and ratified.

Mr. Compton offered the following resolution, which was unanimously adopted:

Resolved, That B. G. Humphreys, Brigadier-General of the late Confederate army, be invited to a seat within the bar of this Convention during his stay in this city.

Mr. Martin, of Adams, offered the following resolution, which was unanimously adopted:

Resolved, That Major-General Osterhaus, Commandant of this District, be invited to a seat within the bar of the Convention.

Mr. Martin remarked, in offering the foregoing resolution, that he felt more pacifically disposed than formerly.

Mr. Watson, of Marshall, offered the following resolution:

Resolved, That a committee of three be appointed by the Chair who shall have authority to employ two competent short-hand reporters, for the purpose of furnishing verbatim reports of the debates in this Convention; and said committee shall be authorized to award a just and equitable compensation for the services of such reporters.

In support of which, Mr. Watson said: I hope, Mr. President, it will be the pleasure of this body to adopt that resolution. The subject has been heretofore brought before the Convention, but in no direct form. This resolution proposes that a committee be appointed charged with the duty of employing two competent short-hand reporters. The cost will not be very great to have an accurate and full report of the debates of this body taken and preserved. Now the question of the publication of these reports is quite an independent affair. The publication of these reports, to be sure, should they be voluminous, would cost a great deal; but that question may be adjourned. I do deem it important, however, that the debates of this body should be taken and preserved, in a permanent form, for future reference.

The questions before this body, sir, are of very great gravity—very great; and it is due to each member that the opinions and views which he may express, should be thus preserved. Our action must be construed in the light of what may transpire whilst we are in session; and then, sir, I believe that the spirit breathed by the members of this Convention will be of such a character as to vindicate the State from the aspersions that are being constantly cast upon her. I hope, therefore, the gentlemen will adopt the resolution. I repeat, that the mere cost of having this report made, cannot be great—cannot exceed thirty-five dollars a day.

MR. MARTIN, of Adams—Mr. President: A proposition somewhat similar to this was voted down yesterday without discussion. I voted in favor of that proposition; but I think it very likely that many members voted without reflection as to what the intention of the proposition was. It is important for us not only that the Constitution which we shall adopt, shall show the spirit of our people, but it is also important to show by the debates the spirit in which these propositions were discussed. That Constitution will go out to the world as the action of a majority of this Convention; and it is necessary to show, as the debates will—by giving in full the expressions uttered on the spur of the moment, of those representing the people of Mississippi—the feeling in this State. It is also necessary and proper that we should show, as was suggested by the gentleman preceeding me, that it is a mistake to suppose that in surrendering, and as a people giving our paroles, we merely did it to gain time, and that there was still a disposition among the people of the State of Mississippi to carry on the war against the Northern States—against the Federal Government. I think it also important, in the present crisis, that whatever can should be done to assure the people of the North, and especially that portion of the Northern people disposed to be conservative and consider that we have some rights at least in the South, to show them, and to show the Government of the United States, also, that having first tried the logic of the schools, and having failed in that, and having then resorted to the sterner logic of arms, and having failed in that, also, we are now honestly disposed to return to our allegiance, and to make out of the disasters that have befallen us the best we can. I think there is no surer and better way of showing the conservatives of the North and the Government of the United States, that we are in earnest and that we are sincere, than by publishing the debates of this Convention. There is no other way in which we can ascertain, with any certainty, the views of the people of this State, whose opinions are supposed to be represented here; and I desire that in some permanent manner these may go abroad in the country to show our action, and to show that we intend to deal fairly in this matter, and that we may, for many reasons, satisfy them that we are not, while we are preparing to return in form to our allegiance, entertaining opinions and feelings hostile to the government of the country. I hope, therefore, as the cost is insignificant, and as the case is an important one, and the questions to be discussed are the most vital in their interests of any that have ever been discussed since the State of Mississippi was organized, that these debates may be preserved, so that it can be ascertained beyond question --not by looking to the contributions of of itinerant newspaper writers—but from the discussions of this body, what is the true spirit of the people of this State and our interests here. I therefore trust that the resolution of the gentleman from Marshall will prevail.

Mr. Houston, of Monroe—Mr. President: I introduced the other day a substitute for a resolution offered by the gentleman from Rankin, in reference to this same subject matter. I was then of the opinion, as I am now, that it was due not only to the members of this Convention, in order to prevent misrepresentation in reference to our future course here, but that it was also due to the people of this State that they should know what was said and done here, that they might properly interpret any action of this body. I think it was a strong proposition, and above either of the last in importance, that the action of the Convention on constitutional questions, will doubtless, and must sometimes become the subject of litigation in the courts of the country. By what light or what means can these courts more rapidly come to the proper interpretation of what was meant by this Convention in its action, and what was intended by this or by that article of the Constitution that may have been amended, than by the light which may be aforded in the publication of the discussions of this Convention.

I think, sir, that if there is no other, this one consideration is in itself of sufficient value to warrant the meeting of any cost which might accrue to the State from the employment of reporters and the publication of our debates. For these reasons, and others which I might give, if the time of the Convention was not too valuable, I shall vote in favor of the resolution.

The question recurring on the adoption of the resolution, it was decided in the affirmative; whereupon the President appointed Messrs. Watson, Martin and Houston as the committee contemplated therein.

Mr. Cooper, of Panola, offered the following resolution:

Resolved, That Brigadier-General Wirt Adams and Judge E. S. Fisher be invited to seats inside the bar of the Convention.

On motion of Mr. Johnson, of Smith, the resolution was amended so as to embrace the name of Hon. John Watts; when it was so adopted.

Mr. Hudson offered the following ordinance, which was read the first time and placed on the calendar:

Be it ordained, That no law shall ever be passed by the Legislature, or law-making power of this state, imposing any civil or political disability, or punishment, or forfeiture of estate, upon any citizen or person of this state, for any participation in bringing on or prosecuting the late war between the United States and the Confederate States, or the State of Mississippi, or for his or her political opinions in relation thereto: hereby declaring that such policy or conciliation, protection or recognition, will soonest and most effectually unite our people in one harmonious and loyal, prosperous and happy community, in all that relates to relative duties as citizens, the state at large, and our peaceful relations to the United States.

Mr. Hudson offered the following resolution:

Resolved, That the several proposed ordinances read and placed upon the calendar this day for a second and third reading, be printed forthwith, to the number of one hundred copies each, and furnished to each delegate of this Convention, that the same may be carefully criticised and understood, preparatory to a wise and judicious action upon and disposition of the same.

On motion of Mr. Simonton, of Itawamba,

The resolution was laid on the table.

On his further motion, the ordinances referred to in said resolution were referred to the select committee of fifteen on ordinances and laws.

Mr. Harrison, from select committee on State Constitution, submitted the following report:

Mr. President: The committee to whom was referred the resolution to amend or alter the Constitution in relation to judges of probate, so that the court may be open at all times for business, have duly considered the same, and after consideration, recommend that the same do not pass.

On motion of Mr. Harrison, the report was received and agreed to.

Mr. Harrison, from the same committee, submitted the following report, with accompanying ordinance:

Mr. President: The committee appointed to inquire into and report to this Convention such alterations and amendments of the Constitution as may be proper and expedient to restore the State of Mississippi to its Constitutional relations to the Federal Government, and entitle its citizens to protection by the United States against invasion and domestic violence, submit the following

REPORT.

The committee recommend the following alterations and amendments of the Constitution of the State of Mississippi, adopted October 26th, 1832, and the amendments thereto adopted prior to the 1st day of January, 1861:

First. That the Constitution shall be amended by abolishing and striking out Sections one, two and three, of Article VII., under the title "Slaves," and amendment number one, approved February 2d, 1846, relative to slaves.

Second. That a provision, in the following language, shall be inserted in the Constitution as Article Eight: That neither slavery nor involuntary servitude, otherwise than in the punishment of crimes, whereof the party shall have been duly convicted, shall hereafter exist in this

State; and the Legislature at its next session, and thereafter as the public welfare may require, shall provide by law for the protection of the person and property of the freedmen of the State, and guard them and the State against any evils that may arise from their sudden emancipation.

Third. That the twelfth section of the Declaration of Rights be amended by the insertion of the following proviso, to-wit: *Provided,* That the Legislature, in cases of petit larceny, assault, assault and battery, affray, riot, unlawful assembly, drunkeness, vagrancy, and other misdemeanors of like character, may dispense with an inquest of a grand jury, and may authorize prosecutions before justices of the peace, or such other inferior court or courts as may be established by the legislature, and the proceedings in such cases shall be regulated by law.

Fourth. That amendment number two, approved March 12th, 1852, being an amendment of the twentieth section of the fourth article, shall be amended by inserting after the words, "matters of county police," the following words, to-wit: including herein the power to make necessary and proper regulations relating to apprentices, and their rights and duties, and also to suppress vagrancy and punish vagrants.

The committee also report the following ordinance in relation to the election of public officers; and the committee are of opinion, and respectfully submit, that it is not necessary or proper, at the present time, to enter into other or further alterations or amendments of the Constitution, or to take it up for consideration upon its general provisions.

ORDINANCE.

SECTION 1. *The people of the State of Mississippi in Convention assembled do ordain and declare, and it is hereby ordained and declared,* That a general election shall be held according to the Constitution and the election laws of the State as they existed on the first day of January, 1861, for Representatives in Congress, and all State officers, and members of the Legislature. The several Congressional Districts shall be the same, and the time of holding the election for Representatives in Congress the same as fixed and established by the Legislature in the year 1857. The Legislature shall convene on the first day of November, 1865, and be organized and classified as the Constitution directs. A special election shall also be held at the time of said general election, (the first Monday in October, A. D. 1865,) for all county, district, judicial and ministerial officers; and the officers so elected shall hold their offices until their successors are elected and qualified, and enter upon the duties of their respective offices, according to the Constitution and laws; and the term of all such State, county, district, judicial and ministerial officers, so elected, shall commence on the first Monday in November, 1865. No person shall be qualified as an elector, or be eligible to any office at said elections, unless, in addition to the qualifications required by the Constitution and election laws aforesaid, he shall have taken the amnesty oath prescribed in the proclamation of the President of the United States, of the 29th day of May, 1865; and immediately after the adjournment of the Convention, the President thereof shall issue writs of election, directed to the sheriffs in the several counties in the State, requiring them to cause said elections to be held according to the election laws in force and existing on said first day of January, 1861.

On motion of Mr. Harrison, the report was received and agreed to; and, on his further motion, the ordinance was laid upon the table, and three hundred copies ordered to be printed.

Mr. Matthews, of Panola, offered the following resolution:

Resolved, That a committee of three be appointed to ascertain and report:

1st. How many votes were cast for delegates to this Convention.

2d. Whether a majority of legal voters, under the laws of this State, voted for the delegates elected.

Mr. Yerger, of Hinds, offered the following amendment:

Amend: And that the said committee also report the number of legal voters there were in the State at the said election.

On motion of Mr. Martin, of Adams, the resolution and amendment were laid on the table.

Mr. Watson, from special committee, submitted the following

REPORT.

The Committee appointed to employ two competent short-hand writers, to report accurately and fully the debates of this body, have performed that duty by employing for that purpose Messrs. S. W. Burnham, and A. L. Bartlett, of New Orleans, at a compensation of fifteen ($15,00) dollars a day each.

On motion of Mr. Watson, the report was received and adopted.

Mr. Matthews, of Panola, offered the following resolution, which was adopted:

RESOLVED, That the Sergeant-at-Arms be authorized and required to furnish for the use of this Conventlon a sufficient quantity of ice.

Mr. Hudson, of Yazoo, offered the following

ORDINANCE.

Be it ordained by the loyal people in Convention assembled—First, That the High Court of Errors and Appeals of this State, the several circuit and chancery courts of this State, the criminal court of Warren county, the office of Attorney-General of this State, the office of District Attorney of the several judicial districts and criminal courts of this State, and all county officers known to the Constitution and laws of this State on and before the 9th day of January, 1861, be and the same are hereby revived, re-established, and declared to be in existence, full force and operation, and that the several persons elected to the said offices by the people at the last election therefor, in this State, and holding said offices at the time of the suspension of their functions and powers in May, 1865, be and the same are hereby re-instated, restored and elected to their said several offices and positions, upon their taking the amnesty oath, if not already taken, and the proper oath of office, and giving bond and security, to be taken, conditioned and approved according to law in the case of bonded officers, for and until the end of the unexpired terms for which they were severally elected: *Provided,* That any such office now filled and held by any appointee of Gov. W. L. Sharkey, shall be held and filled by such appointee for the unexpired term of said office; and in case that any of said offices are or may become vacant by the death, removal, re-ignation, refusal to qualify or act, or other legal cause, such vacancy shall be filled, in cases of district and State officers, by executive appointment, and in case of county officers, by election, according to existing laws in such cases, for the unexpired term thereof.

On motion of Mr. Yerger, of Hinds, the ordinance was laid upon the table.

On motion of Mr. Maury, of Claiborne, three hundred copies were ordered to be printed.

Mr. Johnson, of Marshall, offered the following ordinance, which was referred, under the rule, to the committee on ordinances and laws:

ORDINANCE.

The people of the State of Mississippi in Convention assembled do ordain and declare, and it is hereby ordained and declared as follows, to-wit:

SECTION 1. That an ordinance known as the Ordinance of Secession, declared and established by the people of Mississippi in solemn convention, at the city of Jackson, on the 9th day of January, 1861, dissolving the connexion between the State of Mississippi and the United States of America, be and the same is hereby repealed and abrogated, and all obligations on the part of said State, or the people thereof, to observe said ordinance of secession, or any of the laws or institutions growing out of the same, are annulled; and that the said State of Mississippi, doth hereby assume all the obligations incumbent upon the State as a member of the Federal Union of the United States of America, as fully as if they had never been renounced; and all laws and ordinances establishing and defining said obligations and relations between the said State and said United States, are hereby declared valid, renewed, and in full force and effect.

2d. That so much of the first section of the 7th article of the Constitution of the State as it stood previous to said ordinance of secession, requiring the officers of the State—legislative, executive and judicial—to take an oath to support the Constitution of the United States, is hereby declared to be still a part of said Constitution, and a fundamental part of the organic law of the land.

On motion of Mr. Simontion, the Convention adjourned until 4 o'clock, P. M.

FOUR O'CLOCK, P. M.

The Convention met pursuant to adjournment.

Mr. Johnston, of Hinds, from the special committee on ordinances and laws, made the following report:

Mr. President: The committee appointed "to inquire into and report to this Convention such action as is proper and expedient to be taken relative to an act commonly known as the Ordinance of Secession, adopted and approved on the 9th day of January, 1861, by a Convention of the delegates of this State; and also what action should be taken for the purpose of ratifying such legislative, executive and judicial acts, not in conflict with the Constitution of the United States, as were passed and adopted by the authorities acting in the State in a legislative, executive and judicial capacity, since the 9th day of January, 1861," beg leave respectfully to report: That they have given to the subject committed to them that calm and deliberate consideration which their great importance demand. The result of the deliberations of your committee is embraced in two ordinances herewith submitted—one entitled: An ordinance to legalize and support the legislative enactments of the State of Mississippi, passed since the 9th day of January, 1861, and for other purposes; the other entitled: An ordinace in relation to the Ordinance of Secession and other ordinances and resolutions adopted by a former Convention of the State of Mississippi. held at Jackson on the 9th day of January, 1861, and on the 25th day of March, 1861." Your committee pray that this Report, and the accompanying Ordinances, be received; that said Ordinances be adopted by the Convention; and that your committee have leave to sit again, having other subjects submitted to their consideration.

Ordinance No. 1.

AN ORDINACE in relation to the Ordinance of Secession and other Ordidinances and Resolutions, adopted by a former Convention held in the city of Jackson on the 7th January, 1861, and on the 25th day of March, 1861.

Section 1. *Be it ordained by the people of the State of Mississippi in Convention assembled*, That an ordinance passed by a former Convention of the State of Mississippi, on the 9th day of January, 1861, entitled "An ordinance to dissolve the union between the State of Mississippi and other States united with her under the compact entitled, 'The Constitution of the United States of America,'" is hereby declared to be null and void.

Sec. 2. *Be it further ordained*, That the following ordinances and resolutions, passed by said former Convention of the State of Mississippi, which assembled in the city of Jackson, on Monday, the 7th day of January, 1861, and on the 25th day of March, 1861, be and the same are hereby repealed, viz:

"To raise means for the defense of the State, (said ordinance having no date.)

"To regulate the military system of the State of Mississippi." Passed 23d January, 1861.

"To amend the Constitution of the State of Mississippi in certain particulars." Passed January 26th, 1861.

"Concerning the jurisdiction and property of the United States of America in the State of Mississippi." Passed January 16th, 1861.

"Supplemental to an ordinance concerning the jurisdiction and property of the United States of America, in the State of Mississippi." Passed 26th January, 1861.

"To provide for postal arrangements in the State of Mississippi."' Passed January 12th, 1861.

"Further to provide for postal arrangements in Mississippi." Passed January 26th, 1861.

"To provide for the formation of a Southern Confederacy." (No date thereto.)

"To regulate the right of citizenship in the State of Mississippi." Passed 26th January, 1861.

"Providing a Permanent Council of three for the Governor of this State." Passed 26th January, 1861.

"To provide for the purchase of arms, munitions and military equipments, and for other purposes." Passed 26th January, 1861.

"To provide for the representation of the State of Mississippi in the Congress of the Southern Confederacy." Passed 26th January, 1861.

"To provide for surveys and fortifications of military sites within the State of Mississippi." Passed 26th Janu-ery, 1861.

"To authorize the Governor to borrow a sufficient amount of money to defray the expenses of the troops now in the field." (No date thereto.)

"To provide for the formation of a Southern Confederacy." (No date thereto.)

"To adopt and ratify the Constitution adopted by the Convention at Montgomery, Alabama." Passed March 29th, 1861.

"In relation to lands in the State of Mississippi belonging to Indian orphans." Passed March 29th, 1861.

"To define the power of the Legislature of this State in relation to ordinances and resolu ions adopted by the Convention." Passed March 30th, 1861.

"In reference to the Marine Hospital at Vicksburg." Passed March 30th, 1861.

"To provide a Coat of Arms and Flag for the State of Mississippi." Passed March 30th, 1861.

"To authorize the entry and sale of waste and unappropriated lands in the State of Mississippi." Passed March 28th, 1861.

"To revise and amend the law in relation to foreign insurance companies." Passed March 27th, 1861.

"To provide for the appointment of Electors of President and Vice-President of the Confederate States of America." Passed March 30th, 1861.

"To alter and modify the ordinance entitled 'An ordinance concerning the jurisdiction and property of the United States in the State of Mississippi." Passed March 30th, 1861.

"Supplemenal to an ordinance entitled 'an ordinance to raise means for the defense of the State,'" passed March 29th, 1861.

SEC. 3. *Be it further ordained*, That this ordinance shall be in force from and after its passage.

ORDINANCE NO. 2.

AN ORDIANNCE to legalize and support the legislative enactments of the State of Mississippi, passed since the 9th day of January, 1861, and for other purposes.

SECTION 1. *Be it ordained by the people of the State of Mississippi in Convention assembled*, That all laws and parts of laws of said State enacted since the 9th day of January, 1861, when the Ordinance of Secession was passed, so far as the same are not violative of the Constitution of the United States, or the Constitution of the State of Mississippi, or not in aid of the late revolution, except "an act to enable the railroad companies of this State to pay the monies borrowed by them," approved December 7th, 1863, be and the same are hereby declared to be legal, valid and binding, to all intents and purposes, from the respective dates thereof, until repealed or changed by the Legislature of said State.

SEC. 2. *Be it further ordained*, That all the acts of all public officers of the State of Mississippi, done and performed under and pursuant to the laws of said State, whether these offices be legislative, executive, judicial or ministerial, since the aforesaid 9th day of January, A. D. 1861, shall be held as legal, binding and obligatory, to all intents and purposes.

SEC. 3. *Be it further ordained*, That all the orders, judgments, proceedings and decrees of all the courts of the State of Mississippi, rendered and done since the aforesaid 9th of January, A. D. 1861, are hereby declared to be legal, valid and binding in every respect, subject only to such right of appeal, writ of error, supersedeas, or review, as may be allowed and provided for by the statutes of said States, and the rules of practice prevailing in said courts respectively.

SEC. 4. *Be it further ordained*, That all official bonds executed by all public officers of the State of Mississippi, and the bonds of all executors, administrators and guardians, and all bonds executed by parties in the progress of legal proceedings, made since said 9th January, A. D. 1861, and which were executed conformable to any statute of said State, be and the same are hereby declared to be valid, binding and legal, to all intents and purposes.

SEC. 5. *Be it further ordained*, That all contracts and engagements between citizens of the State of Mississippi or other persons, as well as all deeds of conveyance or other contracts for land or other property, made and entered into under the laws of said State, enacted since the 9th day of January, 1861, and which contracts and engagements are in conformity with those laws, and the common law principles relating to such transactions, be and the same are hereby declared to be valid, legal and binding, between the contracting parties, and all persons concerned therein, to all intents and purposes.

SEC. 6. *Be it further ordained*, That no debt, demand, contract, obligation, bond, deed of trust, mortgage or other pecuniary liability or engagement, made or entered into in the State of Mississippi, shall be barred or in any manner affected or impaired by reason of the time elapsing without suit or proceeding commenced thereon, or demand made therefor, since said 9th day of January, 1861.

SEC. 7. *Be it further ordained*, That all sales of executors, administrators, guardians, commissioners in chancery, and ministerial officers, and persons acting in a fidicuary capacity, made conformably to the statutes of the State of Mississippi, or decrees of courts, and made since said 9th day of January, 1861, are hereby declared to be valid, and legal and binding, in every respect, from their respective dates; and all such sales which may hereafter be made under the laws of said State enacted from and after said 9th day of January, 1861, shall also be held and maintained as legal, valid and binding.

SEC. 8. *Be it further ordained*, That no debt, claim or demand of any person against the estate of any deceased person, shall be impaired or barred in consequence of such debt, demand or claim not having been probated and registered since said 9th day of January, 1861.

SEC. 9. *Be it further ordained*, That all marriages celebrated in this State since the 9th day of January, 1861, are deemed and declared by this Convention to be valid and binding to all intents and purposes, from the respective dates of their celebration.

Mr. Trotter of Marshall, submitted the following

MINORITY REPORT.

Mr. President: The minority of the committee have directed me to report the following ordinance and substitute for the one adopted by the majority, to-wit:

Be it ordained, That the Ordinance of Secession, adopted by a Convention of the people of this State on the 9th day of January, 1861, be and the same is hereby *abrogated*.

Mr. Goode, of Lawrence, submitted the following

MINORITY REPORT ON ORD NANCE OF SECESSION.

WHEREAS, A Convention of the people of the State of Mississippi, assembled at the Capital on the 9th day of January, 1861, adopted an ordinance of secession from the United States Government, and declared that the State resumed her sovereignty; and in a war resulting therefrom with the United States Government, which refused to recognize the legality or validity of that ordinance, the State failed to maintain her asserted sovereignty, and is now willing and ready to resume her station in the Union as before the passage of that ordinance; therefore—

Be it ordained by this Convention, That said Ordinance of Secession be and the same is declared to be henceforward null and of no binding force.

E. J. GOODE, of Lawrence.
RICHARD COOPER, of Rankin.

On motion of Mr. Goode. the majority and minority reports were received, and three hundred copies of each ordered to be printed.

Mr. Wier, of Yalobusha, moved to reconsider the vote by which the majority and minority reports were ordered to be printed. Which motion was lost.

On motion of Mr. Harrison, the Convention adjourned until to-morrow morning, 9 o'clock.

FIFTH DAY.

FRIDAY, AUGUST 18TH, 1865.

The Convention met pursuant to adjournment.

Prayer by the Rev. Geo. A. Smyth.

Journal of yesterday read and approved.

Mr. Watson offered the following resolution, which was unanimously adopted :

Resolved, That the Hon. A. H. Handy be, and is hereby invited to a seat on this floor, during his stay in this city.

Mr. Hudson offered the following resolution :

Resolved, That a committee of five be appointed by the President of this Convention, to take into consideration the propriety of this Convention memoralizing the President of the United States to grant the release of Jefferson Davis and Charles Clark, citizens of this State, from prison, upon their respective paroles of honor, and for their ultimate pardon, or either ; and if said committee shall deem it proper so to memoralize, they are hereby requested and instructed to report to this Convention a suitable memorial in that behalf as early as practicable.

The motion to adopt was declared carried by a *viva voce* vote, when Mr. Yerger, of Hinds, called for a division.

MR. WATSON said :—

Before the division is counted, I desire to offer a suggestion or two. Sympathising with President Davis and Governor Clark as deeply as any other gentlemen, I am prepared and ready to do anything in my power calculated to ameliorate their condition, but I doubt the wisdom of sny action in their behalf on the part of this body, as a Convention. As Mississippians, as individuals, it may be right and expedient for us to make an effort to do something for them. In this form, our action can at least, I think, do no prejudice, and will doubtless be as efficacious as any action which we could take as a Convention.

We have been convened for a specific object of great importance to the people of the State; and nothing should be done, which could even contingently or remotely prejudice this object. Our proceedings should be characterized by moderation and prndence; and no step whatever of a doubtful character, should be hazarded. Many members of the Convention have contemplated personal action in their private character, as citizens of Mississippi, and in this character, I hope we may all unite in a memorial expressive of our sympathy and the sympathy of the people of the State, for the two distinguished gentlemen in question; but lest harm might result therefrom, I ask gentlemen to deliberate well before they do more than this. Under the influence of these views, I shall be constained to record my vote in opposition to the proposed resolution.

Mr. Yerger.—I concur fully with the sentiments and views of the delegate from Marshall. As an individual and a citizen of this State, I am ready, at any and all times, to join in any movement that may have a tendency in any way to mitigate the condition of Mr. Davis and Gov. Clark. I am satisfied that if we were to undertake action as a Convention, under the circumstances in which we were called, we should not only prejudice, to some extent, the action which we desire to take in behalf of the people of the State, but that we should prejudice the cause of Mr. Davis and of Gov. Clark.

Our motives might be misconstrued, and it would certainly be charged that we had proceeded beyond the purposes for which we were convened. Under such circumstances, I shall be constrained to vote against the resolution, being ready, as I remarked before, to join members of this Convention in my private, individual capacity, in any memorial, or any other act that they may see fit to take, that will tend to mitigate the condition, or relieve these gentlemen from their confinement, or any penalties that might possibly be inflicted.

Mr. Johnston, of Hinds.—I intend to vote against the resolution on the division ; and I wish to say a few words in explanation of my reasons and motives for that course. I know that I have as active sympathy both for the late President of the Confederate States and Governor Clark, as any member of this Convention, or any citizen of the State of Mississippi. I feel this in my heart, and know it to be so—that I would do anything, or make any reasonable sacrifice—almost any sacrifice, to be of service to either one of these distinguished gentlemen. But I am impressed with the belief, Mr. President, that the official, authoritative action of this Convention on that subject, would, in the language of the gentleman who has already spoken, tend to defeat or embarrass the very object we have in view. I think it would tend to defeat and embarrass the great object for which this Convention was called—the restoration of civil rule, the destruction of military rule, and the full representation of this Sate in the Congress of the United States. I think that action, so far from mitigating the sufferings of these distinguished gentlemen, would perhaps have the very contrary effect. But we ought to do something, and must do something, and it seems to me the proper action to pursue would be this:

The members of this Convention, as private individuals, might frame a memorial to the proper authorities at Washington, setting forth our views, and asking for the relief we all so much desire. That could not be objectionable, and would have the same weight, with no injurious consequences, that the official action of this Convention might possibly have. I have nothing more to say—my only motive being to express the feelings and sentiments which actuates me in the course I pursue. I hope gentlemen will consider this and act with prudence in the matter.

MR. MARTIN, of Adams.—I yield to no one in the strong desire I feel, to see some such action taken as suggested by this resolution. Having since I arrived at manhood, invariably been in opposition to the school of politics of our late President, I have said in conversation with personal friends, before coming to this place, that I intended, if no one else did, to request the members of this Convention to express—not as a Convention, but as individuals—to the President of the United States, the desire we all felt, that neither Mr. Davis, nor any other person should suffer for our sins; that if many of us had opposed the secession of the State of Mississippi at the outset, many of us had considered it to be our duty to oppose the movement made in the South with a view of asserting and maintaining a separate government—still, I presume all of us are more or less guilty, having afterwards sympathised with the movement, and aided it; and I am not willing that the sins of us all shall be visited on the head of one man. I am, therefore, willing to go as far as the farthest in endeavoring to mitigate the punishment that may be thought proper to be inflicted upon the late President; but I regret very much that a resolution like this has been offered, for I know any action this Convention might take in furthering the object of that resolution would be misconstrued; and I think that gentlemen, after a moment's reflection will agree with me. What is sympathy for the individual would be construed into sympathy of a different kind. I hope it will not be necessary for us to vote on this matter, and that the gentleman will withdraw it, for I think this action will come with better grace from us as individuals.

MR. HUDSON, of Yazoo.—Mr. President, I proposed this resolution, simply as an act of humanity—as one coming from the State in which the distinguished gentlemen mentioned therein, resided, and as coming, perhaps, from the proper source.

4

In the first place, the resolution does not require that the committee should report a memorial to the President of the United States, but only calls for the appointment of a committee, by the Chair, to inquire into the propriety of memorializing the President upon the subject. In the event of that committee deeming it proper and prudent to do so, a proper memorial could then be presented with their report.

If, however, it is deemed obnoxious, and that such action on the part of the Covention would prejudice us in the eyes of the administration--in the eye of the United States Government,--I shall certainly withdraw the resolution.

But, in regard to this subject, sir, the President can only regard us either as loyal or disloyal. What is the evidence of loyalty--so far as regulating the government itself? It is that certain parties shall comply with certain requisitions pointed out. I believe this Convention is almost entirely composed of gentlemen who hold opinions, politically, the very opposite of those of Mr. Davis; and it seems to me that, without a very unusual and extraordinary construction of this resolution, the President could not suppose it to emenate from any political sympathy or agreement with Jefferson Davis.

I merely introduced the resolution that enquiry might be instituted, but, upon the suggestion of members that it would be obnoxious even in the sense of an enquiry upon the part of this committee, I will now withdraw it.

Mr. Harrison, of Lowndes, from select committee on State Constitution, submitted the following report:

MR. PRESIDENT :

The Committee on Constitutional Amendments, to whom was refered the resolution, in relation to the expediency of authorizing the Legislature to confer jurisdiction on Justices of the Peace, in actions of debt where the principal of the amount in controversy does not exceed one hundred dollars, upon an open account, and two hundred and fifty dollars upon a promissory note or writing obligatory ; ask leave to report, that they have duly considered said resolution, and are unanimously of opinion that it is inexpedient at this time to enter upon any such changes or alterations of the Constitution, and accordingly recommend that said resolution do not pass.

On motion of Mr. Harrison,

The report was received and agreed to.

The following communication was read, and ordered to be spread upon the Journal :

HEADQUARTERS NORTHERN DIST. OF MISSISSIPPI,
August 17th, 1865.

HON. J. S. YERGER,

President of the Convention:

SIR:—I am in receipt of your favor of this A. M., enclosing a resolution of the honorable body presided over by you, inviting me to a seat within the bar of the Convention.

I feel the honor conferred on me deeply, and cannot suppress a feeling of justifiable pride and pleasure, that my humble self was destined to be the first officer of the National forces, to receive such a friendly invitation from our returned brethren. No man can more earnestly desire that all the States of the Republic may again be encircled by one bond of harmony and confidence, and that the noble stars and stripes be recognized by all men, as the emblems of the "home of the brave, and the land of the free."

Be pleased to accept, and to express to the members of the Convention, my heartfelt thanks for the high distinction expressed in your resolution, and believe me to be, with great respect, Your obedient servant,

P. JOS. OSTERHAUS,
Major General Volunteers.

On motion of Mr. Harrison,

The report of the Committee, appointed to "inquire into and report to this Convention, such alterations and amendments of the Constitution, as may be proper and expedient to restore the State of Mississippi to its constitutional relations to the Federal Government, and entitle its citizens to protection by the United States against invasion and domestic violence,"

Was taken up.

Mr. Simonton, of Itawamba, moved that the report of the Committee and accompanying ordinance be considered section by section,

Which was adopted.

The first section of the report having been read,

On motion of Mr. Harrison, it was adopted as follows, to-wit:

First. That the Constitution shall be amended by abolishing and striking out sections one, two and three of article seven, under the title "slaves," and amendment one, approved February 2th, 1846, relative to slaves.

Mr. Barr, of Lafayette, offered the following as a substitute for the second section of the report:

"Slavery having been abolished in this State by the action of the Government of the United States, it is therefore hereby declared and ordained, that hereafter there shall be neither slavery nor involuntary servitude in this State, otherwise than in the punishment of crimes, whereof the party shall have been duly convicted, and the Legislature, at its next session, and thereafter as the public welfare may require, shall provide by law for the protection and security of the person and property of the freedmen of the State, and guard them and the State against any evils that may arise from their sudden emancipation.

Mr. Yerger: Mr. President.--I do not propose to enter into any discussion on this substitute, but simply to state that in my opinion, the tendency and effect of the preamble thereto, will be prejudicial to the purposes and views which I think a majority of this Convention entertain.

The preamble undertakes to assert as a fact, what may or may not be true, to-wit: That slavery has been abolished by the act of the United States Government. I think it has been abolished by the war--and that its abolition is the consequence of the war, carried on between the United States and the belligerent authorities--known as the Confederate States. The result of the war has been the destruction of slavery.

It is true, that the President of the United States, by a proclamation, issued as a war measure, on the 1st day of January, 1863, declared that slavery was thenceforward abolished. But that proclamation, being a mere declaration, did not abolish it. Something more was necessary. Before the issuance of this proclamation, the President, in September, 1862, had issued another proclamation, calling upon the people of the Seceded States to lay down their arms, and return to their allegiance to the Government of the United States--assuring them, that if they would do so, they would be protected in all their rights to person and property, including slaves, guaranteed to them by the Constitution; but warning them, if they did not do so, he would, on the first day of January, 1863, declare, by proclamation, that all slaves in the insurrectionary States should be free. This proclamation was derided--the warning was disregarded--the insurrection continued--and the war was carried on until the armies of the United States entered into every State, and compelled the surrender of all the forces arrayed against them—and thus carried into execution the proclamation of emancipation.

Hence, as a fact, slavery has not been abolished by the sole act of the United States—but its abolition has been produced by the joint action of the Government, and the people of the Southern States. The Southern States seceded—attempted to withdraw from the Union—and a war ensued.—During the war, the President warned them, if they would not discontinue the war, and return to their allegiance, their slaves would be emancipated. They declined the proposition, and continued the war, until they were overcome, and slavery was destroyed. How has it been destroyed? Unquestionably, its destruction has been produced by the war, and is the consequence of the war which was carried on between the two sections, in which the abolition of slavery become one of the issues involved and decided.

I, therefore, oppose the preamble, because it asserts as a fact, what I do believe is historically untrue, and because it can have no other tendency or effect, than to impair the usefulness of the section to which it is proposed as an amendment. It would create useless discussions, North and South, and would prejudice hereafter the condition of this State, by ceaseless wrangling over an immaterial issue, which should be left to the historian—and which this Convention is not called on to determine—and should not therefore undertake to decide. If the fact be, as all admit, that slavery has been destroyed, then we should deal with that fact in a practical way, and for practical purposes, and not impair the usefulness of our action, by the assertion of things as absolutely true, which some assert and others deny—and which, whether true or not, can make no practical difference in our action.

I, therefore, without pretending to argue the question, will be compelled to cast my vote against the substitute offered by the gentleman from Lafayette

Mr. Jarnagin, of Noxubee:—Mr. President: I agree in part with the last gentleman, and do not rise for the purpose of making a speech or entering into a debate upon this subject—a thing I do not expect to do, in regard to any matter, during the sitting of this Convention.

We are all satisfied that slavery is abolished. It has been abolished by some power, and I think it nothing but right to inquire into it, and we can certainly come to some conclusion how it has been abolished in Mississippi. It surely has not been abolished by the unrestrained action of this State, as a voluntary act. This system has in some manner, been forced upon the State, and I, as a delegate upon this floor, wish to see this Convention assert, if we can arrive at it, how it is that we are willing to declare that slavery shall not hereafter exist in the State of Mississippi, for certainly in the view and opinion of the civilized world it will be well known that this was not a voluntary act on the part of the State of Mississippi. If we had had no war, there was no compulsion, force or power the world knows, so far as this State is known to the world, that could have obliged us to take this step, and there would not have been a delegate upon this floor, that would have said: "Abolish slavery in the State of Mississippi." I, for one, am willing to concede and recognize the fact that slavery is abolished in this State. I am not here to advocate slavery among us, or to plead for its restoration; but I think it due to our constitutents, that in our constitutional amendments upon this subject, we should set forth distinctly how slavery was abolished. I believe it was abolished by the proclamation of the President of the United States and the fortunes of war, and what possible harm can there be in setting forth that fact? I am opposed to the naked fact of the abolition of slavery going forth to the world as the action of this Convention, and I am in favor of stating the facts and setting forth the condition in which we were placed, and which has changed our views in regard to this thing, causing us to accept this alternative.

Mr. Barr, of Lafayette—Mr. President:—The question has been raised by the delegate from Hinds, as to whether the statement that slavery has been abolished by the action of the Government of the United States, is in point of fact true. Now, sir, each delegate in this house has taken an oath that he will abide by and faithfully support the acts of Congress and the proclamations of the President of the United States, in reference to the emancipation of slaves, and each voter in the State of Mississippi, by whose authority we are here, was required to take that oath also. When the Federal Government asked us to take this oath that we will abide by and faithfully support the acts of Congress, and the proclamations of the President of the United States in reference to the emancipation of slaves, what proposition did the Government submit to us? It submitted to us this proposition: That the laws of Congress and the proclamations of the President of the United States in reference to the emancipation of slaves constitute the authority of the Government, by virtue of which, and in pursuance of which slavery has been abolished and abrogated. The Government of the United States in making this proposition to us required us to accede to the proposition as plainly admitted, as plainly, if you please, dictated to us, that by its official authority, the Government of the United States has abolished slavery. We know that the laws of Congress and the proclamation of the President of the United States in reference to the emancipation of slaves, declared the slaves of the State of Mississippi to be free. I have taken the oath to abide by and faithfully support these laws of the Congress and the proclamations of the President of the United States. I stand to that proposition; I shake hands with the Federal Government in this way. I came here to stand to that proposition, and I propose to stand by it in the Constitution.—I propose, sir, to put the language in the Constitution, that I have agreed under oath that I will stand by. I ask the gentleman from Hinds, if there is any escape from the proposition? Does not the Government itself admit that by its authority, by the authority of the laws of Congress, by the authority of the President of the United States, slavery has been abolished? Does not the Government take upon itself the responsibility, the credit and the honor, if any there be in abrogating and abolishing slavery in the State of Mississippi? Is it not true, then, in point of fact, that the proclamations of the President of the United States, together with the laws of Congress on this subject are the authority of the Government of the United States by which slavery has been abolished, and is it not consequently true that by the action of the Government of the United States, slavery has been abolished in the State of Mississippi? No other hypothesis is true. The ordinance reported by the committee says, without any explanation, that neither slavery nor involuntary servitude shall hereafter exist.—What do we mean by saying "shall hereafter exist?" The implication, and the only inference is, that up this point of time it does exist, and that in point of fact, is untrue. Let me illustrate this thing. Suppose the Convention should pass an ordinance saying that hereafter the Sabbath should not be observed as a day of rest. What is the implication and the inference? That up to that time—up to the very moment when the ordinance was passed—the Sabbath had been observed as a day of rest. Is it not also true here? Is it not stated by implication as strongly as if it had been stated expressly in words, that up to this time slavery does in fact exist? Do we not, therefore, ignore the action of the Government of the United States, and we do not therefore say that what we have sworn, is not, in point of fact true? I assert that my proposition states the truth of the subject, whereas the ordinance of the committee does not state the whole truth. I have heard gentlemen say, it is not prudent to always tell the truth. I agree to it with this qualification: if you are under no obligation to speak, if you are not bound to speak, if you are not called upon to speak, then you are not under any obligation to speak the truth; but if you are called upon to speak as we are bound to speak on this subject, then I hold that we are bound to speak the whole truth, and that a *suppressio veri* is tatamount to a *suggestio falsi*. Having come here to speak on this subject, we are bound to speak the truth, the whole truth, and nothing but the truth. I propose to state it here, relying upon the justice and magnanimity of the powers that be in Washington, that the truth will give no offense. How can the thing give offense? How can the statement of the whole truth be prejudicial to the objects we desire to accomplish? Is it not a fact that the whole world knows that the Government of the United States has proclaimed to the civilized world upon the face of every Northern newspaper—is it not a fact, patent upon the Freedmen's Bureau—is it not a fact patent on the whole action of the Government of the United States, that the Government of the United States claims the responsibility and honor, and credit, and in their language, "the immortality of having wiped from this great and free country the stain of slavery."

I somewhere read a document, issued, I believe by a delegate from this county, in which he undertakes to tell the people of this county—if I am quoting correctly—that the President of the United States suggested to him and another gentleman, that it was proper that the State of Mississippi should recognize in her Constitution, that slavery was gone. How then can the statement which the President suggested should be made in the Constitution of this State, be prejudicial to us, when this Constitution goes there? Did not the Governor, when he issued the proclamation calling us here, tell us that slavery was gone, and by the action of the Federal Government? Does that prejudice us? In view of the truth—in view of what is due to us as men—we should state the truth, and the whole truth on this subject.

MR. POTTER, of Hinds.—Mr. President:—I am sorry to

see sir, that important proposition, suggested for the consideration of this body, in relation to this subject, meet with a sort of whispered objection. If the delegates of this State, sitting here in their sovereign capacity, shall choose to declare what they believe to be the truth, or to act according to the dictates of their deliberate judgement for the good of the people of the State, and the country, they should not be thus softly silenced, with a whisper, that their sentiment may offend somebody out of the State; that it may prejudice their interests somewhere. I had hoped, sir, that every member of this Convention came here with the view of acting as this people acted in days of old—for the good of the people, and the good of the country—regardless of considerations, whether parties outside might take exceptions to our proceedings. There is a right course sir, and there is a wrong course; and in my judgement, the right course is to act and do as one thinks right, regarding the position of this as a State in the Union. I am, therefore, in favor of independent action on this subject. I am in favor of exercising to the fullest extent, that ancient liberty of speech, which prevailed when those stars and stripes floated over us and guaranteed a freedom which is older than the Constitution, and secured by it.

Now, sirs, what is the condition of affairs here? Gentlemen say, that slavery is dead. Well, I say that practically, it is dead—the fact, however, being yet a subject for legal decision. But if it be dead, how was it destroyed? Has there been any Convention of the State of Mississippi in session, during the last four years. which has abolished it? No, that is not the case. Has any authority competent to bind the State of Mississippi by any ordinance or action, abolished it? No, sir! Is it by any action of the people of Mississippi? That cannot be. Who claims, then sir, to have abolished it? Is there any such claim? I think, sir, that as to the historical question, there can be no manner of dispute on this subject. Members of this house recollect that Gen. Hunter, of the United States service, when commanding on the coast of Georgia, issued his proclamation, asserting, among other things, that slavery and martial law were inconsistent with each other; a paradox in my estimation. Asserting that, however, he went on to declare that slavery was abolished within his military department. On the 19th, of May, 1862, President Lincoln issued his proclamation, correcting that little proceeding of Gen. Hunter's, but the President in his proclamation, reserved the right thereafter, to declare whether the exercise of such a power was a necessity indispensable to the maintenance of the Government. Now when he came to issue that emancipation proclamation, on Sept. 22d, 1862, he commenced the document with the following preamble: "I, Abraham Lincoln, President," &c., "commanding" &c., "hereby proclaim and declare that hereafter, as heretofore, the war will be prosecuted with the object of practically restoring the Constitutional relations between the United States, and each of the States and people thereof, in which States the relation is or may be suspended or disturbed." He then goes on to declare that unless the people, by the first of January ensuing, shall establish such relations, he will issue a proclamation abolishing slavery in the States and districts then in insurrection. Accordingly, on the first day of January, 1863, he did issue the threatened proclamation. He goes on to recite the previous proclamation, and declares that the insurrectionary States and districts, excepting certain specified parishes in Louisiana, and excepting therefrom any slaves in the State of West Virginia, in certain counties of Virginia, occupied, I suppose, by Federal forces at the time—were free; and sir, he declares this to be "an act of justice, warranted by the Constitution, upon military necessity." I think, sir, in view of these declarations of the President, and what has been insisted upon by the Federal Government since, in relation to this proclamation, there can be no doubt that the Government, of the United States has asserted, and now assumes that the slaves in some States, and in this, had been freed by virtue of the proclamation of the President. How is it that the General Government is now acting upon this matter? Is it not, sir, by force of the acts of Congress enacted before the military occupation of this State by the Federal forces? Was not this Freedmen's Bureau put in operation before that time, the jurisdiction of which extends to all persons of color, in the State of Mississippi?

There you have the action of the Federal Government on the subject, and one provision of the act of Congress requires the military authorities, to yield such aid as may be necessary, on requirement of the proper officers of that Bureau.

If then, sir, it be true, as gentlemen say, that slavery is dead here, in the State of Mississippi, I think no man can deny, as a historical fact, that that extinction has been produced by the action of the Federal authorities.

The only point is this—whether that action is legal—

whether the courts of the country will sustain it. President Lincoln regarded the matter in this light. In his annual message succeeding the issue of the second proclamation, he said the courts of the country might overturn all his action upon this subject; but he throughout the whole course of his administration, by his public declaration and official acts, held that this population was free.

Let me call the attention of the Convention to certain acts of Congress, on this subject. An act to define and punish treason, declares that slaves belonging to every traitor in the South, he being duly convicted, shall be free. It further declares that slaves taken or captured, in any fortified places occupied by the military power in rebellion, shall be free.—It declares that slaves permitted to labor on any public work in the South, or engaged on any ships of the insurrectionary power; or in its arsenals, or in any manner aiding in the military operations of the power opposed to the Federal Government, shall be free.

Well, sir, when gentlemen who conceived themselves to be liable to the pains and penalties of treason, as declared by the act of Congress I have referred to, applied for amnesty and pardon under the proclamation of his Excellency, the President, what did they do? Was any one sworn to recognize the fact that slavery is "rubbed out by the friction of war"—to use semi-official words? Were they required to swear—in the language of my friend—that the "thing is dead by a sort of mutual friction, or crushing out," caused by the rush of contending, opposing hosts?

No sir! They were reqnired to abide by, and faithfully support the Proclamation of President Lincoln, declaring these people free.

They were required to abide by, and pledged to support the acts of Congress for the emancipation of slaves—and what sort of a pardon do they get sir? They get full amnesty with restoration of estates—excepting property in slaves. Now, sir, how does the government look at it?—It looks upon it in this light—that it has accomplished the abolition of slavery in the South, by, as President Lincoln declared, a military necessity—to uphold and sustain the Government.

What sort of policy does the President require us to pursue in the estimation of certain gentlemen? Why sir, it is to admit the fact in relation to this subject. If slavery be abolished here in Mississippi—and if the truth be that it was abolished by Federal action—the gentlemen comes forward and blink that fact, refuse to acknowledge what they assert the President requires of them, and cooly adopt an amendment in our organic law, abolishing an institution of the State, which existed before the days of our sovereign capacity—an institution regarded as the foundation of our prosperity; and we are to do it now for State reasons, and not because of outside reasons, or outside pressure, but purely as a matter of State policy.

This Convention, professing to act as a free Convention of free people, proposes to declare it a matter of policy; in other words, it proposes to declare that the prosperity of the State does not depend upon this great source heretofore of its productive industry and prosperity. Although as I have said, this is perhaps the public declaration, we know there is something behind it. And I ask gentlemen who are disposed to regard such suggestions from abroad, and to take suggestions as they come from Washington, to admit frankly the true reasons for their action. It has been declared over and over again, by the whole North, that they had wiped out slavery here in the South. If that is the fact, act on your own policy gentlemen, and frankly admit it.—If that is not the fact, then let it alone. I beg of the gentlemen of this Convention to consider what is due to the character of the State, and what is due to themselves. Do we adopt this as a measure of public policy, best adapted to promote the material prosperity of the State of Mississippi? Do we consider it necessary as a matter of policy, and for the prosperity of the State, to change our labor system?—If we do, let us frankly declare that; but sir, in any event, let it appear why it is that this amendment was adopted.

Mr. Jarnagin, of Noxubee, moved to postpone the further consideration of the report until to-morrow morning, 9 o'clock.

Which was lost.

Pending the further consideration of the substitute,

On motion of Mr. Barr, the Convention adjourned until 4 o'clock, P. M.

FOUR O'CLOCK, P. M.

The Convention met pursuant to adjournment.

The substitute offered by Mr. Barr, for the second section of the Report of Committee, was then taken up; when

Mr. Hall, of Covington, offered the following amendment:

Slavery having been abolished in consequence of the war, resulting from an Ordinance of Secession, adopted 9th January 1861 ; therefore,

It is hereby ordained by the people of the State of Mississippi in Convention assembled, That neither slavery nor involuntary servitude, otherwise than in the punishment of crimes, whereof the party shall have been duly convicted, shall hereafter exist in this State ; and the Legislature at its next session, and thereafter, as the public welfare may require, shall provide by law for the protection and security of the person and property of the freedmen of the State, and guard them and the State against any evils that may arise from their sudden emancipation.

Mr. Cooper, of Rankin, moved to lay the substitute and amendment upon the table.

Mr. Barr, of Lafayette, asked that the substitute and amendment be voted upon separately : which not being entertained by the Chair,

The question was taken upon the motion of Mr. Cooper, and decided in the affirmative, by yeas and nays, called for by Messrs. Barr, Compton and Lewers, as follows, to-wit :

YEAS.—Mr. President, Messrs. Byars, Bond, Blackwell, Billups, Binford, Brandon, Cason, Cooper, of Rankin, Carter, Crawford, Cummings, Duncan, Farley, Gaither, Gulley, Griffin, Hemingway, Hamm, Houston, Harrison, Horne, Hill, Jones, Kennedy, Lindsey, Loper, Lewis, Martin, of Adams, Montgomery, Mayson, Morphis, Niles, Owens, of Tunica; Owen, of Scott, Pressley, Peyton, Rives, Rushing, Sanders, of Attala, Simonton, Sparkman, Stanley, Wallace, White, Wooley, Webb, Wylie, Wier, Yerger.—51.

NAYS.—Messrs. Barr, Bailey, Brown, Compton, Cooper, of Panola, Crum, Dowd, Franklin, Goode, Gowan, Hurst, Heard, Hall, Hudson, Jarnagin, Johnson, of Mashall, Johnson, of Smith, King, Lewers, Lambdin, Marshall, Martin, of Sunflower, Maury, Malone, Matthews, Potter, Phipps, Quinn, Reynolds, Reid, Sanders, of DeSoto, Swett, Stone, Slover, Trotter, Tate, Wall, Watson, Wade, Woodward, Wilson.—41.

Mr. Johnson, of Smith, offered the following, as a substitute for section two :

"Amend, by striking out section two, and insert the following :

WHEREAS, African slavery in the State of Mississippi, has been abolished by the power and authority of the United States Government, and the loyal people of the State having been sworn to abide by, and faithfully support the proclamations of the President of the United States, and the laws of Congress, in reference to the emancipation of slaves ; and the people of the State of Mississippi, being desirous of acting in good faith ; therefore,

It is ordained and declared by the loyal people of the State of Mississippi in Convention assembled, That African slavery shall never be restored in the State of Mississippi, by State action ; and involuntaty servitude shall only exist, as punishment for crimes or misdemeanors, whereof the party has been duly convicted ; and the Legislature at its next session, and thereafter as the public welfare may require, shall provide by law for the protection and security of the person and property of the negroes and mulattoes of the State, and guard them and the State against any evils that may arise from their emancipation.

Mr. Harrison moved to lay the substitute upon the table,

Which was decided in the affirmative, by yeas and nays, called for by Messrs. Potter, Barr and Phipps, as follows :

YEAS.—Mr. President, Messrs. Byars, Bond, Blackwell, Billips, Binford, Brandon, Cason, Cooper, of Rankin, Carter, Crawford, Cummings, Crum, Duncan, Dorris, Davis, Dowd, Farley, Gaither, Gulley, Griffin, Hemingway, Hall, Hamm, Houston, Harrison, Horne, Hill, Jones, Johnston, of Hinds, Kennedy, Lindsey, Loper, Lewis, Marshall, Martin of Adams, Martin of Sunflower, Montgomery, Mayson, Morphis, Niles, Owens, of Tunica, Owen, of Scott, Pressley, Peyton, Rives, Rushing, Sanders, of Attala, Simonton, Sparkman, Stanley, Slover, Wallace, White, Wooley, Webb, Watson, Wade, Wylie, Wier, Yerger.—61.

NAYS.—Messrs. Barr, Bailey, Brown, Compton, Cooper, of Panola, Franklin, Goode, Gowan, Hurst, Heard, Hudson, Jarnagin, Johnson, of Marshall, Johnson, of Smith, King, Lewers Lambdin, Maury, Malone, Matthews, Potter, Phipps, Quinn, Reynolds, Reid, Sanders, of DeSoto, Swett, Stone, Trotter, Tate, Wall, Woodward, Wilson.—33.

Mr. Jarnagin offered the following as a substitute for section two of the report of the Committee ;

The State of Mississippi, fully recognizing the laws of Congress, and the proclamation of the President of the United States, in reference to the emancipation of slaves, and hereby ordains : That neither slavery nor involuntary servitude, otherwise than in the punishment of crimes, whereof the party shall have been duly convicted, shall hereafter exist in this State; and the Legislature at its next session, and thereafter, as the public welfare may require, shall provide by law for the protection and security of the person and property of the freedmen of the State, and guard them and the State, against any evils that may arise from their sudden emancipation:

Which, on motion of Mr. Harrison, was laid upon the table.

Mr. Potter, of Hinds, offered the following as a substitute for section second:

WHEREAS, Certain authorities of the United States, do claim, that, by force of certain proclamations of the President, and of certain acts of the Congress of the United States, all colored persons, heretofore held as slaves, in this State, are, of right, free; which said claim is now enforced by military power, against children of tender years, and other innocent persons, as well as against those implicated in the recent rebellion; and

WHEREAS, The Government of the United States has, by acts and resolutions of Congress, and otherwise, acknowledged the obligation and duty resting upon it to make compensation to proper parties, for their slaves, emancipated by its authority; but has neither paid, nor promised, to any party entitled as aforesaid, such just compensation, as by the Constitution it is bound to render; and whereas, the constitutional validity and operative effect of said a ledged acts and proclamations are questions proper for the decision by the appropriate judicial tribunals; and

WHEREAS, The good people of this State, reserving to parties entitled, full power to assert in the proper forms, any of their rights and claims in the premises, do at present submit to the said claim, asserted and enforced by said authorities: and in so submitting, do now treat said portion of said colored population as if free, and will continue so to regard and treat them until the said alledged acts and proclamations are annulled by the proper tribunals, or are otherwise lawfully vacated.

Be it further ordained, That the Legislature of this State be, and is hereby authorized and required at its next ensuing session, and from time to time, as may be proper, until such time as said alledged acts and proclamations are lawfully annulled or vacated as aforesaid, to enact all needful and proper laws, rules and regulations, to secure to said colored population, protection and just'ce ; and to regulate their labor, secure industry and sobriety, prevent vagrancy, idleness, pauperism and crime among them ; and promote the peace, order and prosperity of the State.

Mr. Potter, of Hinds—Mr. President: In arising to present my views, and to urge the adoption of this proposition, I trust that I do so with a full sense of the obligation and responsibility cast upon me as a delegate to this Convention. I desire to express my views plainly and freely, as I believe the adoption of them would be for the best interest of the State; and, in doing so, I shall regard, not the things that may be approved outside, but the great good of the State and the country. Before, sir, I proceed to discuss directly the propositions contained in this substitute, I wish to examine a little the condition of the State after four years of disastrous war.

If we are to judge from expressions used by delegates, by official personages, and by citizens in the community, it is plain that a great contrariety of opinion exists as to the *legal* condition of Mississippi at this time. I, sir, adopt the public position of the President of the United States, as avowed in his published official documents, and addressed to this people for their information regarding the true condition of Mississippi. The condition therein indicated is, that our State to-day, notwithstanding the acts of secession, notwithstanding the war of rebellion, is still a State of the Union, with all her rights and privileges under the Constitution, precisely as she stood in the day when she was admitted in the year 1817. She stands, under that Constitution, the co-equal of every other State in this American Union. So regarding her, and feeling myself under special, solemn obligations to regard and support the Constitution of the United States—that obligation being higher and above all others—I am not disposed to submit to any conditions imposed upon this State as conditions to the admission of her Senators and Representatives into the National Congress, that are not authorized by the National Constitution. I am sworn to support that Constitution, and will not be a party to any action pursued in submission to dictation, from any source whatever, imposing conditions precedent to such admission. I cannot regard it as lawful that our Senators and Representatives shall be first required to take a special oath contained in the acts of Congress—a sort of test oath of loyalty—the sum and substance of which may be stated in this wise: that no man can present himself there, as a

Representative of a State, who has even smelled the recent rebellion. I say, I cannot recognize the constitutional right of Congress, or any other body, to impose that oath upon the delegation that Mississippi may choose to send to the Congress of the United States. I cannot recognize any authority in the General Government, or any of its departments, to impose upon the people of Mississippi a condition that she shall present herself there with any special or particular clause in her State Constitution, before her delegates shall be permitted to take their seats.

As I understand the position of the Président of the United States, he takes precisely this view of the subject. He holds that Mississippi is a State in the Union, under the Constitution, and entitled to the full enjoyment of its benefits and guarantees. In his official proclamation for re-organization and the re-establishment of civil government here, he has affirmed these truths, and has conceded our right of representation in the Congress of the United States. He has prescribed no terms or conditions such as seem to be assumed by gentlemen in speeches out of the house, and by their votes here, regarding this slavery question. I state his position to be, that he is willing to admit our delegation with the Constitution just as it stands. I know there has been a contrariety of opinion on this subject, which has arisen, in no slight degree, from incorrect reports of the address of the Federal Executive in his interview with a certain delegation from the State of South Carolina. I hold in my hand a report of those proceedings, contained in the "National Intelligencer," of the 27th of June, and will read an extract to show you his exact position:

"*Delegate*—Can our admission or rejection depend upon our adopting, or not adopting, what you think right?"

"*President*—No, I only *advise*—I would have you understand me more correctly.

"*Delegate*—Then is this a *sine qua non* to our being restored?"

"*President*—You must see that the friction of the rebellion has rubbed slavery out, and I assume it would be *better* for the people, through their Convention, to make it legally and constitutionally dead. The people, in coming forward, would better recognize that fact.

I take it, sir, that this report contains a correct statement of what passed at the interview between the President and the South Carolina delegation; and the tenor of his language is purely advisory. Another portion of this

5

report represents the President as advising the delegation to adopt a free State Constitution, and the proposed amendment to the Federal Constitution abolishing slavery wherever the jurisdiction of the United States extends. The The President says: "When you have done all this—when you have adopted a free State Constitution, and the proposed amendment to the Federal Constitution, it remains for the Government to admit you, or leave you out in the cold, to use a common expression." He neither promises one thing or the other, and gives us no hope, even though we do adopt all these amendments. All we can say, then, as to the position of the Executive, on this subject, is that he *thinks* it would be *better* to do this; but he imposes upon us no condition precedent. Such a condition, imposed by him, would be in direct contradiction to his public declarations. He asserts that the people have, from the beginning, possessed the right to determine who shall constitute the voting population of the State. After making this declaration, he cannot interpose against a State, and change the law relative to voters. How contradictory would it be for him to attempt to dictate to the people of a State what particular sort of a Constitution they should have—to dictate to them that their delegates should not be admitted to Congress, unless the people of the State, in Convention assembled, should adopt a clause forever prohibiting slavery in that State! No, sir! The position of the President is exactly the reverse of that; and the inevitable legal conclusion from his proclamation for the re-organization of this State, is, that he is in favor of the admission of her senators and representatives, if qualified under the Constitution, without any other terms or restrictions being imposed upon them.

I say, further, that were we inclined to submit to dictation from any quarter, I should insist that the dictation should be plain and explicit beyond the possibility of misapprehension. I say, sir, if the President has any purpose to exact of this people—the insertion of a free clause in her Constitution—it is his duty so to declare publicly, in a formal document addressed to them for their information. It will not do for it to be given out that the President desires this and desires that, when he is dealing with the people of a sovereign State. I cannot consent to receive Executive *hints* on this subject. I wish the thing plain and outspoken on his part, that I, in my capacity of a delegate of the people, may be able to respond in like manner, by way of answer.

I will not receive hints even from him in a matter so important to the interest of the States. It does not become the delegates of a great people to listen to *hints merely*, from *any* quarter. I can say, sir, if the President of the United States is ashamed publicly to declare his wishes, then I am ashamed to consent to any wishes he may convey to me by way of *hint* or *inuendo*. Let him take *his* share of the responsibity, and I take *mine*, as a representative of the people; and when gentlemen talk me about the wishes of the Executive, let them show them to me in a public document issuing from him and addressed to us as a people; for I can believe none not thus coming from him.

Inasmuch as the President of the United States has not officially notified this people that he insists upon this amendment as a condition to the admission of their delegation, I must say that no such desire exists on his part. He will insist on no such condition. I say it from the fact that he has not notified the people that he would so insist. Can I be guilty of injustice so monstrous against the Executive of a great people as to assume that he will declare his wishes by private telegraphic dispatches or hints to one gentleman, and inuendoes to another, that may or not reach any other citizens of the State; and will then hold this people liable if they fail to come up to proposals and conditions that he keeps secret in his breast—conditions of the existence of which they are in no manner or form publicly notified? I cannot assume it. I cannot do the National Executive that great injustice. I therefore say, in view of the circumstances, that the President exacts no such condition from this people. I say further, sir, that, although he may suggest by way of advice to certain individuals, that it is politic to adopt a free State Constitution—politic to adopt the amendment to the Federal Constitution which would give to the Congress of the United States jurisdiction to legislate over the freed population, in spite of the desire of the people of the State —I cannot say, I cannot assume, that the President of the United States even advises this to be done. He has not notified this people in any official form whatever that such is his advice. No, sir, the Executive of the United States knows better what becomes himself, as an individual, and as the great Executive officer of the nation—better what is due to a great State of the Union—than to assume any such function as adviser to a sovereign State. I say then, that in my view, so far as regards the National

Executive, we stand entirely unrestrained—we stand entirely without advice in this particular. His purpose in issuing the Proclamation is, that the people of this State may enjoy speedily the benefits of a republican government, and the blessings of liberty, regulated by law. How does he propose this shall be done? He proposes to appoint a Provisional Governor, and that Governor has to take the initiative. In his interview with the South Carolina delegation, he says the Executive can only do this, leaving it for the people to carry out for themselves the objects had in view. The Provisional Governor can issue a call for the Convention, can see that the delegates are properly qualified according to the terms of the Proclamation, and then the functions of the Provisional Governor, or of the Executive, as connected with them, cease. It is then for the delegates of the people to go on, and, by new provisions, organize civil government in the State of Mississippi.

It is one of the great purposes of the proclamation to re-establish here in the State the functions of civil government, which have been suspended during the recent war of rebellion. What other object has the Executive in view, as indicated by his proclamation? It is, that steps should be taken by the people of Mississippi for their due representation in Congress, according to the Constitution of the United States. These are all the purposes indicated by the President with regard to this matter; and now I desire, gentlemen of this Convention, to bear in mind this especially: that there is no suggestion from any quarter, or any threat, or any hint on the part of anybody, that the Government which may be organized through the labors of this Convention, and put in operation for the State of Mississippi, will be overturned or suspended in its operations, whether we adopt a Free State Constitution or not. I say, I have yet to hear the first intimation of a threat from any quarter, that the Government which we shall establish and organize here, will be interfered with in any manner whatever. That is not the danger which gentlemen on the other side suggest to the apprehensions of delegates. They do not venture to say the Executive will overturn a State Government, established in accordance with his own invitation, through the agency of his own Provisional Governor, and in accordance with the regulations he has prescribed. There is no suggestion of that kind. As I said before, there is no danger that the Executive will interfere in regard to the admission of our delegation into Congress. That is not the danger. What is the danger? I ask gentlemen to consider, and not mingle one thing with another; nor confound the innocent Executive with any who may become guilty parties in this respect. I admit, sir, there is a party at the North, and I think it probable there is a large party in the Federal Congress, who will insist upon imposing on the State of Mississippi, through her delegation, illegal restrictions. They will say: your delegation shall not be admitted into Congress until the people of the State have complied with certain conditions. One of these conditions is, that they shall have adopted what is called the Free State Constitution. Another of these conditions is, that the population lately occupying the position of slaves in this State, shall be raised, by State action, and that immediately, to the position and dignity of equals with the white population. There the danger lies. And let me warn gentlemen, that in adopting this Free-State clause with a view to secure the admission of our delegates into Congress, there is exceeding danger that we yield too much, because they do not yield enough. I say, sir—paradoxical as it may seem—they yield too much, because they do not yield enough. They yield so much as will encourage, as will incite, as will prompt and invite to further aggression; but they do not yield enough—their sacrifices are not large enough to appease the appetites of those to whom they offer them.

So soon as you are prepared to come up to the standard; so soon as you will make in this State a perfect equality between the two races, I will guarantee that your delegation will be received; its admission will be hailed by the parties whom you seek to propitiate; but I cannot guarantee that it will be hailed by any national, constitutional, conservative man, who may happen to be in the councils of the nation. It seems to me, Mr. President, that gentlemen, in presenting this matter, lose sight altogether of human nature, and especially of depraved political human nature, so to speak.

There is a controlling party in Congress at this time that sees, as we see, that its political existence may depend upon the rejection of the delegations from these Southern States; and it is for delegates to consider the probability whether these gentlemen will consent to this species of political suicide—the extinction of their party, by permitting the admission of these delegations. It is a great question of party with them—the continuance in power as a party; and, in our deliberations here, we should never lose sight of this and other facts connected with the subject. Whether that extreme party which insists upon free suffrage and perfect equality, now controls the legislation of Congress, I cannot tell; but I say this to gentlemen of the Convention, that if it possesses the majority, and insists upon the duty of the government to raise this population to equality with the white citizens of the State, then we may assume it as certain that our delegation will not be admitted. On the other hand, if we are in the majority—if the majority consists of men of just constitutional views on this subject—then we will be admitted under the terms of the Constitution, whether we have a free Constitution, or present ourselves as the members from Mississippi have presented themselves since the year 1832, upon this old Constitution. If the party in power desires to impose this condition of free suffrage upon us, we cannot avoid it by any submission short of that. If the party in power in Congress is a constitutional party—if it regards the right of the States to regulate their own domestic concerns in their own way—why, then, it will admit our delegation as in times of old. What, then, do we gain on the question of expediency, by the policy suggested by gentlemen on the other side? Can they give to this house any assurance whatever, that if we do as they propose, our delegation will be received? No, sir!

But, they say, if this be done, the President will probably remove from our midst these bayonets! Well, Mr. President, I believe it is an historical fact, for something like a year, that a free State Constitution has existed over the State of Tennessee. They there did, a year ago, what it is now said the President desires we should do; and I ask gentlemen to inform me how it is, and why it is, that the military forces of the United States still exercise sway in that State? If it is probable, if it is to be hoped even, that the President will remove them from Mississippi when we adopt this proposed amendment, why is it that he has not, within this past year, removed those troops from the soil of Tennessee?

I had an order which I have not at hand now, issued by Major General Slocum, on the 3d of August, which recites a recent order issued by the controlling officer of the Freedman's Bureau at Washington, which order was approved by the President of the United States in the month of June last. According to the recital of this order, (in order No. 10,) by General Slocum, it directs that the officers of the Freedman's Bureau, and the military officers of the United States, shall so act and conduct themselves in relation to this negro question, as to convince everybody not only that the negro is free, but of the necessity of adopting such legislation as will prevent further interference of the military authorities on behalf of the negro. That order, according to the statement of Gen. Slocum, was approved by President Johnson himself in the month of June last. I wish the house particularly to bear that in mind. Here, then, is an order, and its direction to the military authorities is, that they are so to conduct themselves as to convince the people down here of the absolute necessity of adopting such laws as are considered necessary and proper in relation to this matter—not such laws as this people, acting as a free people in their legislative capacity, or in their sovereign capacity, would freely adopt; but such laws as the Federal authorities may regard in the premises. In the order there is this further declaration, that so soon as the courts of Mississippi recognize that the black man has the rights of the white man, then the military will not interfere. I regard it an important matter, and I take occasion to say now that I will look up the order and have it read to the Convention. Now, sir, here is the public position of the President of the United States—a bureau order approved by him; and it requires more than is proposed in the ordinance reported by the committee—more than they are required to grant. Gentlemen have not come up to the requirements of the President's order in this respect. Then, sir, if we regard this order as an indication of the purpose of the National Executive, I ask how can gentlemen assume—how can they flatter themselves, that the proposed ordinance will prove satisfactory; or that its adoption will in some way result in the removal of the armed forces from the State? Until you recognize the negro as your equal in the courts of justice, you cannot hope it; until the act of Congress in relation to freedmen is repealed, we cannot expect the removal of these forces. It is known to the members of this Convention that wherever the officers of the Freedmen's Bureau go, there go the bayonets for their protection and the enforcement of their orders.

The act of Congress provides that this bureau shall be

continued for one year after peace is declared. Now, Mr. President, although it be true that the Executive authorities of the United States have declared to the nations of the earth that peace exists here in Mississippi—that peace exists through all this Southern country—that peace exists through all the United States—they have not declared that fact to us in such a way that we can realize or appreciate it. We are the only portion of the people on God's earth, sir, that have not been informed that peace exists throughout the United States. Military operations still go on here. although there is no clashing of arms. Our people are at peace, as they were in times of old. When will come that time when peace shall be declared by the Federal authorities as existing in these States? I cannot say; but when that time does come—when the Executive chooses to declare that peace exists in Mississippi—then in one year from that day, under the express terms of the acts of Congress, the Freedmen's Bureau is to be continued in the State. I have heard it said by gentlemen—that they understand the President has promised that as soon as we got right in certain particulars, this bureau shall be removed; but the act of Congress will interpose and prevent what he might desire in this respect. Unless he can procure the repeal of that act, he cannot carry out any pledges he may make in this particular.

Looking to the acts of Congress, and to the executive orders for the employment of the military to pursuade the people to the enactment of supposed proper laws, there is no present prospect of the speedy removal of the military forces from this State. I ask then, Mr. President, that gentlemen will explain to us what is sought—what is expected to be gained by pursuing a course of supposed subserviency to Executive views in regard to this matter? Is there a reasonable prospect—is there a hope even, that our delegation to Congress will be admitted any sooner if we adopt the proposed amendment to the Constitution? Can gentlemen give us any reason to expect the military forces will be removed one moment sooner if we pursue that policy? If the gentleman can give no reasonable ground for assurance in either of these particulars, what can they offer to induce us, as delegates from an independent people, to pursue a course of subserviency, to gratify the wishes of any party or person, outside the State of Mississippi? Until they do this, their plea of expediency utterly fails them.

They come to me and say, "your views of the subject is

legal—it commends itself to the reason of every one—it is constitutional—it is just—but you have outlived the Constitution; you have outlived the palmy days of the Republic, are are a sort of an old fogy waking up in a new era of new ideas. You insist on these terms and conditions for your State, which would have been just and proper, and have met the approbation of everybody in the days of old, before the rebellion: but they are now entirely out of order." Well, Mr. President, it is my sworn duty, to regard this slavery matter, and do right and justice concerning it; but, sir, it is also my duty, my sworn duty, to maintain the Constitution of the country. It is my sworn duty to vindicate and maintain the liberties of the State, and of its people.

Some gentlemen with whom I have conversed, who have taken an oath that is not very popular in the State, but very common, consider that the party taking it becomes bound to abide by and faithfully support the acts and proclamations passed during the war with regard to the emancipation of slavery; and they think that is the whole of the oath they take; but, sir, it is only a part of it—according to my legal apprehension, the minor part. We are solemnly bound "to support, protect and defend the Constitution of the United States, and the union of States thereunder."—Now, sir, you may raise a suit regarding the validity of the Federal Constitution, and bring in the weight of law and musty law records, and law rolls; you may employ any amount of logic and ingenuity, but you can get from no legal tribunal the declaration that your Constitution is illegal or void; but, sir, if you start a suit which involves the validity of these laws and proclamations for the emancipation of slaves, you may, or you may not, as the mind of the court may be constituted, procure a declaration that they are unconstitutional.

Now, to show which is the superior part of the oath we have taken, let me suppose the Supreme Court of the United States declares that the proclamation, and laws referred to, are null and void, as repugnant to the courts of the United States. I ask any gentleman on this floor, to say, if he can, that after the Supreme Court had thus annulled these laws and proclamations he would still support them, against his oath to support the constitution? No, if the court of the United States should declare these things void as against the Constitution, you could no longer abide by and support them: for the oath to protect that Constitution would still be of binding force. This shows, beyond dispute or cavil, which is the superior and paramount obligation contained in the complex oath that the people have been required to take. Let me offer another suggestion in regard to this oath—and I do it from what I have heard in conversation with a member of this house. Because he had taken this oath, he considered that he must vote for the free State amendment—that he must support this clause in the report of the committee. Let me say, in all candor, without intending to wound the feelings, or touch the sensibilities of any citizen attempting to support or abide by the amnesty proclamation, that he who votes for a free clause in the constitution on that ground, gainsays the validity of the laws and proclamations he has sworn to uphold. Why vote for this constitutional amendment? It is because slavery is not abolished? The proclamation you are sworn to abide by and support, declares that it is abolished. Do you assume that it is yet not abolished? Then you do not abide by the proclamation—you do not abide by its words, by its purpose, by its terms. You assume it is null; and therefore you go on, by your own will and in your own power, to vote the abolition of slavery; and when you return to your constituents, acting with that view, you cannot say, "I have abided by and faithfully supported the proclamation regarding emancipation;" but you can say, "I and my associates, representing the majority of the people of Mississippi, have abolished slavery." No, sir! A man who takes that oath is not bound to support such an ordinance as that proposed; nor to prop up either proclamation or laws, or do anything of the kind, that would raise a doubt in the minds of the people, whether those laws and proclamations are of any force or validity of themselves. I say then, sir, that legally every member is perfectly free to vote for or against the amendment, according to the dictates of his judgment as to what may be for the best interest of the State; and in taking either course he equally abides by the obligations he has come under in taking the amnesty oath.

He lets those laws and proclamations stand as they are, and abides by them and supports them in all their extended operation whatever that may be, for better or for worse. If we do thus abide by those laws and proclamations and continue to so do, so long as they are neither annulled or vacated by judicial proceedings or other lawful authority, do we not, in spirit and in truth, abide by our oaths? Until thus declared to the contrary, we propose to continue to treat them as valid, and to consider these colored people as if free. Do we not in that respect, sir, come up exactly to what gentlemen have proclamed were the wishes of the President? Recognizing the present condition of affairs, I propose to go on, and by solemn ordinance to authorize and require the Legislature of this State, at its next ensuing session, and from time to time, as it may deem necessary, until such time as the action of the Federal Government is lawfully vacated--to pass all needful and proper laws and regulations in regard to this population, to secure to them protection and justice ; and regulate their labor ; prevent idleness, pauperism and crime among them; and preserve the peace, and promote the general welfare. Does not the proposition I suggest cover the whole ground? all that can be asked or wished, and is it not done in perfect good faith?--Why, sir, what did the late President Lincoln declare on this subject? He admitted that the courts of the country might annul his emancipation proclamation and the acts of Congress passed in aid of it. The truth is, that these acts present great judicial questions, proper to be decided by the courts; and there is no possibility of evading a decision.—Well, there is just where I propose to leave the question.—We submit to the proposition that these slaves are free, for the present, and, perhaps, for all time to come, subject only to a determination, by the appropriate judicial tribunal, of the questions involved.

Suppose the Supreme Court of the United States should declare these acts and proclamations to be utter nullities and void, as repugnant to the Constitution, then, gentlemen, what have you done in vain here! Suppose, on the other hand, that the Supreme Court, as it is said will probably be the case, shall declare that those acts and proclamations were, under the circumstances, legal and obligatory, and that by force of them, slavery was abolished in this State. When the Supreme Court does that, it declares in a manner not to be denied, that the whole work of abolishing slavery in the State of Mississippi, was the work of the United States! It casts upon the United States the whole responsibility connected with this great question; and among those responsibilities, in my judgment, Mr. President, there is one of no small moment. That government having set free the negroes in this State, having cast loose in the State, a large population, among whom were thousands and tens of thousands of the aged, helpless and infirm, made paupers for somebody to support. In such case, every sentiment of justice, duty and honor, would dictate that the Federal Government should make adequate provision for the support of the large pauper population they have brought into this condition, by taking them from those from who, by law, were obliged to support them. Suppose we act upon the abolition of slavery, and adopt this ordinance declaring slavery abolished here, what would be the result? You may make appeals in vain to the Congress of the United States, to incur the expense of supporting this vast and needy throng. It will point you to your own State Constitution, declaring the abolition proposed, and will tell you that those are the paupers of Mississippi, and that we should be taxed for their maintenance. Unless gentlemen can evade this conclusion, which I deem to be a logical one, I ask them to oppose the amendment reported, or count the extent of additional tax they will impose by an opposite action, upon an impoverished people.

There is another matter, Mr. President, in connection with the proposed action of the Convention, to which I ask the attention of gentlemen, and that is, the effect their action will have upon the question of compensation for slaves liberated and freed by the course they wish to pursue. Whatever may be said of the mass of the population of this State, it is certainly true, and beyond controversy that there are innocent parties here, who heretofore have been owners of slave property; in many instances the helpless women and orphans of the State, had their all invested in this species of property. By no possibility can any of them have been implicated in this rebellion. No argument can be raised to relieve the Federal Government from making compensation to this class of our citizens. Let gentlemen reflect upon the consequences of their action in connection with these unoffending parties, as regards their claims, for compensation. Whenever they come forward and present their claims to the Congress of the United States, and demand payment for the slaves taken from them by the Federal Government, if they are met by the ordinance proposed by the committee, what will become of those claims? Is it not certain that Congress will respond to all appeals of that sort by saying, "whatever may have been the legal effect of the proclamations and laws of Congress regarding emancipation, one thing is certain—the State of Mississippi has adopted a valid ordinance, abolishing slavery throughout the State; and whether these slaves were free by act of Congress or Presidential proclamation, or not, they are freed by a sovereign State. We will not stop to discuss the question, but we say to you, the petitioners, go back to your State, look to your State Constitution, and apply to the authorities of that State, for such compensation as they may deem proper." I wish to leave this question of compensation entirely open, unaffected by the action of the Convention: and thus while we do all that we ought in the premises, so long as these acts and proclamation continue annulled by judicial proceeding, we leave open all claims to compensation presented by any of our citizens.

But I am told that this claim for compensation amounts to nothing—that we are not to suppose that the government of the United States will, in any time to come, pay it—that it will not recognize what all the world must declare to be a solemn obligation and duty. Let us see whether the federal government has given our citizens any reason to suppose that it will fail to recognize right and justice in this respect. Why, sir, how was it after what we used to called "the late war with Great Britain?" The British armies took Southern slaves from plantations, and after the war the authorities of the United States demanded compensation from the British Government, and that compensation was made to the owners of those slaves. They were slaves taken, in time of war, by the public enemy. Again, when the late President of the United States was considering the propriety of employing our slaves to aid in suppressing the rebellion, he took the advice of the judge advocate general of the United States upon the legal questions involved—and was advised by him that the Government might legally take these slaves upon one of two grounds. One was, that they were property, and could be, as such, appropriated to public use, upon making due compensation to the owners, as required by the Federal Constitution. The other ground suggested by him was that they were recognized as persons as well as property; "but" said the judge advocate general, "if you take them on the plea of their being persons, the constitutional obligation rests upon you still to make compensation."

When the late President of the United States came to issue this proclamation regarding the emancipation of slaves in the insurrectionary States, he had this same matter of compensation upon his mind. In the proclamation of September 22d, 1862, is the declaration, that at the proper time the President would urge upon Congress, the duty of making compensation to loyal men for property lost in the South by reason of the war, including slaves. During the war, the Federal Government abolished slavery in the District of Columbia, awarding compensation to the owners of the slaves thus set free. During the war, also, both houses of Congress adopted a resolution declaring it the duty of the Government, whenever any State adopted a policy of gradual emancipation, to give pecuniary aid as compensation. I say, then, Mr. President, that the Federal Government has acknowledged itself, over and over again, bound in duty to make compensation to proper parties on account of their slaves emancipated by its authority.

The debt of the country is great, and it may be some time before such claims are paid; but we need not wait; for the

Government can, even now, make compensation to this people. It can, for years to come, relieve us from the burden of taxation. Let the Government say to the people of Mississippi, "we relieve you from taxation for a series of years, in consideration of this debt for compensation due your citizens; and in consideration that we so relieve you from taxation, you shall pay over what you owe the government to the proper parties among your population." Would not that present relief be of great moment to this people? Would it not be more to them than thousands or tens of thousands would have been but four years ago? A mere pittance of what is righteously due on account of this emancipation, would be much, very much, to our impoverished people. I say we have no right to assume, without an appeal made for a fair compensation, that our right will be denied; or to assume that, against the interests of those whom we are, of all others, solemnly bound to protect—innocent children, women, and orphans—our government will do this great injustice.

I will submit for the consideration of gentlemen of the Convention, whether the plan I propose does not meet all that could be required of us by anybody, if gentlemen persist to act upon suggestions of that kind. It proposes to acknowledge for the present time, and through all time, until the proper tribunals shall declare this claim of the government to be invalid, all that can be required; and is not this policy better than that which gentlemen propose; inasmuch as it secures to those who are undoubtedly entitled to compensation, an unrestricted opportunity to come forward and demand from the proper tribunals, compensation for the property they may have lost during the war.

Mr. Harrison moved to lay the substitute upon the table,

Which was decided in the affirmative, by yeas and nays called for by Messrs. Potter, Marshall, and Johnson of Marshall, as follows:

Yeas.—Mr. President, Messrs. Barr, Byars, Bond, Blackwell, Billups, Binford, Brandon, Cason, Cooper, of Rankin, Cooper, of Panola, Carter, Crawford, Crum, Duncan, Farley, Gulley, Griffin, Hurst, Hemingway, Heard, Hall, Hamm, Houston, Harrison, Horne, Hill, Jarnagin, Jones, Johnston, of Hinds, Johnson, of Smith, Kennedy, King, Lindsey, Loper, Lewis, Lambdin, Martin, of Adams, Martin, of Sunflower, Montgomery, Mayson, Morphis, Niles, Owens, of Tunica, Owen, of Scott, Pressley, Phipps, Peyton, Quinn, Rives, Rushing, Sanders, of Attala, Simonton, Sparkman, Slover, Wallace, White, Wooley, Webb, Watson, Wylie, Wier, Yerger.—63.

Nays.—Messrs. Bailey, Brown, Compton, Cummings,

Dowd, Franklin, Gaither, Goode, Gowan, Hudson, Johnson, of Marshall, Lewers, Marshall, Maury, Malone, Matthews, Potter, Reynolds, Reid, Sanders, of DeSoto, Stanley, Swett, Stone, Trotter, Tate, Wall, Wade and Wilson.--28.

On motion of Mr. Potter, the Convention adjourned until to-morrow morning, 9 o'clock.

SIXTH DAY.

SATURDAY, AUGUST 19th, 1865.

The Convention met pursuant to adjournment.

Prayer by the Rev. John Hunter.

Journal of yesterday read and approved.

Mr. Watson, of Marshall, asked leave of absence for Mr. McBride, of Madison, on account of illness.

Which was granted.

The Convention proceeded to the consideration of the regular order, to-wit: The second section of the report of the committee on State Constitution.

Mr. Hudson, of Yazoo, offered the following as a substitute for said section:

That neither slavery nor involuntary servitude, otherwise than in the punishment of crimes, whereof the party shall have been first duly convicted, shall hereafter exist in this State; and the Legislature at its next and succeeding sessions, as the public welfare may require, shall provide by law for the protection and security of the persons and property of the free negroes and mulattoes of the State, and guard them and the State against any evils that may arise from their sudden emancipation: *Provided*, That this clause of the Constitution, and all legislation based upon it, shall be suspended and inoperative, until the several persons hereafter elected and commissioned to represent this State in the Congress of the United States, at the next session thereof, shall have been duly admitted to seats and all the rights and privileges of representatives in the said Congress, and until the civil authority of this State shall have been duly restored, according to the Constitution and laws thereof, upon said representatives and civil authorities taking the amnesty oath, if not already taken, and the oath of office, required by the Constitution of the United States, of the former, and by the Constitution of the State, of the latter; and their admission to such seats, rights and privileges, and such restoration of the civil authority, shall be evidenced and declared by the proclamation of the Governor of the State; but nothing herein contained shall be construed to prejudice any right to compensation from the United States for the loss of any slave.

MR. HUDSON, of Yazoo—Mr. President: In contemplating the probable labors of this Convention, I had concluded to abstain from a participation in the public discussion of those great, important and fundamental questions, which would likely be presented for our determination and final action, and to content myself with the exercise of the greater power and privilege of silently voting upon them, at that stage of action. I would, still, Mr. President, if left to my own feelings and pleasure, adhere to that line of policy; but finding many of the most prominent and able members of the Convention battling for results, and asserting a policy, so antagonistic to those I hold, I feel it due to myself, to this Convention, and the country, to briefly present the reasons that control my action, and I think, should mark the action of this Convention. I therefore, Mr. President, ask the kind indulgence of the Convention, while I present my reasons and convictions upon this important, and to me, unpleasant question.

In the discussion of this question, the first duty is, to settle in our minds the nature and character, power and authority, of this Convention. Whether it is a Convention of the people of the State, in their sovereign capacity and power, exercising the greatest privilege of freemen—the framing of her great organic chart of liberty, with no restriction upon its action; or whether, as insisted by many, it is saddled with unusual and extraordinary restrictions and disabilities? I hold, sir, that this is a Convention representing the sovereign power of the State, with no restrictions, fetters or shackles, save those imposed by the Constitution of the United States and the laws passed in pursuance thereto; otherwise it is no Convention, and does not represent the people, but rather the President of the United States, or the Federal Government. It is true that this Convention was called by the Provisional Governor of the State, acting under the authority and sanction of the President of the United States, but of whom and what is he Governor? It is of the people of the State of Mississippi, and of them only. Who elected and sent us here? The people of Mississippi, who, by the rule and test of the federal authorities were and are loyal and liege subjects of the State and the United States. The State existence has never been denied.—She wears from the Federal Government and all her authorities the title of "State." This is a Convention of the State, and not the Territory of Mississippi. The President of the United States and the Governor of this State, both address the State of Mississippi. When and by whom have we been declared not a State, but a Territory? For whom can we legislate or ordain? For the people of this State only. It is solely for them that we can make or unmake an organic law; and no Convention of a State can do that unless it represents the sovereignty of the State. The creation or amendment of an organic law is an act of sovereignty of the highest possible grade and dignity. I feel reponsible to the people of the State, and to them only for my action here, for they alone must wear the iron yoke or soft crown of all we ordain. Every delegate here fully knows this. We can make no law, no rule, no action, no Constitution, for any other State, nor for the United States. I no know of no mandate from the President of the United States, or the Governor of this State, as to what we shall or shall not ordain. Would they hold us in duress, and extort from us, by force and bayonets, an organic law, not required by the people of the State, or the Constitution of the United States? If so, then this is a bastard Convention, and represents nobody.

It is said here that this Convention, being called and suffered to sit here by the mercy of the President, we are responsible to him and him alone, for our action or inaction, and that he expects and requires us to walk a chalk line; that our path is narrow and straight, and that is to abolish slavery. This requisition, if it exists, is not on visible paper, but is in pairs or parcels. Is the Government of the United States a "Constitutional Government?" It has ever been so declared. Then where does the President get the power and authority to call a Convention of the people of any State, for any purpose?—Where does he find his rightful authority in that civil government and Constitution to require the Convention to ordain his pleasure, and not the will and pleasure of the Constitution? Where does he find in that veteran Constitution, the authority to *make*, or *make us make*, a Constitution not required by, but at war with that Constitution? Sir, I think this must be a mistake. The President, in his conference with the South Carolina delegation upon this very subject, and in answer to an explicit question, said, "let us proceed rather upon the idea of *right*, and *not of power*." "I speak not peremptorily, but merely *advisory*." This language, sir, of the President repeats the idea of *force*, *duress*, or mere *power*. It may be unpleasant to the nostrils of the administration, as I know it would be to the taste and prejudices of *party*, for us not to abolish slavery; but it cannot be so to the Constitution of our fathers, and of our own, as it came from them—and which was purchased with seas of blood. I must insist that this is clearly a Convention of the people of Mississippi, with no overseer or dictator; but the plain and plebeian Constitution of the United States, as it is this day, and was on its birth-day, upon this subject. There is no war, or war-feeling element in this country. A profound peace prevails; the Constitution of the United States is over us—or it is dead everywhere. If we are in the Union, it is a Constitutional Union.

In presenting the substitute for the report of the committee, which I have here offered, I do not present what I would prefer for our adoption—nor have my votes on the various questions voted upon here, represented my convictions of the duty and policy of this State—but my own opinion, and such, I believe to be the judgment of the intelligent of those I have the honor to represent, that slavery being declared by certain authorities of the United States, already abolished and there being no clause of our Constitution creating or perpetuating slavery, it is a work of folly and superorogation—a work of inhumanity—a desecration of the dead and the grave, to exhume the negro, merely to celebrate anew the funeral ceremonies over his putrid body, and the stench of his cold and icy grave, and to register the fact, and his re-interment in our Constitution. Why not simply repeal the two provisions in our Constitution, prohibiting the introduction of slaves into this State, and the emancipation of slaves in this State—the only clauses therein having any mention of, or reference to slaves, and then repeal our slave legislation? What objection can there be to this policy and course? What conflict would there then be between the State, and the declaration of freedom by the authorities of the United States? There would be none, but it would be an acceptance of the fact, that if slavery was abolished, it was done by the United States, and not by us; and that we offer, and would offer no forcible resistance to such declaration of freedom to the negro—but might legally, peaceably and constitutionally, enquire into the validity of their freedom in the Constitutional, judicial forms of the United States, where we could not expect anything more than law or justice in our behalf on this subject. This is all I ask, and every man in the State would be satisfied with it. I do not believe that slavery has been abolished in this State, legally or constitutionally—nor even by the laws of war. If the President thought it was abolished, why did he prescribe certain provisions in the amnesty oath on that subject? Why does he deny us access to, and close the Courts against us upon that subject? Why does he urge the proposed amendment to the Federal Constitution, abolishing slavery? Why does he advise South Carolina to "legally and constitutionally" abolish slavery? If this Convention thought slavery abolished, why does it propose to abolish it, or why did the President call us here to abolish it? Mr. Lincoln, in his inaugural of March 4th, 1861, declared that he neither had the intention or constitutional power to abolish slavery. Mr. Seward assured the French Government, through Minister Dayton, even after the bombardment of Fort Sumpter, that the United States had no Constitutional power to abolish slavery in the States. In fact, every prominent man of the abolition party have frankly declared the same thing. The question does not admit of debate in legal minds. While I admit that slavery, in point of *fact*, is abolished, I cannot admit, but deny, that in *law*, it is abolished. Slaves were not surrendered with the Confederate army. Only the soldiers and property of the Government of the Confederate States were surrendered, and not the private property of individuals; but so far as the negroes were actually captured and held by the military of the United States, during the war, they were, by the laws of war, free, but no others. It is now, however, proposed that we do now kill all these questions very and perpetually dead, beyond the power of resurrection. It is said that this course will secure us the exercise of civil authority, the exit of the Federal army from our State, and representation in Congress. Then I understand that this is a forced measure, and that we can have no such rights until we do so. Truly sir, this speaks volumes, colossal and potential, for the sovereignty of a State; for the Constitutional Government of the United States, and for the freedom of the great plebian people and freemen of the Republic. This is no longer a Government of the people, holding their agents ameanable to them and the Constitution; but one in which the people are down-trodden by their agents. But, sir, where do these promises come from? who makes them? where is the record thereof, or the witness? The President could not make them—for he has no right to admit or reject from Congress, any member. Congress has that sole power by the Constitution. Congress can control the army and navy, over the President. Congress can increase or diminish here the garrisons; and shorten or lengthen their stay; and certainly they have made no such promise; but the leaders of the dominant party of the Congress, are openly declaring in public speeches and fourth of July orations, even at the very Capital of the Government, that we shall enjoy no such right or privilege, until we sanction the proposed amendment to the Constitution of the United States; until we confer upon the Congress the right to legislate for the negro in the States; and until we enfanchise the negroes with the highest political status, power and freedom of the country; and that they already have drawn and prepared such bills, for the immediate action of the ensuing Congress. Look, sir, at the fate of Maryland, who never had even a bogus ordinance of secession; and who, by her people, abolished the institution of slavery three years ago; and the Federal armies are thicker upon her soil than upon ours. Look, sir, at Tennessee, who abolished slavery over one year ago; and yet she is more sadly oppressed by the heel of military power and rule than we are. They have not reaped the harvest, nor caught the golden image promised to us as equivalent for the abolition of slavery, and I ask why we should hastily lay the flattering unction and earnest to our poor hearts and bosoms, that we will be an exception to the rule, and a peculiarly favored people? Let us not deceive ourselves, nor be deceived by others. Let us not give ourselves away, nor be "sold."

Finding that the Convention is resolved to re-abolish slavery; to do that which the Federal army and bayonet, and the President, and Congress could not legally do; I propose by the proviso offered, that while we make the concession, we make its effect and operation dependant upon the Congress, who can secure to us the pleasing reality of civil authority and civil liberty; and at the same time, secure to the negroes of this State, the boon of freedom; placing the sole power and responsibility upon them to do both; and if they do the one they must so instanter necessarily do the other.—Could they ask more, or could we offer more than to submit the whole question and power to their own pleasure and judgment? If they decide wrong, it cannot be our fault; nor can they complain at us for having been so generous and confiding. Why reject the proviso, for it simply provides for that which delegates so fondly hope will follow without it? What harm can it do? Sir, I prefer to do nothing, unless we can settle all the questions involved. Why leave any question unsettled that closes the door of civil liberty against us? Why be quartered by piece-meals, and protract our lingering, tortured lives in the fiery crucible of the hour, only to be scorned in the last agonies of conquered and expiring nature? Why concede, without reservation, to one aggression, when others equally great and more intolerable are being pressed? It but invites, nay, stimulates and rewards the pressing of any and every aggression their folly or malevolence may indict. I want peace of mind, peace of persons, peace of State and nation; and that we can only have by a settlement of all these firebrands at once. Sir, we have been, are now, and I believe ever will be, a persecuted people. If we abolish slavery, make witnesses of negroes in all cases; allow them to vote, hold office, and stand par excellent with us in all that appertains to us as individuals, or state, socially, religiously, and politically, we shall then be tormented and tortured upon other and new exactions. Party is ever contending for power, and its retention, and is ever fruitful in new questions and demands for its elevation and maintenance. There is no relation that it will not invade and crush for its hold upon the Government. It has for forty years past kept this Government in a fearful tempest and unholy wars—the elements of their creation and life—and rather than disband or give up power, would strike down the Government itself. Sir, why is it, that we hold a representation in Congress so indispensible? Why is it that a party at the North deem it so indispensible to defeat that representation? It is, sir, because there is no confidence, no fellowship, no good in store between the two sections, and great *party* purposes are thereby to be accomplished. Neither section is willing to trust the other, to make laws for a common Union and Government. Sir, until these evils shall have passed away, there can be no quiet and harmony between the great family of States, either in their own Capitals, or that of the General Government.

My proviso, simply suspends the operation of the proposed Constitutional amendments, until the Federal Government shall have shown by the action of her Congress, now soon to meet, a reciprocity of duty on her part. It is no dictation or threat, but an affirmative response to and acceptance of the assurances which delegates here say have been whispered by the Government, so that while slavery would be certainly abolished, we would at the same time, certainly secure those whispered benefits that are otherwise uncertain. We make the great and extraordinary concession and sacrifice to attest our devotion to the Union, and to its true and proper Government in parting forever with all the labor, economy and wealth, for which we not only have labored, but for which our fathers and mothers have toiled and labored through long and eventful perils, and lives; and in death transmitted to us under the Constitution as it is. We do this in the hope of future quiet and harmony, and to enjoy the full and undisturbed benefits of the re-establishment of civil authority in our own land. The proviso presents two features to the Congress of the United States. It fixes the next Congress as the time for the admission of our representatives in the Congress. I propose this Congress, for the palpable reason that the great questions, in which we are most deeply interested, will and must be settled by that Congress. If their admission is postponed to a later period, all the great mischief we apprehend, without representation, will have been accomplished; and our labors and sacrifices, hopes and expectations, forever blasted upon this subject. The other is the oath to be taken by our representatives in Congress, enacted in 1862, commonly called the "test oath." From the birth-day of the Republic to the creation of this extraordinary oath and bill of discovery, the only oath required of members of Congress, was that provided in the Constitution; but this additional oath, created during the rebellion, and in party bitterness and proscription, is to be administered hereafter to all Congressmen from these

States. I hold that the oath of the Constitution is ample and sufficient, taken in conjunction with the amnesty oath, of May 29th, 1865. If I understand this "test oath," it excludes from office, every man, who, in any way, sympathised with the late rebellion, and that would behead every man in this State, mentally capable of representing the great and various interest of the State, in the Congress of the United States. While there are many men in our State who opposed secession and the war, and not only deeply regretted, but denounced them; still, sir, there are but few, if any, of such capacity, who did not under some circumstances, during the terrible conflict of arms, sympathise deeply with our cause and success. The war, carried on upon our institutions, our friends, our relatives, our homes and native land; the involuntary wails of the wife, and screams of the child, rising up to heaven, in view of the devouring flames of their only earthly tenement, and last daily bread; the flowing of the last best heart's blood, drawn by the assasin and robber; the shrieks of the brutally ravished sister, daughter, wife, or mother; the sad scenes and desolation in the track of the invading army—all excited a sympathy and judgment which was impossible for the best human nature to repel—and which the God of nature has indelibly written upon the tablet of every manly heart. It is therefore insisted that no good and competent man—such only as this State would honor and trust—shall be crucified by the grand inquisitions of the "test oath," but shall be permitted to take his seat as our representative, upon taking the oath required by the Constitution, from its creation to this hour, and which has been administered in every age of the Republic to the unhappy moment when this "test oath" was illegally sired, and unfortunately swaddled. The whole proviso, to the report of the Committee, is designed as an earnest appeal, and to obtain some certain security that we obtain the benefits which some hope may follow our action without the proviso, but which all must be admonished does otherwise depend upon the mere caprice of political and partisan foes in power. We thus throw at the same time, upon Massachusetts, Maine and New England, the final and delicate responsibility of the operation of this ordinance. If they desire to have it settled, and that forever, if this matter of slavery is the great obstacle between the right of civil authority in this State and the general government, it is by this proviso, in their power to remove and silence it forever.

As was well remarked by the gentleman from Hinds, (Mr. Potter,) on yesterday, Mississippi has never been out of the Union—there is no such thing as "re-union" or "re-construction." Those terms are as replete with humbuggery as that of "peaceable secession." We are in the Union to-day, if we ever were in it. The ordinance of secession was a nullity, and did not put us out of the Union. We failed to fight ourselves out of the Union, and the Federal Government has no legal power to expel a State from the Union. Mr. Lincoln at all times held us to be in the Union, and refused to receive or treat with the Commissioners sent by the Confederate States, upon the sole ground that secession was a nullity, and that he could only look upon us as States in the Union, in rebellion against the rightful authority and jurisdiction of the United States. The Congress of the United States has uniformly pronounced secession a nullity; and that we were a part and parcel, and a State in the Union. President Johnson, in his speech in the Capitol of Tennessee, accepting his nomination for the Vice Presidency, declared emphatically that secession was a nullity, and every State adopting it was as much in the Union as if no such ordinance had ever been adopted. This State, in her sovereign Convention in 1851, declared that the State had no right to secede from the United States, and this Convention will doubtless declare the ordinance of secession of 1861 a nullity. The weight of the great statesmen and jurists of the Republic largely preponderate with this opinion. If anything has been settled better than another, by the late war—by a resort to arms—the weakest resort for the protection of our rights and liberties, in my opinion, (at least it has so proved,) it has *settled* this one, that there is no such right as secession. Any difference of opinion on this subject must now be silent, as it is certainly wrong and impotent. It is silent and impotent, and no man now controverts the fact so fully determined, and, so far as we are concerned, settled forever by the leaden messengers of death.—The State is in the Union. We cannot vote her any further in, nor can we vote her out. Our civil rights and authorities are simply suspended for the present, by military power and force—in order, it is said, to purge us of our treason, and fit and prepare us for loyal subjects—and until the multiplied questions about the negroes are settled. As far as I am informed and understand, those who have taken the amnesty oath, as the late elections will show, constitute a majority and the power of the State. They have taken the oath in good faith—with pure resolution—a proper and obedient purpose and spirit—and with a determination to cast no obstacle in the way of harmony, and the restoration of all our civil rights and authorities; at the same time, as powerless as they are in a military sense, they should do nothing cowardly and from fear either against themselves, or for any other power, but do their duty as the Constitution directs. The State, by the action of her people, in taking the amnesty oath, stands today redeemed and disenthralled, so far as the executive judg-

ment and sentence of treason is concerned—and is entitled to the whole armor of any State in the Union. She has passed through the ordeal and crucible, established by him, who sits in judgment, and declared her guilty of treason: and through the crucible erected, to cleanse and purify her from treason; and we do not stand here to day, as intimated by some, an abject and powerless set of criminals and traitors. I must be permitted to say, Mr. President, that the idea so often advanced here, and even practiced upon elsewhere, that a State, a corporation, can commit treason, is miserable law, bad logic, and poor politics. If it proceeds upon the idea that by the sins of our first parents, the judgment of condemnation come upon all men, then the same remedy should be applied for the salvation of all. I know no other precedent or law sustaining such an idea; and I think it would tax the best ingenuity to make that applicable to a corporation.

Again, Mr. President, the Constitution of the United States is the same now that it has always been upon the subject of property in man. It remains untouched entirely in this respect. The first law book I ever read, was Blackstone's Commentaries—a standard work of the highest merit and authority, in which I learned what is certainly true, that there were four great kindred subjects and relations in life, so nearly the same that they could be treated under one head, and the laws applicable to the one, were the laws of the other. Those relations were husband and wife; parent and child; guardian and ward; *master and servant.* I maintain that the Federal Government has no more power to intervene between *master and servant*, until the relation is legally and constitutionally dissolved, than between that of husband and wife, parent and child, guardian and ward. Indeed, sir, it never occured to me in reading the Declaration of Independence, the Bill of Rights, and the Constitution of the United States, asserting the right of a free people, to *alter, change* or amend their *form* of Government, that it was ever intended to confer upon the General Government, the power, even by way of amending the Constitution, and certainly not without it, the right to invade and destroy these great private and domestic relations between mere private and mutually dependent creatures. The Government can neither take or destroy the private property of the citizen, or appropriate it to public use, without fair compensation first paid therefor. By our laws, and the recognition of the Constitution of the United States, and by the Government of the United States until now, our servants were property, not belonging to the States, the Confederacy or the United States, but to mere individuals. The relation of *master and servant*, is a mere private one, regulated by themselves in a great degree, and protected by the State, as in the relation of husband and wife, parent and child, guardian and ward. The right to change, alter or amend the *form* of Government, certainly did not mean the right to amend, change or alter, so as to seize upon and destroy the mere property of the citizen, and the relation of owner and property. If such is the case, then, sir, the sacred relation subsisting from time whereof the memory of man runs not to the contrary, between husband and wife, parent and child, guardian and ward, may be violently invaded and hopelessly destroyed at any time. They exist at the mercy only of the Federal Government. If this right is her's, then, sir, she has the right to seize upon our little homes, our land titles, the only remnants of our labor, industry and economy of long and constant toil, that now survive this abortive revolution. No property of any kind, upon the same principle, is secure. Soon the question will be forced upon us, that the lands must be divided, not by purchase or sale, nor upon compensation; but by an act of violence and self-constituted authority. There is already a party in the land, advocating this doctrine, and you and I may yet live to see the home of our youth and old age thus desecrated. The Federal Government has no Constitutional jurisdiction or power over these questions, and the people of the United States have no right by the laws of nature—or of nature's God—nor by the great moral political code of mankind to even amend the Constitution, so as to confer such power and jurisdiction. Sir, there is a great principle that underlies this whole question, and with me, overrides and buries into insignificance all others. I am in favor of standing up wherever we may be permitted to assemble, and discuss these great questions and wrongs, presenting our views, and insisting upon our rights, and the preservation of the Constitutional Government; otherwise we can have no Constitutional Union, and if overpowered, we can but submit as the victim bows to the highway robber. The idea prevails, sir, that the military power of the Government can do any thing, and is above all restraints upon any and every matter. This may be so in fact, but not rightfully or legally so. The military arm of the Government, is by the Constitution, in subordination to the civil authority; and the civil authority, the President, Congress and the Supreme Court, in subordination to the Constitution and Constitutional laws. The military can rightfully do nothing not authorized by the civil authority, and the civil authority can rightfully do nothing, not authorized by by the Constitution, and Constitutional enactments. Any other conduct must be illegal, and amount to an overthrow of the Constitutional Government and Union, and bring upon the country, the laws of the wild, savage and unbridled nature, in its worst and most malignant passions. That this proposition is true, who can deny? If it is true, has slavery been legally abolished? Let him who can, answer the question in the negative.

In the Revolutionary war of 1776, when the British Government offered freedom to the slaves of New England and the South, if they would join the British army, and fight the rebels of that day, murder our fathers, and burn their homes, who denounced the act? Sir, one loud and universal indignation and denunciation went up from Massachusetts and all the States of that day, against the infamy and shame of the deed. The historians of those events, have never failed to note it as a most extraordinary and nefarious, black and diabolical act. The school room histories of this day, written by Northern authors, denounce it. Sir, there is some settled law of war growing out of this very thing to which the United States was a party, that does not sustain the views of some delegates here, but may be considered good authority against them, and I hope will be recognized by the United States, now as binding upon her—and if not, she will find that her history and consistency upon this subject is not as lovely and unspotted as the "Alpine rose that leaves it cheek upon the bosom of the eternal snows."

It has been questioned here whether the Government of the United States liberated the slaves, or whether Mississippi did it? Sir, I confess my surprise at any such proposition, for two reasons: first for the want of foundation upon which to make the query? and second, the insult offered to the United States, in proposing to abate or diminish her glory upon that subject. So far as that is concerned, permit me to express my surprise, with all deference to opposing opinion, that any one should seriously controvert what the Government regards as one of her settled and most immortal glories.—I have not recognized the fact that we have voted for it, or fought for it, or contributed anything to that end of doubtful glory or humanity, but on the contrary, the claim that the unclouded and undivided festoon, and imperishable wreath of everlasting honor and undying glory, should encircle the Federal head and temples for the liberation of the slaves—and that whatever part we had in the affair, was in ignoble and barbarian opposition to that god-like, glorious and happy end. I am not willing to rob them of the proud title and sacred distinction, nor permit another to do so; but freely and frankly concede the bloody work; the unfading chaplet of undying fame, and the springtide festoons of perennial renown, as their exclusive title and estate; and that Mississippi had no hand in that grand and pround achievement. Sir, this joy should not be dimmed or marred by the suspicion that all the work and immortality was not theirs. It is a star of the first magnitute in their political firmament—the brightest jewel in their national existence—the most glorious achievement of their life—and by the resplendent blaze of which, even the blind shall read her title clear. They are now, and for all time, the sole heir, the lawful potentate, the great high priest, the immaculate conceptor, progenator and Ajax of the whole deed; and I solemnly protest in the name of truth and history, justice and title, that the virgin and holy temple of the Government, shall be encircled with the ever-living and undimmed—the blazing and god-like halo of still higher, deeper and expanding glory, as she claims, for what is upon her and us to-day, upon this subject.

Permit me, Mr. President, to say, in conclusion, I oppose the report of the Committee. I do so, because we have no clause in our Constitution, creating or perpetuating slavery; and I know, that the State approves no such thing. There could and would be no conflict between us and the General Government upon this institution, and this would simply leave our people, the liberty to revise in the Supreme Court, the action of the Government in this matter. This would satisfy everybody, whatever that decision might be, for they will feel that the true and Constitutional tribunal will have passed upon it, and will bow to its solemn judgment. What objection can the Government have to such a course? Why should it decline to meet the citizen in its own court, and there give him the courtesy and benefits of litigating the question upon legal principles? If the Government thinks it has done right, if it has legally deprived the citizen of his property, why not allow the issue to be made up and settled in the Courts? She is powerful—she can afford a generous magnanimity, and re-impress the citizen with the happy belief, that he lives in a civil land—a free country—and above all—in a Constitutional Union and Government. Mr. President, I have been frank, but I trust respectful. I have no concealments, nor can I do violence to my convictions of duty. I shall gladly sustain the President of the United States, in all things, and at all times, in whatever commends itself as right and proper; to do less, would be dishonest and unmanly; to do more, would in effect, be treason. I trust, sir, that whatever may be the result of this question here, it will be conformed to with the deep earnest of filial duty, and that our poor, crippled and emaciated people and country, will emerge from the ocean of trouble, and the bane of distress, and yet live to see, when they behold for the last time, the sun pass below the western horizon, a free, happy and united people and country.

Mr. Johnston, of Hinds.—Mr. President, in considering the substitute offered by the gentleman of Yazoo, I propose to submit a few of the reasons which have influenced me to oppose it. I shall not, at this stage of the discussion, submit all the reasons which might be presented in support of the position I assume, but simply advert to one or two prominent considerations which, in my judgment, are conclusive of the whole question. I am free to concede that it is the object of the gentlemen on the other side of this question, to promote the glory, prosperity and happiness of our State. I attribute to them as much sincerity as I claim for myself in any course which I feel constrained to pursue. But, as all minds cannot see propositions in the same light—and perhaps it is well it is so—and inasmuch as some of us must be in error as to the course we are pursuing, it is but right and proper that discussion may be brought to bear, that it may be demonstrated where the error lies. Without having any great faith in my judgment of public matters of this character, and without urging my opinion as a standard for the opinion of any gentleman, I nevertheless declare at the outset, that it seems to me as clear as the beams of the sun that shines upon us to-day, that the course recommended by the Committee is the only course that can conduct us to the end which we desire to obtain. But before I attempt to answer the arguments of these gentlemen, permit me to take a brief glance at the present condition of our country, and ask what is the great object which animates us all at present. There is danger that in a multiplicity of propositions we may lose sight of the great work we have in view. I propose, therefore, to refer to them, before I proceed to the general argument.

I will not attempt to draw before this intelligent body, the melancholy picture of the condition of our State. That condition is already too apparent—too well known. Suffice it to say, that having gallantly and nobly, but unsuccessfully, struggled, we find ourselves a mere wreck of our former grandeur and prosperity, standing amidst the ruins of the most prosperous country that the sun ever shone upon. Our fields are desolate; nothing but the charred remains of our homesteads are to be found wherever we travel. The spirit of desolation, like a funeral pall, broods o'er the land of the South. The arm of industry is paralyzed; poverty and privation meet us on every hand; and lawlessness stalks abroad unpunished, and almost unrebuked; our people are vanquished, overcome, trodden down, oppressed and ruined in their public and private fortunes; and many of them, even yet, are strangers and refugees in foreign lands, perhaps never to return again. Disguise it as you may, Mr. President, whatever may have been the former power and glory of the State of Mississippi, to-day she stands vanquished, without power, without will, without volition—absolutely without any choice as to the course she may pursue. Let us, as philosophers and men, look stern realities in the face. We are here this day, subject to the dictation of the powers that be, however grossly that dictation may violate the principles of justice and the guarantees of the Constitution. Gentlemen propose acting here in this Convention as if they had a choice—as if we might do this, or that, or the other thing, and pursue this, that or the other pathway; when it is perfectly manifest that there is but one course that can be pursued, and that is the road marked out by the dictation of the powers that have vanquished us. That is our situation—the obvious and inevitable situation—and I hold it no humiliation to concede it. It is, in my humble opinion, the part of true dignity, and true manhood, and elevated moral courage, to have a conception of our inevitable destiny, and at once to realize this idea, distasteful as it may be, and act in accordance with the soundest and best policy that can be devised. It is not wise, in this sad extremity, to act by impulse. Mere obstinacy would prove our utter ruin. Let us all endeavor to do that which is best for ourselves, and the coming generations of our posterity. Now, Mr. President, what course has been dictated to us? What is the only road we can pursue, in order to obtain our great object of securing the blessings of peace and civil government? It has been dictated to us, by the powers at Washington, in every conceivable form and shape, that there is no hope for the restoration of civil rule and representation in Congress, except by the adoption in the State of Mississippi, of a free Constitution. If we desire to resume our former political status, with all of its rights and privileges, we must conform to that dictation. There is no other alternative.

If we refuse to submit to that dictation, the necessary result then is, that we stand out for long and lingering years of misery and suffering as a conquered province, under the stern, inexorable control of military rule, with one oppression to-day and another oppression to-morrow, until there will be no life and prosperity left in the prostrated State of Mississippi at all. If we do not conform to the indications of the powers at Washington, we must submit to be garrisoned by negro troops. What is the great object which we have in view? What is the great object which the honorable members of this Convention have in view? What is the great object which our constituency have in view? The popular feeling undeniably is to make almost any sacrifice—to pursue almost any course which will have a tendency to restore civil rule in the State of Mississippi—to put the beautiful machinery of our State Government in operation in all of its departments; to have our representation in the Congress of the United States; and banish from our midst every vestige of military rule and military power; withdraw all of the bayonets which gleam around us, and be no longer disturbed by the *reveille* at the dawn of day; to have amongst us no remains of that sad and desolating war which hath swept over our country; and so to shape our public policy that the remnant of our poor down-trodden people may come together, weak and despondent though they be, and sit down in quiet amid the ruins of their former greatness—at least to plant a vine and tree and rear a cabin, where they may repose themselves under the downy wings of returning peace. This is the object—my object, at least—and to that I shall strain every energy of my mind. I am prepared to make any reasonable sacrifice, that I may secure my constituency and the State at large, at least in the enjoyment of some of the many privileges which were once enjoyed by us, in the departed days of peace and prosperity. Did not the President of the United States (who is our friend on this subject, and whose administration I intend to support,) declare it in so many words to our commissioners when they visited Washington? I have said that the only hope of the restoration of civil rule in Mississippi, and our representation in Congress, was in framing for the State of Mississippi a free Constitution. Has not the President made the same declaration to the South Carolina delegation—indeed to every delegation that has waited on him from the revolted States? Do we not know, independent of that declaration, that that is the only course left for us to pursue? Without impugning the motives of any gentleman, I say that the effect of the proposition offered by the gentleman from Yazoo, will be to defeat this end, and keep us from returning to the Union. I know it is not so intended; I am satisfied that the proposition originates in a spirit of patriotism, and perhaps in a spirit of wisdom; but I cannot see it in the light of wisdom myself, and I entertain no earthly doubt, as I before remarked, that the adoption of the substitute to the report of the Committee would have a tendency to prevent our representation in Congress, and keep us as a conquered province or territory, perhaps for a series of years. Are gentlemen prepared for this? Have they weighed the sorrows and miseries that would inevitably visit our constituents, as the inevitable and natural result of protracted military rule? Sir, let gentlemen pause and reflect, before they act on this momentous proposition.

It has been argued, Mr. President, that we are not out of the Union; and I agree with gentlemen when they assert that the right of secession never did exist under the Federal Constitution, and ought never to have been exercised. Such have always been my views, from the time I first uttered a political sentiment, to the present. My opinions were formed at least as far back as the days of the South Carolina nullification, during the reign of that noble Roman, Andrew Jackson, who expressed the true theory of this Government in his celebrated South Carolina Proclamations. I shall not, however, be so indiscreet, and exercise such bad taste, as to attempt here and at this time, a stale repetition of the thread-bare arguments for and against the right of secession. I content myself by a simple statement of my views in reference to that question.

I think, Mr. President, that to accomplish the great object we have in view, it is indispensably necessary that we should insert a free clause in the Constitution of Mississippi, unencumbered by any preambles—unencumbered by any proviso—unencumbered by any extraneous language. Let it be a cheerful, frank, definite avowal of our sentiments upon that subject. I shall, therefore, oppose all the propositions which have emanated, or which may emanate from this body, tending materially to change the language and principles embodied by the Committee which has just reported. If we pursue that course, I have no doubt of our success—if we manifest that spirit, I have no doubt of the speedy restoration of civil law in Mississippi and our representation in the Federal Councils of the nation, at the next session of Congress in December.

What is the effect now of adopting this substitute? By this substitute the honorable gentleman makes the actual reception of our Congressional delegation a condition precedent to the operation of the clause for freedom which we are about to insert in our State Constitution. In other words, we, a vanquished people, under the power and rule of dictation, propose to say we will do thus and so, if you do thus and so; we will not perform our part of the bargain until we have received a guarantee that you will perform your part. The effect of this is, in the first place, to discourage the President of the United States, who sides with us on this great question—to discourage the great conservative party of the North and West, coming up to our aid against the radicals, and place in the hands of the radicals a weapon with which they will successfully carry out their favorite doctrine of negro equality and negro suffrage. So sure as we fail to obtain representation in Congress, so sure will the radicals pass, and rivet upon us the disgusting doctrine of negro suffrage, which would, indeed, render this country no longer an abiding place for the white man. I hold that we are bound, every man, woman and child, to come up boldly and promptly to the support of the President of the United States, and the conservative party, against the power and influence of the Northern radicals. All that party in the North called the Copperheads are with us on this question; and even from the ranks of the

Black Republicans, there springs up many conservative patriots, armed for the coming struggle on this great question. The President of the United States is committed emphatically and plainly against the doctrine of negro suffrage; and I understand that every member of his Cabinet, with perhaps one exception is with him on that great question. If we can get back speedily into the Union, all the revolted States with their representation, united with the President and those members of his Cabinet friendly to his doctrine, and leagued with the great conservative party of the North, we at once form a great party, irresistible in its power, and sufficiently efficacious and strong to control the next Presidential election, to defeat the radicals, and place some conservative Northern man in the Presidential chair of the United States. There is no chance for a Southern man to occupy the Presiidential chair. We should be well satisfied with a Northern President possessed of conservative sentiments, and willing to accord to the revolted States their political rights and civil privileges. We should expect nothing beyond this. The adoption of this substitute would, in my opinion, defeat this very end and object, and would give to the Northern radicals an irresistible argument against us. They would say, look at the people who have been in rebellion against the constituted power of the Government; they have not even yet subdued their rebellious spirit, and are talking about having their rights guaranteed as a condition precedent; they are talking about the right to compensation for slaves, and manifesting a spirit which cannot be trusted. You cannot admit them to representation in Congress, while that spirit exists; keep the bayonets over them, and let the tramp of soldiers be heard by day and by night, a garrison in every town and village, and hold them until they quell that spirit. Do you not see, Mr. President, how fatal to our prospects and our hopes the proposition under discussion would prove, if adopted by this Convention? Would not its success prove a death-blow to Mississippi?

Now, as to this right of compensation which is so much harped upon, I hope I may be indulged in a remark or two with reference to that. In the first place, I most freely concede, that the destruction of so many millions of property, by any means, was a great wrong to our people. I admit that the right to property in slaves was guaranteed to our people by the Constitution. I believe it was an institution sanctioned by God himself; and I shall always believe that its destruction was unwise in every particular—a curse to the very race sought to be benefitted. For thirty years, or more, I fought the battles of slavery against the attacks of Northern abolitionists; and if the battles were to be fought again, which never can be, I would not recede from my position. This institution, such as it was, is, as every sensible man must know, not only wounded, but dead, dead, *dead*, to all intents and purposes, beyond the power of resurrection, except by the miraculous interposition of the Most High.

It would be vain to inquire how the institution was killed; and there can be no good in asking whether the blow which felled it to the earth was constitutional or unconstitutional. There can be no utility in debating *how* it was destroyed, whether by the emancipation proclamation, by the result of the war, or by the outside pressure from all christendom; or by a combination of all those forces and influences. That slavery is dead, is a fixed fact. Let us, like sensible men, entertain that idea, and shape our new policy with reference to another system of labor.

There is not a gentleman here who believes in the possible resurrection of slavery as an institution. It is gone, and however much we were attached to it, or however much it benefitted us—being dead, let us indulge in no useless regrets over its demise, but bury the carcass, that it may no longer offend our nostrils. Let its fœted remains be speedily conveyed to the grave. But gentlemen say there springs out of that dead institution, a right of compensation for our property—that minors, orphans, innocent persons, and helpless widows, having never been guilty of participation in this revolution, their rights must be saved, and they must be compensated. This places the matter in a strong and pathetic point of view; but I have this to say in regard to the matter, that whatever right of compensation there may be—however good—the adoption of a plain, free Constitution by this Convention, unclogged by any proviso or preamble, would not, as a legal question, interfere, in the slightest degree, with such rights, but leave them untouched and unimpaired. Such were my impressions when I first examined the legal proposition for myself; and those impressions are fortified by the concurrent opinions of the most able and distinguished men that grace the State of Mississippi; one of whom—without mentioning his name—has an almost world-wide reputation for his sagacity as a lawyer, and for the depth of his comprehension of judicial questions. The institution of slavery was destroyed by certain war measures, and by the operation of war, without any concurrence on our part. This wrong was consummated when the Federal power entered our territory, divested us of our slaves, took them from the fields, and converted them into soldiers under the stars and stripes, or enticed them away from us, carrying them off by hundreds and thousands, employing them and proclaiming them free. Those acts, by which our property in slaves was destroyed, created whatever right of compensation we may have.—Should we now say in our Constitution, that, hereafter slavery, or involuntary servitude, shall not exist in the State of Mississippi, does it not leave untouched the question of the preceding wrong? If we choose to say that we will have slaves no longer, does not the amendment as reported by the Committee, leave untouched entirely, this great question of compensation, according to every principle of law and common sense? There are a great many of my profession in this Convention, and I ask them, as lawyers, to consider of this, and say if this opinion is not correct—that the right to compensation would not be interfered with by the adoption of the report of the Committee; or in other words, the framing of a pure, free Constitution, untramelled by any conditions.

But what is this right of compensation, about which we hear so much in this hall, and amongst the people? It is vague, shadowy, indistinct, unsubstantial, ideal. It is an airy myth, floating in the imaginations of certain gentlemen; a mere expectation or desire that "something may turn up" in the great history of future events, by which dollars and cents can be obtained for the property thus destroyed. Mr. President, I would not give this glass of water before me, for the right which I possess to compensation for my former slaves; and I believe there is no gentleman in this Convention who relies upon realizing, for himself or his posterity, a single cent of compensation for this property. It is not reasonable to suppose that the Government of the United States will ever recognize any right in a claim of this nature, or appropriate a single dollar in payment of slaves taken from us; and this for two great reasons. The first is, that the people who destroyed this institution and who were its implacable enemies for half a century, would never consent, if in power, to give up one picayune of the public treasure to compensate a single individual; and secondly, if they were ever so willing, they are so bankrupt that the attempt would hopelessly involve the General Government in pecuniary embarrassment. Besides, can it be supposed, Mr. President, that the people who sat down with the avowed purpose of destroying slavery; who expended vast sums and hundreds of thousands of lives during the last four years, in accomplishing the fall of this institution, would turn round and say that, "having destroyed it, we will pay a just compensation to those interested therein?" There is not a Black Republican Radical in the North who would consent to such a thing; and I, for one, believe that this talk about "compensation," has no real foundation. Compensation may come to some portion of our people hereafter, but it will not embrace me, or any one occupying my position. Perhaps, in the lapse of years, when justice shall once more hold aloft her unerring scales in the land, and a returning sense of justice animate the masses: when the overwhelming excitement of war shall have passed away, and everything is quiet in the land, under a new organization, Congress may say it will pay the orphans and helpless and innocent widows who have been reduced to beggary by this war, and who had no agency in its inception or maintenance. *Their* rights, such as they are, will remain unimpaired, by the adoption by us of a free Constitution.

Gentlemen talk sometimes about an adjudication from the Supreme Court, touching compensation. Are not gentlemen aware that there is nothing to hope from a Supreme Court composed of Black Republicans and Radicals, with a Chief Justice traveling the country as a disgusting itinerant preacher of the doctrine of negro suffrage?

But you cannot get there with the question, and cannot sue the United States in any court for any claim. You cannot get the question of compensation before a legal tribunal for adjudication, in any way which I can perceive. If any of my legal brethren can suggest a way, I would like to have them do so. The only manner of preferring the claim, is to submit it, with the evidence in support thereof, before the court of claims, and let that tribunal pass upon it. If that court recognize the claim as right, it is referred to Congress, and Congress may or may not, grant an appropriation to pay it. If Congress makes the appropriation, pursuant to the judgment of the Court of Claims, all is well; but, if the appropriation be refused, the claim is defeated. If we now proceed, and make a free Constitution, and unite with the Conservatives of the North and West, we can elect a Conservative President, and a Conservative Congress, who will unitedly give the question of compensation a fair consideration. Thus, widows and orphans may procure indemnity for the destruction of their slave property; and, if the future should produce that result, certainly it would be gratifying to all good men.

A few words more, Mr. President, and I shall have concluded. It has been contended, that there is a disposition not to receive our members in the Congress of the United States next winter, although the President of the United States appointed a Provisional Governor and ordered him to call this Convention, to be composed of loyal men, as it is, and ordered him to take means for the speedy election of members of Congress, with a view to put our suspended civil government in operation. Notwithstanding all this, it is contended that our Congressional Delegation is not to be received, and that although these promises have been held out, they are to turn to ashes upon our lips. For myself, Mr. President, I sincerely believe, that if we adopt the report of this Convention, and assimilate all our action here to the spirit of the report of the Committee, without change or qualification, that when we shall have elected our delegation next fall, and they present themselves before Congress, their claims will be so irresistible, that, through the influence of the President of the United States, and the conservatiwe pressure brought to bear, the door of the national council will fly open, our members be received to their seats, the voice of Mississippi be once more heard upon the floor of Congress, and our interests again represented. I do not doubt it, but feel sure of it. At all events, the course we propose to pursue, in adopting this report, is the only hope we can reasonably cherish for consummating this most desirable end. If we trammel the free clause with proviso and preamble, rendering it equivocal and ambiguous, we shall certainly close and bar the only door left open for representation in Congress, and the restoration here of entire peace and unfettered civil rule.

It is said, however, that there is an oath prescribed for members to Congress, which will render it impossible for any citizen of Mississippi, though elected, to take his seat in the National Council. I have not myself scrutinized that oath, so as to be fully satisfied of the character thereof; but, Mr. President, who does not know that, when our members are elected by a loyal constituency—when the powers at Washington see that we have conformed to their dictation, and done all they have required of us, and made a Constitution, entirely free, and swept from the statute books every vestige of revolutionary legislation and revolutionary action; that the spirit of rebellion is quieted in our midst; that we realize the situation and accept our destiny—who does not know, I ask, that there will be moral power and virtue enough in the Congress of the United States to modify that oath and admit our delegates? At all events, how can the proviso save it? If you send up your free clause, with a proviso attached, suspending its operation as an instrument for freedom, until actual representation is accorded, is it not manifest that seats would be denied to members coming with such a Constitution, breathing the spirit of rebellion and distrust?

How can the proviso preserve the institution of slavery? Suppose our representatives go there and are refused admission—this proviso having been adopted? Suppose they reject that Constitution and its proviso—have we saved the institution of slavery and brought the dead to life? Don't it leave it where it was—dead to all intents and purposes? Although you may refuse to insert a free clause in the Constitution, yet your institution of slavery is still dead and you gain nothing, and it will be doubly dead;f or before you get from under the power of military rule the amendment to the Federal Constitution will be irretrievably fastened upon you, by which every vestige of slavery is swept from every inch of our soil from the Atlantic to the Pacific. The powers at Washington, and the Northern people know perfectly well that the institution of slavery has been killed by their influence, by their power, and the unanimous influence of all the Christian world; for it is a fact that nowhere upon this spacious globe we inhabit, is there a single advocate of African slavery, except among the very people who have cherished the institution. Is not all Christendom bitterly opposed to slavery? Undoubtedly, such is the fact. I sometimes think that if the war had not come, this continual moral pressue would have, in time, destroyed the institution by a slow but sure process, rendering the continuance of slavery, a mere question of time, independent of the warfare made upon the institution here at home.

Let us do nothing that will clog our admission to the National Congress. Let us look straight forward to the road marked out for us to travel, with firm steps—assuming, here and elsewhere, the responsibility cast upon us. If, men, in their ignorance, choose to say we are abolitionists in pursuing this course, let them say so. One thing is certain: if we pursue this wise and prudent course, we will have the consciousness of having discharged our duty to our suffering country; and when the records of your Convention will be read by generations yet unborn, they will rise up and call you blessed for having conducted them out of the wilderness in which this question now places us. Let the institution of slavery go, and the question of compensation—everything—until we relieve ourselves and our posterity from this present pressure, and get some little guarantee at least, that the children whom we are rearing up, will have a land to live in and the privileges of freemen.

Though I have no great confidence in my opinion on these great public questions, and my attention has been distracted by private matters, yet it is true that by day and night, not only for days and weeks, but for years past, I have meditated upon the situation we are in and speculated as to the mode of relieving ourselves. Again and again have I pondered upon this during the vigils of the night, while all others around me were wrapped in slumber. My faith was matured by myself, and I feel and know that I am right—perhaps that is too strong an expression—but I am satisfied that I am right. I beliewe that other gentlemen who oppose me are honest, but I do them no injustice in saying that I think they are mistaken in their views. If the policy of framing an unclogged clause of freedom for our Constitution, prevail in this Convention, all will be well. If the opposite view prevail, I see nothing for us and our posterity but absolute misery and ruin. Thus considering the question, it presents itself to my mind as one of overshadowing importance. I shall say nothing more, Mr. President, as other gentlemen are to follow in this discussion, far more capable than myself of enforcing the views I have attempted to elucidate.

Mr. Watson—Mr. President: I feel unwilling, at any great length, to protract this debate, but at the same time, I desire to explain the views which I entertain upon the subject before us.

The representatives of the people here assembled, have assumed duties not only of responsibility and importance, but of novelty and delicacy. Sir, for myself, I feel greatly embarrassed by the circumstances which surround us. We all, no doubt, have in view the same object. We desire to emancipate ourselves and the State from military rule, and at the earliest practicable period to place the State in her Constitutional connexion with the United States, and thereby to restore her to the exercise of her legitimate functions under the Constitution of the United States, as a free, sovereign and independent State of the American Union, subject only to the constitution and laws of the United States, as the supreme law of the land.

But here, Mr. President, allow me to advert to our present condition, and to some of the circumstances which we should keep steadily in view in marking out the line of policy which this Convention should adopt. Have we assembled as the representatives of a people who possess and enjoy all the rights and privileges which they inherited from their fathers, or are we in circumstances which, to some extent, impair our representative independence and freedom of action? The distinguished gentleman from Hinds, (Mr. Potter) said on yesterday, that he stood on this floor the independent representative of a free people; he denied, with emphasis, that any dictation had been attempted in any quarter; he asserted that the President of the United States had given us no intimation as to what, in his opinion, was necessary or best to be done, in order that the State of Mississippi might be enabled "to resume her place in the Union;" but before he took his seat—indeed, almost in the very same breath—he read an order sanctioned by the President, and which he declared proved that terms had been imposed upon us which it was impossible for us ever to accept. Looking to these terms, he expressed the belief that we could not now do enough to reconstrnct the Union as it once was, and that therefore it seemed to him almost unnecessary for us to attempt anything. I shall, at least, Mr. President, endeavor to steer clear of what seems to me so glaring an inconsistency.

It has now been more than four years since a Convention of the State passed an ordinance entitled "an ordinance to dissolve the union between the State of Mississippi, and other States united with her under the compact entitled the Constitution of the United States of America." As a consequence of this act, which as yet remains wholly unrepealed by any direct action of the State, we have just passed through a bloody, devastating, gigantic and bloody war—a war, which for the number of troops employed, and the many great battles fought, has not, perhaps, its parallel in history. This war was terminated by the surrender of our gallant armies to the overwhelming armies of the United States. Our soldiers have laid down their arms and been disbanded, and all of the Southern States are now in the military occupation of Federal troops, and are under the government of military rule; those whom we represent, as well as ourselves, have sworn allegiance to the Constitution of the United States and the Union thereunder; and moreover, that we will not only abide by, but support, the proclamations and laws made by the President and Congress, during the rebellion, in reference to the emancipation of slaves.

These, Mr. President, are facts with which we are all familiar, but to which, it seems to me, some gentlemen on this floor are very unwilling to give due and proper weight.

Now, Sir, the ordinance of secession was either constitutional, operative, and obligatory upon the citizens of the State, or unconstitutional, null and void. If the former, the State of Mississippi ceased to be an integral part of the United States; and as this ordinance, as already stated, still remains unrepealed, the State continues to sustain to the United States the relation of a power foreign thereto. On this hypothesis we are now endeavoring to effect the readmission of Mississippi into the Federal Union, and this being the case, does it belong to us to dictate the terms of our readmission, or is it not the right of the Government of the United States, within certain limitations, to prescribe these terms? These limitations, however, in the case supposed, do not grow so much out of the constitution of the United States, as out of the great and immutable principles of right and justice. Rightfully or otherwise, the Government of the United States has the power to prescribe these terms, and most manifestly, looking to passing events, this power will be exercised by that Government.

And now, on the other hand, let it be conceded that our ordinance of secession was unconstitutional, null and void, that in unfurling the flag of the Confederate States of America we violated the constitution of the United States, and waged a war against that Government, whilst we owed allegiance thereto. On this hypothesis, is it so very clear that we have not forfeited our rights as citizens of the United States, and incurred the pains and penalties of the laws in such cases made and provided? As a condition precedent to a pardon, by the President of the United States, we have all taken the amnesty oath prescribed by his proclamation of the 29th of May last. The terms of this oath I have already repeated, and by its very terms we have certainly affirmatively and directly sworn to support the proclamations of the President and the laws of Congress with reference to emancipation.

Then, Mr. President, viewing the case in whatever aspect we may, the conclusion still seems to me inevitable, that slavery stands this day practically abolished with us; but at the same time, sir, that I make this statement, I must avow my belief that by the abolition of slavery a great wrong has been done us—that a heavy blow has been inflicted upon the material resources and prosperity of the South, and upon the wealth and resources of the country at large, if not of the civilized world. I deprecate, sir, this blow as much as any one can, but there was no way to escape from it; and so too, in reference to our lands, aye, in reference to the very homesteads to which the gentleman from Yazoo (Mr. Hudson) so feelingly alluded, it is no less true, that unless they have been, or are saved to us by what purports to be an act of clemency on the part of the President, they too will be taken from us, and we shall be turned out almost penniless upon the cold charity of the world. I wish, Mr. President, not to be misunderstood; I do not undertake to decide the right or wrong involved in the several very grave questions which I have briefly discussed, but I do insist upon it, that whether we are here representing a people who sustain the relation of foreigners to the Government of the United States, or who have involved themselves in the consequences of the violation of the laws of the United States, we should take counsel not from our prejudices or passions, but only from our judgments and reason. Our constitutional rights and the liberty which we inherited from our ancestors, and our determination to live freemen or die, are indeed very popular themes; and, if I expected to play the demagogue in future, I should certainly mount so available a hobby and ride it daily through this hall; but I feel, sir, the full weight of the responsibility resting upon me, and my duty conscientiously and faithfully, I shall endeavor to discharge. I desire earnestly to know what this Convention can do that will best advance the true and permanent interest of the people whom I represent, and of the State to which I owe so much; and in deciding this question, I shall not alone consider what my constituents may have thought upon the subject before I left home, or what may now be their views. I stand here bound by the most solemn considerations to avail myself of all the lights within my reach, and on every question of public duty to yield obedience only to the dictates of my conscience and judgment.

The direct question to be decided, is, shall the report of the committee of fifteen, or the substitute proposed in lieu of it, be adopted? The report simply proposes that the Constitution of the State be amended by adding thereto a section declaring that "neither slavery nor involuntary servitude, otherwise than in the punishment of crimes, whereof the party shall have been duly convicted, shall hereafter exist in this State;"—the substitute proposes the adoption of the report, with a proviso—the effect of which is to suspend the operation of the proposed constitutional amendment until our Representatives have been admitted on the floor of Congress, without having been previously required to take the test oath recently prescribed by that body, and to declare that by said amendment our claim to compensation for our slaves is not intended to be waived or in anywise affected.—My own firm conviction is, Mr. President, that if wisdom and enlightened statesmanship are brought to bear upon the subject, our Representatives will be admitted to their seats on the floor of Congress when they present themselves, and that the obnoxious oath referred to, is in conflict with the Constitution of the United States, and therefore null and void; but conceding all this, I cannot hope that any practical good will result from the adoption of the substitute. By that, slavery is abolished by your own act—on the admission of our Representatives to their seats in Congress. This, (that is the abolition of slavery by ourselves) is at once the effect of the adoption of the report of the committee. But sir, practically, as to slavery, the effect is the same, whether the report or the substitute be adopted, or whether our Congressional Representatives be received or excluded. We all know and admit that the institution of slavery in the Southern States has been destroyed, and that its resurrection is as little to be expected as the physical resurrection at the present time of the dead bodies that have been sleeping in the grave yard of this city for the last quarter of a century. Slavery, then, having already been abolished, the effect of our action, whether we adopt the report or the substitute, will be no more than a declaration that it shall not hereafter be revived. Whatever we may say, we have already been deprived of our slaves by the act and authority of the United States, and therefore our right to compensation, if any, is now an existing vested right, which will remain unimpaired, by the proposed prohibition of slavery for the future. On this subject we have all employed language not entirely correct—we have spoken of the abolition of slavery by the State, when only its prohibition for the future was intended.

Slavery was the issue involved in the war, at least since the President's emancipation proclamation was issued, and that issue has been decided by the bayonet against us; and whatever else we may think about the bayonet, we know that in human affairs its decisions are usually so potential as only to be reversed by a paramount physical power; and who, for one moment, believes that it is in the range of possibility for any such paramount power to be within our reach, for any such purpose, either now or at any future time? For the purpose of preventing the restoration of slavery, the bayonet is still present in our very midst; and it is in the opinion of us all, I believe, the fixed purpose of the United States Government not to remove the military power from any Southern State so long, as by its constitution, slavery has not been abolished, and the agitation, even of the subject, put at rest.

Then, Mr. President, as to the longer existence of slavery there is really no issue before us. we do, however anxiously desire the restoration of the State to all her rights under the Constitution; and in what possible way can the adoption of the substitute, in preference to the report, promote or tend to promote this important object? Indeed, might not its adoption have a contrary effect, by intensifying Northern radicalism? We should remember that the continued agitation of the subject of slavery promises no relief to us. Let the existing state of things in our midst be kept up for a very few years, and we shall all witness, I fear, the enfranchisement of the negro. The very power, sir, which convened this Convention can disperse it, and issue another proclamation calling another Convention, and prescribing other qualifications for voters and for eligibility to a seat in the body, without regard to race or color.

We are without the slightest possible control over the subject, and our condition is manifestly such that we have no alternative but to accept tfie best terms that can be obtained, whatever these terms may be. Let it be kept in mind that I am not now discussing any question of right or justice, or constitutional power: I am considering facts as they are, and not as I would have them, or think they should be. There is a large and growing party in the North, clamoring, not only for the enfranchisement of the freedmen, but who demand equality between the races, before the law, in all things, and there is not any party in the North, or any wing, or fraction of any party there that, in its demands, stop short, at this time, of the unconditional abolition of slavery by the Southern States themselves. There is a party, however, in the North, respectable for its numbers, who insist only upon the freedom of the negro, with the right of person and property guaranteed, and at the head of this party stands, I believe, the Presideut of the United States. He is, I hope, the friend of the Southern States—as a statesman and patriot he must desire the speedy reconstruction of the Union, upon just and honorable principles—the downfall, everywhere, of mere military rule, and the permanent re-establishment of civil power throughout the length and breadth of the land. Let us, then, do everything in our power to strengthen his hands, and carefully avoid whatever is calculated, in any way to embarrass or weaken our friends. Let us place them upon that position upon which alone we have any reason to believe they can successfully do battle in our behalf. The position of the President is one of commanding influence, and we certainly know what his views and wishes are, since they have not only been openly expressed again and again, but, as we must suppose, practically applied in the case of his own State. In the new constitution of Tennessee, we find unconditional, unqualified emancipation, but neither negro suffrage, nor in a controversy to which a white person is a party, negro testimony. The Tennessee constitution is now receiving the cordial support of the President, and by modeling our own after that, so far as the freedmen are concerned, we may confidently expect that those who advocate the former will also advocate ours.

But, Mr. President, should we adopt the substitute, may we not thereby place the administration and its supporters at a great disadvantage. It would, at least, give the prominent radicals of the land a pretext upon which to base their opposition to the emancipation of the Southern States from their present thraldom. These gentlemen and the party of which they are the leaders are, doubtless, watching our proceedings in the earnest hope that we may play into their hands, and afford them plausible grounds upon which to support a policy already fully determined upon, and the success of which will only be defeated by the utmost prudence on our part.

We should, sir, avoid even the appearance of any wish or purpose to dictate the terms on which we propose to consent to what is already an accomplished fact, and as to which, whatever our rights and wishes may have been, we know we are powerless and without the slightest expectation or hope of change or redress in the future. It affords me, sir, no pleasure to make these remarks. To me this theme is anything but agreeable. But as practical men—as statesmen, we cannot shut our eyes to the truth, or (to use a somewhat hackneyed phrase) close them to "the stern logic of events."

Let us then, Mr. President, vote down the substitute and adopt the report of the committee; and on all kindred subjects, let our action be so shaped as to give aid and comfort to our friends rather than to our enemies. By so doing, there is every probability that the State will be speedily restored to her federal relations, and to the exercise and enjoyment of the constitutional rights to which she will then be entitled. Should we, however, adopt an unwise policy, or, one not altogether satisfactory to the administration, I shall tremble for the result. The indications plainly are that there is a numerous party at the North who are conservative in their views, and who will rally to our support, if we place ourselves in such a position before the country as to afford them reasonable grounds to hope, that by their assistance, we can maintain the right and uphold the cause of constitutional liberty.

Mr. President, our constituents are tired of agitation; what they most want, and what our interest imperatively demands, is repose—exemption from all political excitement, whatever. In good faith they have taken the amnesty oath, and their altered condition they have accepted, with a fixed determination to give it a fair trial. At this time, I *am* confident that the Federal authorities may safely confide in the loyalty of the people of Mississippi, and that the true policy to be pursued toward them by the Government of the United States, is one of confidence, and not of distrust of their fidelity and allegiance.

Mr. Brown, of Yalobusha:

Mr. President:—I had intended offering a substitute for the second section of the proposed amendment to the Constitution, but the one offered by the gentleman from Yazoo, and now before the House, embracing, as it does, to a very great extent, the main features of the one I designed submitting—I may withhold it altogether; and will, unless the sentiment of this body undergoes a material change on the subject before the House from what I conceive it now to be. In giving my views in support of some of the features in the substitute, or in the adoption of the substitute as a choice between it and the second section of the amendment, it is not my purpose, Mr. President, to trammel the proceedings of this Convention, nor to embarrass the prospects for "*reconstruction.*" Conscious of the great responsibility resting upon me, I shall act from a sense of duty I owe to the Government of my allegiance on the one hand, and to an exhausted and oppressed people on the other. I favor the "*substitute*" because while it concedes every *requirement* of the Government; every requirement of Proclamation, and with every requirement, even *unofficial*, it proposes to reserve to the people some scanty privilege that does not come in conflict with these requirements, and which we have not been required nor authorized to surrender. I am obliged to the gentleman from Smith,* in the course of his remarks to-day, for calling the attention of the House to the position taken by certain gentlemen in regard to the "discretionary power" of this Convention. This was occasioned during our first day's proceedings, by a resolution offered by myself, to solicit official communication, from the Provisional Governor, who had called, or ordered, the Convention. Its object was to receive instruction or advice, had his Excellency any to communicate. I thought there was a responsibility resting somewhere in regard to a certain important step we had to take, and are now taking; and I wanted to know where that responsibility rested. I did not think it rested upon this body. But it was assumed by gentlemen that it did, and upon nobody else, and the action of the House, you will remember, Mr. President, sustained the assumption. I thought it a mistake then; I think so yet. I conceive this Convention to be the creation of Military order—that we meet to-day by virtue of permission, and that permission contingent upon the humor of our conqueror's clemency. I regret that the Convention evinced a disposition, by that action, to shift responsibility upon a wrongful quarter. I regret that it did not leave it where we found it, and where it does belong, and where I shall insist that it yet be saddled.

Mr. President, however we may differ about other things—there is one point, at least, on which we agree: we agree that reconstruction is the paramount object of the Convention. Its consummation is the mission of these delegates. In its adjustment are involved questions of vast and vital moment—questions of the greatest consideration that ever claimed the attention of any age. The history of the past can furnish no precedent to guide or direct us—no light can beam upon our way—but gloomy and unexploded is the path that carries us towards our ancient allegiance. We know not whether the old Union will open wide her arms to welcome back her prodigal daughters, or whether the door will be closed against us, and be left to wander in the darkness and confusion that war has provoked, and left us.

But we know this, Mr. President: we know that, as we proceed, we have to comply with terms that conflict with feelings we have long indulged—that restrict us in the exercise of privileges we are unwilling to surrender. But let us bear in

*The remarks of Mr. Johnson, of Smith, referred to by Mr. Brown, were not furnished by Reporter.

mind that reconstruction was the paramount condition of surrender—the paramount object of the Convention—that it is the mission of the delegates here. Bear in mind, too, that reconstruction is a nation's destiny: it is a great question of government, over and above the individual. It is a nation's fate, and we should not let our private feelings carry us in contact with its advance, nor drag us in its dangerous wake. It is to me, as an individual, an irresistible consequence; I must deal with the fact as it is, and must make the best of my condition that I can.

One of the terms of the condition is the oath of amnesty. I place a more liberal construction upon the last injunction of this oath, than prevails, I believe, with the majority sentiment of the Convention. I do not believe that my obligations to that oath—which I shall certainly observe, abide by and support, in good faith—require me to vote for a free Constitution; and if I do vote for such a Constitution, it will not be because I feel I am required by my oath to do so, but by the Government, and that, too, unofficial and outside of the obligation of the oath; I do so for the sake of policy. If I do so, it will be because gentlemen of position, whom I esteem for their high private and public virtues, who have lately held personal conference with the central power, tell me that it would be hazardous not to concede a free Constitution. I am open to conviction, Mr. President; and if the distinguished gentlemen, so lately from Washington, are in the same condition, it is left, then, for after argument to decide who shall change opinion. I am not yet convinced of the wisdom nor the propriety of their policy, and may perhaps concede my own position without being so convinced, because, conscious of the oppressed and helpless condition of our people, I may not feel at liberty to hazard opposition to the insinuations that gentlemen report having brought from the Great Central Power at Washington. I am not yet convinced that there is wisdom in their policy—but that it is fraught with injustice and danger; and they must yet bring arguments to support the propositions that have not yet appeared in its defence.

My construction of the obligations incurred by taking the oath to support the emancipation proclamation, is this: That that proclamation, like the Constitution, is the law of the land. But unlike the Constitution, it has yet to pass the ordeal of judicial decision; until then, as we support the Constitution, "in like manner," says the injunction, shall we "abide by and support" the proclamation. Not that we are required to canvass the country and proclaim to the populace that we have taken it—but as it is, that we acknowledge its authority. The President issued this proclamation. He shaped it, I suppose, just as he wanted it; sufficiently comprehensive, in his opinion, to attain its object, and he requires you to so accept it, abide by and support it. The amnesty oath was administered to us as citizens, and we are required, consequently, only as citizens to support it. As members of this Convention, we have taken the oath only to support the Constitution of the United States. We took the amnesty oath at our homes; we took it as citizens, and as citizens only have we been sworn to support it. We came to this Convention for a purpose that has no connection necessarily with the object of this oath. We came "for the purpose," says the proclamation that calls the Convention, "of altering and amending" the Constitution of the State, so that it may be able to resume its place in the Union. Now, what "alteration or amendment" alluded to in the proclamation, that calls the Convention, is necessary, "in order that it may be able to resume its place in the Union?" Why, simply conform the Constitution of Mississsippi to the Constitution of the United States. Alter and amend it, that the Constitution of the United States may operate here in harmony with the organic laws of the State. Alter and amend it, that the Constitution of the United States may operate here in harmony with the organic laws of the State. Alter and amend it that it may not conflict Mississippi with the position she has held in the Union since 1817. Here, in my opinion, end the expressed purpose of the Convention; end the expressed business of its delegates. Consistently, in my opinion, with the proclamation that called the Convention, and with our oaths to support the emancipation proclamation, this Convention could ignore legislation on the subject of slavery—could ignore it, at least, in the Constitution of the State. It would leave the proclamation as the law of the land; it would be legitimately the basis for succeeding legislation on all subjects of internal policy, relative to the rights of property and person of the freedmen. The proclamation could and would thereby be faithfully supported in and by the State of Mississippi, and that, too, in the absence of a free Constitution.

I feel that, in perfect conformity with my oath to support the proclamation of emancipation, I can vote against the establishment of a free Constitution by this Convention, because the very proclamation I am sworn to support, declares to have settled the matter in advance of my legislation. It declares the negro already free. Under that proclamation, which we are sworn to recognize as the law of the land, there is not a slave in the State of Mississippi—and if this be a fact, and we are not allowed to deny it—how can this Convention abolish an institution that has no existence? The proclamation declares already to have abolished slavery; I am sworn to acknowledge it as a fact, but I am not sworn to doubt or to deny its validity, by undertaking to complete the job myself.

This "substitute" to the "amendment," or substitute to the proposition for a free Constitution without any qualification—and which I prefer to the proposed "amendment"—concedes a free Constitution—concedes every requirement that the most strenuous advocates of an unqualified free Constitution can say the Government insists upon as necessary to reconstruction. It is conditional only so far as Congress makes it conditional. It is unconditionally free the moment they admit our delegates. And if they will not receive our delegates without a free Constitution, it concedes the right to receive them with one. If they reject our delegates with the privilege of admitting them with a free Constitution, then we have gained by the reservation we had the precaution to make—because we retain a position that had we abandoned, they would have occupied against us. We would have conceded the freedom of the negro in our organic law. They would then say, concede the franchise, and your delegates may come in. Gentlemen, let us ponder well this question.

But my distinguished friend from Marshall—from whom I have never before entertained an opposing view on a question of public policy—thinks it would look too stubborn, too unyielding, if we hint at any reservation—surrender even the right of indemnity. What! surrender what we have not been required nor authorized to surrender? I thought it was a free Constitution you wanted; this substitute concedes a free Constitution. Now, they say you must also surrender all claims you may have to compensation, should any such accrue from an adjudication of the courts in our favor.

Mr. President, I am willing to do, and to do faithfully, whatever the Government may require me to do, either by its proclamations or insinuations, unofficial, if necessary to reconstruction, and all this is conceded by the "substitute" proposed. But I am unwilling to surrender privileges, the few scanty rights reserved yet to an impoverished people. I have not been required yet to surrender, by anybody, except by these gentlemen, and no other reason offered for doing so, than perhaps we might not appear in the eyes of the government as sufficiently humiliated. I wish the kindly opinion of the Government—I wish its reconciliation, but I do not believe we could conciliate its favor in such a way.

I do not believe in surrendering rights simply to achieve no other purpose than to look humble. I cannot feel that such a voluntary proposition on our part would be becoming overmuch; I do not believe the Government could hardly appreciate such a huge and sudden expression of loyalty from a people who had lately been so beligerent. I do not believe that Mississippi could possibly elevate herself in the estimation or good opinion of the United States by heaping voluntary burdens upon her back, just to show the Federal Government how completely submissive she had grown of late.

I tell you what I do believe—I believe the Government would regard it as a reflection upon her pride for her military prowess, that you had flattered her to cherish when you compelled her to evince her great capacity, in suppressing the resistance you once rendered so formidable and so protracted. I believe that such feigned and slavish submission on the part of Mississippi—claiming no object other than to look humble before the conqueror, would be a lasting stigma upon the arduous struggle we have made—a stigma upon the countless numbers of our slain—upon the maimed remnant of our living. It would be a stigma upon the graves of your sons that mark the fields of a thousand battles. I know that we are humiliated, and must feel so—I know that we are disappointed in our purposes of separation and independence—that our vast armies are disbanded, and that in quiet submission we must bow to fate. But we should remember that on history's eternal page will live the renown of our arms—the chivalry of our people, and the dauntless courage of your sons. Remember this, and tarnish not your memory, by offering to surrender some few little privileges that Government has forgotten and would never think about again, unless to be disgusted at our humiliation when we offer to surrender them. But gentlemen insist that they have no rights. I do not believe that you have committed treason, and I can say this perfectly consistent with the position I held on the subject five years ago.—The distinguished member from Marshall, (Mr. Watson,) will bear me witness that I then denied that a State had the Constitutional right to secede. I denied that it had the reserved or the peaceable right—I doubted the wisdom, and I opposed the exercise of any such policy. Perfectly consistent with that position, I say you have not, in my opinion, committed treason. Because, before a gun was fired; before an army was organized; before a drop of blood was shed, the State of Mississippi, in sovereign Convention, declared you an alien to the Government of the United States. Whether Mississippi had the right to do this or not, was for the United States to decide. But that she did do it, was a fact so far as to you as an individual was concerned, your State assumed the responsibility, you were known no longer in the matter as an individual—you lost your individuality. It became a State action, and you, as an individual, had to submit and obey, or suffer death. There is another argument: the resistance the Southern people made against the effort of coercion, was so formidable, that they compelled the opposing power to recognize them as belligerents—compelled them to recognize their cartel, exchange of prisoners, and flag of truce. I think the resistance

8

made, assumed a dignity above treason. It was a rovolution, and must be, and was so regarded by the civilized nations of the world. But suppose that you have committed treason? It is true that the President would have the power to pardon; but could he pardon you upon that condition which was designated itself as a punishment, and was imposed against you before you had been proven guilty of treason—a punishment which, in my opinion, was the exclusive prerogative of a civil tribunal.

The controling object with me, gentlemen, is, that this great question may be settled *by the law*. The Government of the United States has assumed the responsibility of its settlement —Mississippi is relieved from the necessity. It is now in the hands of a higher power than our own; there let it await its adjustment. Let it be settled by the Constitution, and we will abide that decision, and will support the "proclamation until that decision is made." Let it be settled by the Supreme law of the land; supreme over the States, supreme over the Government. I am unwilling that this Convention shall, by its action, establish the precedent in the history of American jurisdiction, that the Government can *rise above the Constitution* in the settlement of any question. In the name of Mississippi, I protest against it; I protest against it in the name of the North. In the name of the American people and posterity, I protest against it. Let this question be settled, but let it be settled according to *the law*. Let that settlement prejudice a class; let it prejudice a section; but let it prejudice never the integrity of the American Constitution!

But, Mr. President, I am discussing what I conceive to be the merits of a measure that I endorse only as a preference to the proposed "amendment." I hope, however we may differ on this, that harmony may prevail, and that this Convention, in its wisdom and integrity, may extricate our people from the embarrassments that surround them.

On motion of Mr. Niles, the Convention adjourned until 4 o'clock, P. M.

FOUR O'CLOCK, P. M.

The Convention met pursuant to adjournment.

Mr. Montgomery asked leave of absence for Mr. Sessions, on account of illness.

Which was granted.

Mr. Sanders, of Attala, offerred the following resolution, which was adopted:

Resolved, That the Sergeant-at-Arms be instructed to make the necessary arrangements with the Postmaster of this city, for the forwarding of all mailable matter required by the members of this Convention.

Mr. Johnson, of Smith, gave notice that he would move a re-consideration of the vote, by which the report of the Committee on State Constitution was agreed to on yesterday, relative to the expediency of authorizing the Legislature to confer jurisdiction to the Courts of Justices of the Peace, in certain cases.

Mr. Simonton, of Itawamba, offered the following resolution, which was adopted:

Resolved, That the President be authorized and requested to appoint a Committee of five on Enrolled Ordinances and Constitutional Amendments.

The Convention then proceeded to the consideration of the special order, to-wit: The substitute offered by Mr. Hudson, for the second section of the report of the Committee on State Constitution.

Mr. Cooper, of Rankin—Mr. President: I hope that the substitute offered by the gentlemen from Yazoo, will not be adopted. I cannot myself see any good that can possibly result from it. It seems to me that it is simply a proposition on the part of this Convention, to make a bargain with the Abolition party of the North—those who are opposed to the rights of the South. It is a proposition on our part, to say to them: "Gentlemen, you desire to place the freedmen of the country, the negroes or mulattoes, upon a social, civil and political equality with the white man. You have secured his freedom, and ask now that he should be made an equal. We will agree with you to free them, on condition that you will, on your part, agree that our Representatives shall be admitted into Congress." This is the kind of bargain—a mere proposition for a trade between the Abolitionists and ourselves—from which I do not believe any good can come. I am opposed to this, therefore. I think we have but one object now in view. The slavery question is no longer an open question. There is, however, a living question and a living issue, submitted to the people of this country, and that is in reference to the future status of the freed negroes. The great question is now—who shall have jurisdiction—the Federal Congress, or the people of Mississippi? I desire to claim it for ourselves—and now how shall we obtain it? It is not for such propositions as these, in my judgement—it is not by encumbering the record by any "whereas," etc—but by inquiring what the true interests of the country require. What do they call upon us to do? Simply to make such ordinances, and so to regulate the action of this Convention, as to conform our Government in the future, to the new order of things. Take the institution of slavery as abolished—encumber that idea with nothing more, and then present ourselves before the conservative men of the North as a State; and recognizing the result of the war as having abolished slavery, demand all other rights we are entitled to. I am, therefore, in favor of voting for the report of the Committee, as it came before us. I do not care who killed Cock Robin, or by what means, or in what manner, slavery has been abolished; but I concede it as a fact. I propose that we shall deal with it as practical men—as a fact, manifest to practical men, who can draw a correct deduction from premises.

As to the question regarding jurisdiction—if the policy of the gentlemen on the opposite side is to obtain, I can see no earthly hope, but that Congress will continue to legislate and agitate this question, until the last vestige of our rights are taken from us. But, if we act boldly and manfully, meet things as practical men, and pursue the course which I have suggested, I have no doubt that the result will be all we can desire.

I am willing to go this far—to let the institution of slavery be considered as abrogated. I am willing to guarantee that the State of Mississippi will secure to the free negro, those rights which belong to freemen, in all countries—the right of personal security, and of personal liberty, and the right of property. I am willing to do that, without any "ifs or ands," or qualifications, because I believe it best for the country to do it, under existing circumstances; but beyond that, I am unwilling to go. I think it is unmanly for us to make any proposition for a bargain with the Black Republican or any other party. I believe that to be the sentiment of the people of Mississippi.

I did not rise to make a speech, but to give my views, and to advocate the proposition of the Committee, and say that henceforth, there shall be no slavery or involuntary servitude in Mississippi.

MR. JARNAGIN, of Noxubee—Mr. President: There seems to be a strange contrariety of opinion expressed by the delegates of this Convention, in regard to the policy which shall be pursued upon the question of slavery. It is certainly very desirable that there should be as much unanimity as possible. Feeling, impressed with this idea, I think there ought to be something yielded for the purpose of accomplishing the main object of the Convention; that is, the speedy restoration of the supremacy of law in our State, and the restoration of our rights, as regards the Federal Government. I know no individual can be more anxious than myself, that this object should be accomplished; and if I know myself, I do not wish to throw any impediments in the way of accomplishing this object, at the very earliest period possible. But there seems to be a difference of opinion in regard to how this shall be accomplished. As I understand, from the remarks which have made by the various members of this body, there seems to be two opinions on the subject mainly. One is, that we should abolish slavery, as proposed by the Committee, in the amendment to the Constitution, which we now have under consideration. There are others who agree with myself, that we ought to do something more than merely abolish slavery, without giving any assignable cause, or fixing the responsibility, if there be any, upon the proper party. Now, I do not agree with some gentlemen on this floor, and particularly, the gentleman from Marshall, (Mr. Watson.) I do not agree that we are now in a state of rebellion. I do not believe, in the first place, that we ever went out of the Union—that we dissolved our connection with the Federal Government. I think this is too plain to need argument; therefore, I shall say nothing in regard to the ordinance of secession, or what position that placed us in—taking it for granted, that we never have been out of the Union—or that we have been in the Union from the time of secession until the present day. That we were in a state of disorganization and rebellion, I grant. Then the position of the gentlemen from Marshall, seems to be, that we were either out of the Union, by the act of secession, or were in a state of rebellion; in other words, that we were guilty of treason, and he tells this body, we can take either horn of the dilemma. Take the horn that we were in a state of rebellion and guilty of treason, if the gentleman pleases, and what is our condition now? The argument which has been used over and over again, as giving omnipotent power to the President of the United States, as if we were still in a state of rebellion; that even under the invitation of the President of the United States—under the call of the Provisional Governor of this State—unless in our ordinances and amendments to the Constitution, we came up to his ground, he would destroy our State Government. I do not so regard it. I do not look upon the President of the United States, as being vested with this power. What is now our present status? We are here as the representatives of the loyal people of the State of Mississippi, in Convention assembled, for the purpose of amending the Constitution of the State of Mississippi—and from the very words of the President, appointing a Provisional Governor—from the declaration contained in the proclamation of the Provisional Governor of the State, calling us together in Convention. The State of Mississippi has been a sovereign State from the day of secession to the present hour. We are not called upon as if we were out of the Union, for the purpose of forming a Constitution, in order to be admitted back into the Union. We are called for the purpose of amending the Constitution, that which was in existence at the time the President penned his proclamation, appointing a Provisional Governor for the State. He so regarded it; the Provisional Governor so regards it. He proclaims to the loyal people—prescribing who are loyal—that they shall elect delegates to the Convention. For what purpose? Not for the purpose of forming a Constitution. It precludes the idea—if we were a State—that we were in a territorial condition, or in any condition outside of the Federal Government. Then, Mr. President, I assume this position—that we are the representatives of the loyal people of the State of Mississippi—that we have convened as representatives of the loyal people of the State—and if we were guilty of treason, and as traitors, whatever favor was shown us, was a matter of mercy, as declared on this floor; that treason has been wiped out by the amnesty proclamation of the President of the United States. To-day, so far as humility is concerned, we stand as if there had been no rebellion, or if we had been guilty of no treason,. When it has been declared by the highest power of the Government, and the Nation, we have been purged of our treason, and the rebellion wiped out, we stand then as the loyal citizens of the State of Mississippi, with the same Constiutitutional rights as any State is invested with. If not, the proclamation amounts to nothing—we have been guilty of treason in the eyes of the President of the United States. He issues his pardoning proclamation, and as a test of our loyalty, he requires that we shall take a certain oath; and when we have taken that oath, we are restored to our loyalty, and recieve all the Constitutional and political rights, and the rights of property, except in slaves. I cannot see that we are disloyal subjects of the Government of the United States, knocking at the door of the United States for admission, as parties guilty of treason, and claiming mercy at the hands of the Executive of the United States. We stand here as loyal citizens representing the loyal people of our State, and I wish to shape our legislative action so that we may preserve our manhood, self-respect, and the dignity of the State of Mississippi, as a sovereign State.—Then it becomes us to pursue a certain course of policy; and deny it if we may, but the facts stand out boldly to our face, that we are assembled here to-day, as the sovereign people of the State of Mississippi, representing the sovereignty: we stand here not untrammelled, yet without extraordinary or extraneous influence operating on this body. We all know it; but at the same time, Mr. President, I cannot believe with some gentlemen upon this floor, who seem to think, that unless we come up to the behest of the President of the United

States, that he has that omnipotent power by which he can overleap and trample down the barriers of the Constitution, and deprive us of our rights. No, I believe, placed as we are now, as a sovereign State—our guilt, our rebellion, our treason having been wiped out, that we should present ourselves as a free State, and claim the high rights we are entitled to under the Constitution of the United States, and the laws of Congress. But notwithstanding all this—notwithstanding our clear Constitutional rights—notwithstanding representing the people of the State of Mississippi, as we do upon this floor, we are in a situation, in which it may be politic to shape our course, so as to meet the ends which we wish to accomplish. It is certainly very desirable to carry out the grand doctrine which is contemplated by the subject under consideration, that we should have as much unanimity of action on this subject as possible. How is that unanimity to be produced under the variety of opinions entertained upon this floor? I think it might be produced—at least, I have heard no argument on this floor, which precludes the idea in my mind that this harmony can be produced. The fact that slavery is abolished, is not questioned by anybody—practically abolished, at least. That slavery, as remarked by the gentleman from Hinds, is dead, dead, dead, I agree. Under ordinary circumstance, it might be asked, what are we doing here upon this subject? Are we merely burrying the dead, or are we fighting that battle over again, for the purpose of killing slavery more completely than it was killed by the action of the Federal Government? Slavery no longer exists in the State of Mississippi, practically, and to all intents and purposes, and it is not my object, and those who agree with me in sentiment on this floor, to take any action which has a tendency to the restoration of slavery, within the State of Mississippi. There are dangers, it is true, ahead of us, but I do not expect, let the action of the Convention be what it may, that the organization of this State is to be deranged hereafter by the President, or by the Congress of the United States. It is intimated, and I do not pretend to deny the fact, that the President of the United States has given out in unmistakable terms, admitting that he has the power—that there are certain requisites which it will be best for us, at least, to secure that representation in Congress, for the State of Mississippi, in her Convention on this subject to pursue, and that is to present a free Constitution. I grant that the report of the Committee on the section under consideration, does present a free Constitution; but there are members upon this floor, acting with myself, who are not looking alone to the admission of our members into the Congress of the United States; but while they look with anxiety to the accomplishment of that object, at the same time they have an eye to the interests and dignity of the State of Mississippi, and to the interests of our citizens. The amendment which was heretofore introduced by myself and laid on the table, and the substitute which was offered by the gentleman from Layfayette, met my views fully upon this subject, and I think the substitute secures the rights of the citizens of the State of Mississippi. I think at the same time, it leaves the responsibility of the abolition of slavery where it properly belongs, and that is upon the Federal Government. I should state here, that if the section which has been introduced by the Committee, should fail to pass, it would be my purpose, to call from the table the substitute which was offered by the gentlemen from Lafayette.

Now, Mr. President, I think there is a responsibility—a great responsibilty—that rests upon the Federal Government, and the argument which is used upon this floor, that this responsibility will never be met, no matter how just it may be, has no weight upon my mind at all. If it be a just claim —if any portion of the State of Mississippi have a just claim on the Federal Government for compensation, we should take no action that possibly can be avoided; at the same time accomplish the restoration of our rights in the Federal Government—that shall cut off our rights.

It would be useless for me to state my views in regard to the responsibility now resting, or that will rest, upon the Federal Government. That question has been used by learned gentlemen on this floor, and in a much fuller manner than I could do it. Therefore, for the purpose of making my remarks as short as possible, I will pass over the various responsibilities, which I consider resting upon the Federal Government, by reason of the abolition of slavery on our part; and it is my object, in the vote which I shall give upon the report which has been introduced, to secure the rights of all. It will be my object to leave the responsibility, whatever it may be, upon the Federal Government—and the State of Mississippi, shall not, by any action which she may take, assume and take upon herself that responsibility. Now, the amendment which I refer to, accomplishes this precise object, and, as I contend, precisely the object contemplated by the section under consideration. I have heard no argument to show that the preamble which gentlemen speak of, will prejudice our rights, or that it prevents us from presenting a free Constitution. The Constitution, with the substitute, will be as free as the Constitution will be, if the clause introduced by the Committee be adopted. It is equally free. It is a free Constitution, and I would like to have any gentlemen on this floor, show to this body, how it is possible, that by the adoption of the amendment I speak of it is the worse. Slavery has been abolished by the action of the Federal Government. Therefore, we say, "Be it ordained, that hereafter slavery shall not exist in the State of Mississippi." That will meet the views of the President, I think. I merely state the fact, that the President himself states. If there be any honor in the abolition of slavery in the Southern States, it belongs not to us, because according to the declaration, slavery is already dead; and if slavery be extinct in the States of the Union of the Federal Government, which is unquestionably true, then I say, in all action we take, even upon the section under consideration, abolishing slavery, we merely do a work of superorogation, only to appease the North, and meet the views of the President of the United States, and thereby secure our representation. The world knows we met here in Convention by strong pressure, and by the action of the Federal Government; that we were forced almost; we did succumb, and we did abolish slavery, stating it should never hereafter exist. It is not a voluntary offering on our part. It is one that has been wrested from us, and we may say what we please about. It is from compulsion on our part. As slavery is dead, I have no hesitation in recording my vote to the effect, but I want to record my vote, how it was brought about—how it was, Mississippi was abolitionized—how it was, that four years ago, no man would have been in Convention, voting in favor of the abolition of slavery. I want the record to go out with the facts, that is, that the Federal Government abolished slavery. Therefore, the State of Mississippi abolished slavery for the purpose of getting her rights, which she has under the Constitution of the United States. Some unanimity must be produced in this body, and if gentlemen can show that we are to prejudice our rights, and throw impediments in the way of the accomplishment of the object we all have in view. I am open to conviction. I have as yet heard no argument on this floor that has convinced me, that the substitute offered by the gentleman from Lafayette, does not present a free Constitution, untrammelled, and setting forth the facts, and the cause of our action to-day—no argument that has convinced me, if we adopted the substitute, we should defeat our object.

Mr. Goode, of Lawrence—Mr. President: I wish to make a few remarks, for the purpose of removing, if possible, some difficulties, which appear to exist. It seems to be assumed by the gentleman from Hinds, (Mr. Potter,) that so far as the question of adopting a free clause in the Constitution, declaring slavery abolished, the amnesty oath we have taken, has nothing to do with it. He declared himself free to vote for a slave Constitution, or for a free Constitution—that oath notwithstanding. I understood him to declare himself the representative of the sovereign people of the State, authorized to do whatever he thought best, and for the interest of that people, under no restrictions, and accountable to no one outside this Convention, except his constituents. On the first day of this Convention, I took the liberty of suggesting—on motion made and adopted, to advise Gov. Sharkey, that this Convention was organized and ready to proceed to business, and to inquire if he had any communcation to make to us—whether it might not be better, in view of the peculiar circumstances, under which we had assembled, to wait for some communication, in relation to our power and rights as a Convention. The gentleman from Hinds, in reply to that suggestion, and upon the motion, I believe, to re-consider, stated what I have already recounted, as the gentlemen from Smith, (Mr. Johnson,) has remarked. I understood another delegate from Hinds, (Mr. Johnston,) to endorse this position, and to state that he considered himself the representative of a sovereign people, and accountable to no authority outside this Convention, except the people of Mississippi. But whatever opinion is enunciated here, I did not then, and do not now, Mr. President, consider myself the representative of a sovereign people. The voters who sent me here were required by the proclamation, to take a certain oath before they were authorized to vote for a Representative. Before I could take my seat here as a member of this body, I was required to take a certain oath. The difficulty that besets my mind, has not been removed as I desire it to be—otherwise I I shall have to vote against the substitute of the gentleman from Yazoo—in obedience to the terms of this oath.

It has been remarked by gentlemen, that this has nothing to do with the question—that we merely took the oath to abide by the Constitution, and support the Union of the States thereunder, and in like manner, to support all laws mnde during the existing rebellion, in regard to slaves, and that therefore, they have a right to vote for or against a free Constitution. It is my misfortune, sir, to differ from them. One ot the rules for interpreting the meaning of a law, is to satisfy yourself as to the evil intended to be remedied or guarded against, and the object to be acomplished. It is been said by distinguished gentlemen upon this floor, that the President of the United States has not enunciated anything of an authoritative shape, for the guidance of this Convention, but only in hints or inuendoes, by which this Convention ought not to be governed. I have before me the proclamation in which this amnesty oath is contained. After certain recitation, &c., he goes on to say—I think I quote it correctly—"to the end therefore, that the authority of the United States may be established in the State of Mississippi, and that peace, order and *freedom* may be established"—he provides for amnesty and pardon. What freedom? The freedom of the whites? Not at all. Has there been but one class that has been enslaved? If the word *freedom* was put into that proclamation advisedly, and I take it, it was—and has any meaning, does it not mean to the previous slave population here? Surely, and to establish that freedom, he issued this proclamation, and prescribes a certain oath, called the "amnesty" oath. I have been met, out of doors, with this suggestion, that this oath means simply to provide for the acceptance of the proclamation and laws in reference to the emancipation of slaves—that wherever it was placed in my power to defeat that proclamation or support it, then I was bound, by my oath, to support it; and this, of itself, would induce me to vote against this substitute. I do not profess to be a very erudite scholar, but do profess and claim to understand ordinary language.

There are two terms used in the latter clause of this amnesty oath. One is to abide by the proclamation and laws with reference to slaves. I take that to mean acquiescence and submission to those laws—acting simply in conformity to those laws, or abiding by them in a passive manner. There is another term used—to support also those laws. What is the meaning of the word support? I think, that I will aid in upholding and carrying them into effect—giving every assistance in so doing. Suppose, and as is contended, that slavery is not legally abolished in toto—and I take it, that almost all lawyers will agree about this, that slavery has not been legally abolished in the State of Mississippi. Gentlemen say differently, as if it was the conclusion of the argument that nobody contends that slavery is not abolished. I would like to know the meaning that gentlemen intend to give terms, where they use them. I am willing to admit that slavery is impracticable here, and has ceased to exist as a live and vital institution; but there may be a legal slavery still, although it may be but a myth floating in the immagination of legal gentlemen, pretending to understand the rules of law. I am free to admit that President Lincoln had a right to issue the proclamation. I concede it, so far as the United States troops succeeded in giving slaves actual freedom, during the existence of the war, there exists not a doubt in my mind, as to their real freedom; but, sir, at the date of the surrender of this department, and of the armed forces of the Confederacy, when there existed no longer, an armed rebellion, and there was no possibility of the commission of any further acts by the Confederate States armies, or any State composing it, there was a large number of slaves not reached by the military arm of the United States. What is the status of that portion of the slave population?—Is it contended that the mere war measure of Mr. Lincoln, which as a war mea[illegible] terms, is only operative during war, remains operative after the war has ceased? I have the best evidence that the United States Government did not so regard it. I remember reading a speech—a great one, as I thought at the time, and still think—of Mr. Seward, just previous to the nomination of Gen. McClellan to the Presidency. I took it to be an electioneering speech—in which the doctrine was distinctly enunciated and laid down, apparently by authority, that Mr. Lincoln, and the United States Government claimed no virtue for the proclamation, except as a war measure, and he used this emphatic language—that when the war ceased, it ceased to be of force. I saw no disclaimer of this language, on the part of the Government, and nothing to indicate that the Government did not agree with the Secretary of State. Those proclamations, then, being inoperative when the war ceased, I take it that those persons who remained in slavery, at the end of the war, are legally slave. I infer from President Johnson's amnesty proclamation, that he took the same view of this matter. I infer from the proposed amendment to the Constitution of the United States, adopted by Congress, and refered to the States for approval, in February, 1860, such was the view taken of it by the United States Government.

The amnesty oath is proposed. How does that oath propose to treat us? The gentleman from Marshall, (Mr. Watson,) said that gentlemen, who insisted upon the substitute, must take one of the two horns of a dilemma—either that the State was sovereign, and was so treated, or we were traitors. I think we have admitted, by the amesty oath, that we occupied the latter position. President Johnson undertook to extend amnesty and pardon to certain persons, who had been in a state of rebellion, and the members of this Convention accepted the terms, came forward, and by their act in taking that oath, admitted that it was in his power to propose such terms—that it was just and right that he should propose such terms, and that we occupied the position which that proclamation assigned to us—that there was a necessity for us to purge ourselves of this treason and rebellion, before we were entitled to our rights and privileges of liberty and property, and citizens of Mississippi, and of the United States. We come and took this oath, to the end that peace, order and freedom, might be established. He made a certain proposition, as I have said, to certain persons, and left it with those persons to accept it or refuse it, and stand a trial for treason. Every member of this Convention, not only accepted the proferred terms, but so did every one of the constituency, who sent us here. What is our duty in the premises? I believe that this amnesty and pardon conferred upon us, is a sufficient consideration to bind us to the performance of the contract, int[illegible]e entered upon taking this oath.

But, says the gentleman upon the right, what right has the President to affix any condition to this pardon? He had the right of pardon or punishment. but having pardoned, it was a contradiction in terms to impose as a condition, what was, in reality, a punishment. I beg leave to differ from the gentleman here, and say that the President did not inflict this punishment. If it be a punishment, it is self-imposed by the gentleman himself. The President did not, by physical force, compel me to take that oath, but I consider that there was an inducement sufficient to influence me to take it; and, having done so, I consider it before Heaven and this Convention, as a voluntary oath, and I expect to abide by it, as I construe it.

If my position, Mr. President, be correct—if the word "support" means more than mere acquiescence—if gentlemen of this Convention should consider that when we have provided a Constitution, for future time and generations, and people who may not have taken the amnesty oath—if gentlemen consider that this comes under the term "support," when we were called to deal with the question in this shape, I do not see any escape from this oath. I feel myself bound, and have, ever since I was announced as a candidate for this Convention, to vote for a free Constitution; and I consider this Convention, so bound, when by a unanimous vote, they adopted the proposed ordinance, to strike out of Constitution all the provisions, in reference to slaves. We heard of no substitutes or conditions that our Representatives should be received in Congress. We must disregard all these considerations, when we come to what I consider a literal compliance with our oaths. Gentlemen stick it out as if there was a lion in the path; as if there was danger of humiliating ourselves. I am opposed, as much as the gentleman on my right, to doing anything for the purpose of humiliating ourselves. I understand no gentleman to contend for that position. I think we are sufficiently humiliated, and were when we took the amnesty oath; but we prefered taking it, to abide the risks of suffering the pains and penalties of treason; and I think that we intend to act in good faith with the United States Government, in regard to the conditions fixed for our part of the contract. If we have a right to affix conditions, as insisted by the gentlemen from Yazoo, (Mr. Hudson,) and supported by able members, we have a right to refuse to adopt any clause in the Constitution, abolishing slavery—or such as will render it utterly impossible for the Government of the United States, ever to receive it. I consider myself bound—actively, not passively—to support the proclamations and laws made during the existence of the rebellion, in reference to the emancipation of slaves, and I prefer, as some gentlemen have said, that it should appear—as history, if you will, written by the Convention itself—that slavery has ceased to exist as a vital institution—not by the act of the United States Government, (for I do not believe it was the act of the United States Government alone, or that it was produced by the ordinance of secession alone,) but as a consequence of the war. We all know it to be a fact, but I prefer so stating it for this reason.

I am opposed to any further humiliation than is absolutely necessary for the benefit of the people of Mississippi. Not that I am proud and haughty, but I am opposed to humiliation in the sense in which, I suppose, the use of the word upon this floor was intended to be taken—though humiliation is inculcated as a Christian virtue, and in that sense, not to be shunned. I would have been in favor of inserting a few words in this ordinance, as an amendment thereto, to the effect that "slavery having ceased to exist, we provide that it shall not hereafter exist." It might, and will be inferred, that intimidated by bayonets—over-awed by hints or inuendoes, the delegates of the people of Mississippi, who heretofore insisted that slavery was right, by laws both divine and human, have turned a complete sommersault, and have, under this intimidation, being thus over-awed, have suddenly changed their minds, and said slavery was wrong, and therefore should not hereafter exist—said it in substance. It will be insisted that this sudden change which public opinion expresses through this Convention, is the result of fear and of threats. I would, therefore, insert some clause in the Constitution similar to what I have suggested; but if that cannot be done, I will vote for the section as reported.

The gentleman from Yalobusha, Mr. Brown, asserted there was no need, in his opinion, of any provision that slavery should not hereafter exist, in connection with that oath. The gentleman seems to overlook the fact that there may be persons interested in this assertion, for whom we are adopting this Constitution, who have not placed themselves in the state that members of this Convention have—who have not taken the amnesty oath, and who will not be bound by that oath to abide by and support the emancipation proclamation. If we permit slavery to exist, and those persons—they may be in the majority, for all I know—were to continue the institution in the State of Mississippi, in the absence of any claim prohibiting it, would we have fulfilled the obligations which we have sworn to support? I take it we would not. We are providing laws, not for ourselves alone, but for the Government, and the people of Mississippi, whosoever they may be —whether they have taken the amnesty oath, or have not taken it. I think it is our duty—I feel it, sir, so strongly, that I did not consider myself at liberty to vote for the substitute —to vote for some clause prescribing that slavery, or involuntary servitude, shall not hereafter exist. How will it be, on the ground of expediency and policy? If this substitute were adopted, when it went before Congress, this would be urged—and I can see no way of successfully refuting the position, or getting around it—that we left the people of Mississippi at liberty to revive the institution of slavery and continue it, if the proclamation and the laws in reference to the emancipation of slaves, which we have sworn to abide by and support, were decided to be unconstitutional. It would be said that we had not kept our faith with the General Government, and that we could not be trusted, and would not yield the point which we settled—that we had violated our oath, and would not be given the privilege of taking another.

I call the attention of the members of this Convention to the peculiar language used. The whole is not contained in one sentence; but we swore, first, to abide by and support the Union of States, and the laws thereunder, and the laws in reference to rebellion; and then, afterwards, we swore to, "in like manner, abide by and support" these laws and proclamations! Is it usual, in swearing an officer, to say—"You swear to support the laws enacted by Congress; the proclamations issued by the President, and all the decrees rendered by the Courts?" The oath to support the laws, involves all that.

The gentleman from Hinds, Mr. Potter, laid great stress upon the fact that we should not be bound by this oath, in case the courts decided that the proclamations, &c., were unconstitutional. It was within the power of the President, although the proclamation and the laws in reference to the emancipation of slaves were unconstitutional, to prescribe as a condition to our amnesty and pardon, that we should take this oath. How would this whole oath be construed? As one oath? I have called attention to the peculiar language, and it would be considered, in law, as one oath. It would be said that we have sworn to support the Constitution and other laws; in other words, you have sworn to support the Constitution, save and except so far as regards the institution of slavery. If the President did not deem it necessary to swear us to support any other laws and proclamations besides these in reference to the emancipation of slaves—was not that the reason—because doubts did exist in regard to the constitutionality and legality of them? But it was intended to bind the conscience of all those in rebellion to abide by and support them, in any contingency, as the political policy of the country—not as a part of the mere law of the country, but to deal with it as outside the Constitution, in this sense, and to swear us to support it and assist in carrying it out.

In voting, on yesterday, against laying on the table certain propositions, I did not intend to convey the idea—and I suppose other gentlemen did not—that we were in favor of amendments, the tabling of which we opposed. I wish simply to explain that when I cast my vote, I did not mean to be considered as binding or committing myself to vote for them, if put on passage; but I wished to prolong discussion. We came here with the idea of expressing and hearing expression of views on this subject, as the main object and duty of this Convention. My constituents looked at nothing else, and I told them that probably the Convention would deal with little else, at this time. I wished to be enlightened, and was opposed to cutting off debate, by laying on the table, undiscussed propositions, wishing, as I and my constituents do, to have presented for consideration, the different aspects of every question.

MR. CRAWFORD, of Jones.—Mr. Speaker: The principle of the opposition to the section embraced in the report of the Cemmittee, seems to be remuneration. I would agree to that amendment were its provisions broad enough, but in that essential, all the provisos brought up and offered to the original report of the Committee, have fallen short. These provisoes have only aimed at remuneration to certain classes, who have heretofore been the owners of slaves, while I, Mr. President, represent the widows and orphans of the Caucassian race, whose cries are now ascending in my down-trodden county, for bread. Yes, sir, in my suffering county, of Jones, to-day the wails of three hundred and eighty widowed women and starving children are ascending before the God of right, and appealing in tears to the powers appointed for relief. Yet, in the midst of these facts, it appears that the entire sympathies of this body are directed to that class who are presumptively suffering from the passage of the section under consideration. I appeal in honesty to this Convention, to remember the white race, and not to be wholly absorbed in Africanism.

MR. GOWAN, of Simpson.—Mr. President: It is not my purpose, in arising at this stage of the discussion, which has progressed at such great length, to detain the Convention long in discussing the substitute offered by the gentleman from Yazoo, (Mr. Hudson,) or the amendment proposed to the Constitution by the Committee. But I deem it due to myself as a delegate to this Convention, and more especially to those whom I have the honor to represent here, to give expression to the views I entertain, and the reasons which will govern me in casting my vote.

There are some portions of the substitute, Mr. President, which I might consistly vote for, if not taken in connection with other portions; but taking it as a whole, I shall be constrained to vote against it, considering our present relations to the Federal Government. The substitute proposes that if the Congress of the United States will admit our delegates to seats in that body, that in that event we will abolish the institution of slavery in the State of Mississippi, etc., assuming that slavery, as an institution, still exists in this State, notwithstanding the emancipation proclamation, and the laws of Congress, and the results of the war. I cannot see, Mr. President, that the objects contemplated in calling this Convention together, can be accomplished by making such propositions as this to the Government of the United States. In other words, I cannot see that we will succeed in restoring our constitutional relations to the Federal Government, by adopting such a dictatorial policy as this towards that Government. In doing this, sir, we attempt to dictate terms upon which we will be admitted back to our constitutional relationship with the Federal Union. Sir, this would be a novel and exceedingly strange attitude for a vanquished and conquered people, groaning under military despotism as we are, to assume towards those who, after four years of desolating war, have succeeded in wresting from us every means of resistance, and established over us a most grinding military despotism, which we can in no wise get rid of, unless we comply with the terms prescribed by the Federal Government. And what are those terms? As I understand them, they are to strike out the slavery clause of our Constitution, and guarantee freedom to those who have been held in slavery heretofore in this State. As I understand it, we are not to abolish the present institution of slavery in the State of Mississippi, because that has already been destroyed by the emancipation proclamation, and the power of the military forces of the United States; and it is so regarded by the Federal Government; and hence, we are not asked to do that which is already regarded as accomplished by the Government of the United States; but we are required to provide, by our Constitution, that neither slavery nor involuntary servitude shall hereafter exist in the State of Mississippi, unless as a punishment for crime, whereof the party has been convicted. But, sir, some honorable members object to this position, and say that slavery has not, in deed and in fact, been legally and constitutionally abolished in this State. As to the correctness of this assumption, I am rather inclined to agree with those who assumed this position, as it is a matter of doubt in my mind whether the United States have the power to strike down, by executive proclamation, an institution or species of property, recognized and established by the Constitution. But admitting this to be true, I would ask, what conceivable good can inure to us by reason thereof? None whatever, when we con-

9

sider that the Supreme Court of the United States is composed of men, who coincide with the administration, and the whole people of the North, that the Government had a Constitutional right in suppressing the rebellion; to declare the slaves of the South free; and to maintain their freedom, purely as a war measure, And this party being in power, and having our State under martial law and military government, they will maintain the freedom of the negro, until we acknowledge and acquiesce in the fact, that the negro is free; it matters not whether that freedom was brought about by Constitutional means, or not; and having taken this view of the subject—and I conceive this to be the only correct view—we have the alternative left us, either to give up the institution of slavery, and shape our fundamental law in accordance with this truth, or to content ourselves to remain under military Government, as a conquered province, and ultimately have negro equality, socially and politically forced upon us. And I think, Mr. President, that it is far better for this people, not only for their present welfare, but for the welfare of generations yet to come, to secure to us and to them, supremacy over the negro, and the right to give him, by reasonable and just laws, security and protection in his person and property.

These are the terms of adjustment, offered to us by the President of the United States, and the only terms which we can expect to obtain. But there is another question involved in this substitute, which I would favor, if separated from the balance. It is proposed to set forth, by way of *preamble,* the means by which the institution of slavery was destroyed. I think it very proper, that this should be done; as the amendment offered by the Committee, if adopted as it stands, might be misconstrued by the world, so as to cast the responsibility of abolishing the institution of slavery, upon the people of this State. And this I am utterly opposed to. The authorities and Government of the United States have destroyed this institution, and I am in favor of giving them the sole honor. They have fought through a desperate war of four years, for the consummation of this object; and I am in favor of their enjoying the exclusive credit of it.

But there is another question involved in the substitute, Mr. President. This question has reference to compensation for slaves freed during the war. I am in favor of the people having compensation for their slaves, taken from them without their consent, if it is possible for such compensation to be had. But I doubt the propriety of encumbering this proviso of the Constitution with such a proviso as this. If the people have a right to compensation, which I do not doubt they do have, taken in either a legal or equitable light, this right would not be destroyed by refusing to adopt this proviso. No action of this Convention, could either abolish such a right, and I think the proviso wholly unnecessary. And, while it will do no good, it will undoubtedly have a tendency to do great harm, by prejudicing our cause, and I am unwilling to throw any impediment in the way of our speedy restoration to the Union, upon the best terms it is possible for us to obtain; and this amendment would undoubtely have a tendency to impede the progress of our speedy restoration to our Constitutional relations to the Federal Government.

Sir, the object in assembling this Convention, was to remodel our Constitution so as to make it conform to the new condition of things, and it is useless to attempt to evade this main question, by any subterfuge, we may see fit to resort to. We cannot hope to accomplish our object in any other way than by meeting the facts squarely, and adopting the measures which are most likely to give us a civil form of Government, to enable us to regulate our domestic affairs, and which will restore us back to the favor and protection of the General Government. Sir, already there is a large party in the North and West, who are advocating negro suffrage, and the social and political equality of the negro with the white man of the South, and likewise all the leading journals of the North are strenuously advocating this political doctrine. This party are also urging that the Government should hold the rebellious States under military control for a series of years, or until we are willing to confer the right of suffrage upon the negroes of the South, and allow them all other civil political immunities. But the President has adopted a very different policy from this, towards the seceded States, but whether he will be able to carry out his policy, or not, I am unable to determine. But I sincerely hope he will, and think this Convention should do all in their power to uphold and strengthen the Administration, and to aid in turning this terrible tide of fanaticism which threatens to blot out the land-marks which have heretofore marked the distinction of the races. The present condition of this country is lamentable enough; but, sir, if we are forced to this direful necessity, more, far more intolerable will be our condition. I have some very serious fears, sir, that this once delightful country which has heretofore been so prosperous and desirable, would in that event, no longer be a fit asylum for the white race. But, sir, I trust we may be able to avert this great calamity, and once more succeed in restoring civil Government in our State, and that peace and prosperity may again bless our people.

Then let us accept the alternative; acknowledge that slavery has been destroyed by the results of the war and the action of the United States Government, and shape our fundamental law so as to accord or conform with the Constitution of the Union, as the best means of restoring civil government and civil order in our State, and of securing to ourselves and our children the blessings of constitutional liberty and free government.

Mr. Simonton, of Itawamba—Mr. President: I am opposed to the proviso for this reason: it can do no good, and it may do harm. If our members to the National Congress would be received under the substitute, they would be received under the report of the Committee. There is no doubt in my mind but that if the State of Mississippi, through her delegates and representatives in this Convention, show by their action that they are determined to mould or change the fundamental law of the State to conform to the changed condition of affairs—that they are not only determined, but willing, to change the fundamental law of the State and pass such laws as will protect the freedman in his rights, and guarantee and protect other citizens of the State at the same time, we have friends enough left in the North to come forward and say to the fanatics, These people of the South have done all we can ask of them to do; it is nothing but just to receive their delegates. I believe our members of Congress will be received.

I did not get up, Mr. President, to make a speech, but I deem it a duty to myself to show why I vote, as I shall, when the question is put. I believe there is no other means by which the State of Mississippi can be restored to her relations to the Federal Government, but by making the change in the fundamental law of the State which we now propose, and I believe it is necessary to do that without any proviso. By what right do we hold our seats? Do we claim them because we are citizens of the great Commonwealth? No, sir, the right is claimed because we have taken the emancipation oath prescribed by the President's proclamation. That is the test of loyalty to the Federal Government. When we take that oath to relieve ourselves from the crime under which we were suffering, what does the Federal Government charge us with? We have taken that oath and I, as a member of this Convention, expect to carry it out in good faith, as I am conscientiously bound to do.

Before I took it, I looked around me and saw the condition of the State. In the first place I refused to take it, but I saw there was no other remedy. If the people of the State of Mississippi could have left and moved in a mass to a different country, I never would have taken this oath; but that is an impossibility. This people must remain here, at least the mass of them. This people must be governed by the laws or legislation that the State of Mississippi will pass, or they must be governed by laws and officers appointed over them. That is the question. Shall we so change the fundamental law as to enable us and our children, in the future, to carry out our domestic affairs? With this view I determined to take the oath and carry it out in good faith. I shall vote against the substitute, for I believe it falls short of the object it aims to accomplish.

Mr. Marshall moved to adjourn until Monday morning, 9 o'clock.

Mr. Harrison moved to amend by striking out 9, and inserting 8 o'clock.

Tne motion of Mr. Marshall prevailing,

The Convention adjourned until Monday morning nine o'clock.

SEVENTH DAY.

MONDAY, AUGUST, 21ST., 1865.

The Convention met pursuant to adjournment.

Prayer by the Rev. C. Chamberlain.

Journal of Saturday read and approved.

The President announced as the Committee on Enrolled Ordinances and Constitutional Amendments, under a resolution adopted on Saturday last, Messrs. Simonton, of Itawamba; Cooper, of Rankin; Mayson, of Marion; Barr, of Lafayette; and Johnson, of Marshall.

The following communication from the Sergeant-at-Arms was read:

CONVENTION HALL,
Jackson Miss., Aug., 17th, 1865.

MR. PRESIDENT:

Under the resolution this day adopted, instructing me to make arrangements with the Postmaster of this city, for the prepayment of mailable matter sent by members of the Convention, I have the honor to state that I had an interview with the Postmaster on the subject. He informs me that he will forward all printed matter, the postage for which can be afterwards, settled, but that letters must be prepaid; in other words, must have a stamp upon them. The stamps cannot be purchased at present in this city.

I am, Sir, Very Respectfully.
T. C. McMACKIN,
Sergeant-at-Arms, Convention Miss

HON. J. S. YERGER, President of Convention.

The Convention resumed the consideration of the special order, to-wit: the substitute offered by Mr. Hudson, of Yazoo, for the second section of the Committee's report on State Constitution.

Mr. Potter of Hinds—Mr. President: If I did not regard the proviso offered to the amendment, by my friend from Yazoo [Mr. Hudson,] as very important, and well calculated to secure the end which gentlemen seek to obtain through the proposed amendment to the Constitution, I should not delay the Convention by any attempt to secure its adoption.

I think this proviso contains matter of real importance—that the policy it suggests is our true policy, if we desire to secure the early admission of our Senators and Representatives to their seats in Congress. I have listened with attention to the various objections urged against it, and, to my apprehension, they are all founded on erroneous views; in error in regard to our condition as a people; error in regard to the Proclamation of President Lincoln; error in regard to the scope, purpose and effect of the amendment proposed by the committee of fifteen; and error in regard to the probable effect of that proviso.

I seems to me, sir, there are grave errors existing in this bo in regard to our true condition as a people. We have heard it asserted that this people, as a State community—that Mississippi as a State has "forfeited all rights;"—that the State, a co-equal member of the Federal Union, has been "whipped," to use the common expression. The delegate from Marshall [Mr. Watson] insists that one of the two propositions must be true. 1st, If the the ordinance of secession was valid, then it took this State out of the Union, and we stand here to-day as foreigners and subjugated! 2nd, If that ordinance was void, then all stand here to-day as traitors, repsesenting constituencies of traitors. Such is the dilemma in which that gentleman would place us. Now, instead of attempting to persuade the former advocates of secession to adopt more correct views upon the subject, my friend rather urges them to adhere to their heresy, as I term and consider it. As it seems to me, it would have shown more grace, had that distinguished gentleman urged them to come up to the true Constitutional platform; and to admit in their action here, freely and frankly, the error of their former opinions. I think, sir, that all who have entertained those views heretofore, might assume the position of a distinguished citizen of this State—a gentleman as distinguished for frank and manly candor as for gallantry in the field—who now holds and declares that "Mississippi has no such right, as the right of secession."

I hope, therefore, members in acting upon this subject, will disregard the suggestion of my friend, and refuse to consider this people as a foreign people, outside of the Union, and therefore, in military subjection to the United States.

Founding himself upon the proposition that, as a people, we are either subjugated foreigners or domestic traitors, the gentleman gravely asks whether we as a people, can now come forward and assert any rights. It seems to me, sir, that gentlemen, in coming to such conclusions, overlook entirely the fundamental distinction that exists between communities and individuals—between States in their organized capacity, and the individual citizens of the State. I have seen it declared in a newspaper as the true doctrine, that a State of the Union might be guilty of "rebellion;" and that when a State thus committed "treason," the whole population of the State,—those of tender years, as well as grown up men—those incapable of reason and those competent to act for themselves, all become by act of the State, traitors to the Government of the United States. In my opinion, this error and its consequences, may prove more pernicious to our people, than perhaps any other that can be adopted. It is the very position assumed against us by those who assert the power, as well as the duty, of the Federal Government to control the right of suffrage in Mississippi. Their leading proposition is, that Mississippi, as a State, has "forfeited all rights"—that having "no rights" she can claim nothing as a member of the Federal Union; and that so long as she remains in her present condition, the Government of the United States may rightfully deal with the question of suffrage, and perhaps all other questions. Such is the declaration of the Boston committee under the lead of Judge Parsons, put forth in an address from Fanieul Hall.

Such, I believe, is the fundamental proposition of all who assert the right of the Federal Government to control this question of suffrage against us, and to regulate it at pleasure, and even to reduce us to the condition of our former slaves, and make them sole voters in the State. Now, sir, of all things, we should be exceeding circumspect lest we admit this proposition to be true. We should delay long and ponder, painfully, before we proclaim it as a truth. Why, sir, in so doing, we lay for them the very foundation on which alone they can rest their claims. Gentlemen talk of "giving aid and comfort" to those who seek to impose these conditions upon us. I have been told that the policy I propose would, if adopted, end in the imposition of black suffrage upon us, and that therefore, in effect, I was aiding to accomplish that end. But, sir, if we proclaim to the world that we have "no rights"—that we, as a State and people, "have forfeited all," I ask how can we object against the demands of the advocates for black suffrage, or in opposition to any other scheme they may propose for our ruin?

Mr. President, we have been told that we should do nothing to embarrass the Administration; nothing to discourage our friends at the North. I admit that we have friends there; many friends, and I thank God for it. I agree, too, that we should do nothing to embarrass or discourage them, and I urge the fact against this doctrine which gentlemen assert. I say, sir, that the position of the gentleman is in direct opposition to the avowed Constitutional policy of the President, and of the conservative men who sustain him and propose to carry out his policy for the re-organization of the State. Is this true? Is this the position of the President? Let us see whether he regards us, to use the language of the delegate from Marshall [Mr. Watson] as either foreigners or traitors subdued and conquered, and entitled to no rights whatever. I read, sir, from the Proclamation appointing Gov. Sharkey—the first portion of which is in these words:

"Whereas, the 4th section of the 4th article of the Constitution of the United States declares that the United States shall guarantee to every State in the Union a republican form of Government, and shall protect each of them from invasion and domestic violence;" and then follows a recital in these words:

"Whereas, The rebellion which has been urged by a portion of the people of the United States against the constituted authorities of the Government thereof, in the most violent and revolting form, and whose organized and armed forces have been now almost entirely overcome, has in its revolutionary progress deprived the people of Mississippi of civil government; and

Whereas, It becomes necessary and proper to carry out and enforce the obligation of the United States to the people of Mississippi in securing them in that enjoyment of a Republican form of Government."

What, sir, does the President admit here? What does he declare, to us and to the world? "It becomes necessary and proper to carry out and enforce the obligations of the United States to the people of Mississippi, in securing to them the enjoyment of a Republican form of Government." There are "obligations" resting upon the Government of the United States, to do something for these people; and those obligaitons arise out of the Constitution of the United States. The Government acknowledges its duty and declares our right. But, notwithstanding this, gentlemen on this floor would sink us to the degrded condition of a conquered province, in the hope that by some act of theirs the State may emerge and be raised up perhaps, to the position which the Federal Government permits her now to occupy as a State in the Union. I am to be regarded as "crochety," when I, in this hall, assert what the President and Government of the United States declares to be *now* the truth regarding the people!

The Proclamation proceeds: "Now, therefore, in obedience to the high and solemn duties imposed upon me by the Constitution of the United States, and for the purpose of enabling the loyal people of said State to organize a State government whereby justice may be established, domestic tranquility restored, and loyal citizens protected."

Why, sir, the President recognizes the fact that there are other persons here besides traitors; that there are "loyal citizens," here; he goes on to prescribe the mode by which the men of this "State" may increase and multiply; and to that end he prescribes the process of the amnesty oath. Those who are innocent of voluntary participation in the war, and those who have taken that oath, are regarded by the Government as loyal citizens; and we stand here to-day representing them. Why is it, then, that gentlemen persist to argue that this Convention represents only "foreigners or traitors" entitled to "no rights;" and that therefore it would be presumptuous for this people to go before the country upon the proposition of the gentleman from Yazoo [Mr. Hudson]? Is it an act of unparalelled impudence and hardihood to assert, as the President declares, that this people have rights? Will it offend him if we say: "This people, as a people, have constitutional rights, and you, Mr. President, are bound to regard them?"

In that Proclamation, the President asserted, further, the continued existence and binding force of the Constitution and Laws of Mississippi, as they existed prior to the act of secession. He avowed the same doctrine in his public address to the Indiana delegation. When a delegation from South Carolina visited Washington, some of the delegates said to the President: "Sir, we have forfeited all. We have no rights." But the President replied: "It seems, gentlemen that I am a better states-rights man than many of you." Had he been in this hall, and heard language used by delegates here, he might have employed, for our reproof, words of stronger emphasis than he addressed to that delegation. Why sir, here is the President declaring we are a *State* under the constitution, entitled to the immediate admission of our members into Congress; and that it is the duty of the Government to give us all the benefits of republican institutions, in full and free enjoyment; and yet gentlemen who assume to be, *per se*, the supporters of the presidential policy, strive with all their powers of argument to knock from under his feet the Constitutional platform on which his policy rests! Why will not gentlemen permit him to maintain this position assumed for us? Why not permit him, as far as possible, to advance our cause? Why oppose his honest efforts to secure our Constitutional rights, including our representation in Congress? This, sir, is the public policy of the President that I advocated on a former day; and my conviction that it is his policy, is as strong now as before I heard the argument of my friend from Marshall [Mr. Watson.] It seems to me there should be no diversity or opinion as to the views of the President in regard to the rights of these States or as Communities. The Bureau order approved by him, that I read the other day, as recited in the order of General Slocum, does not affect this public position of the President. That order was doubtless founded on erroneous views of right and policy in the treatment of negroes in our midst. The President seems to think they are not practically free, under the Proclamation, if not on an equal footing with the white persons of our country. This order certainly is inconsistent with the right of the State to enact and regulate for herself the laws of evidence; but it does not further affect his avowed doctrine in regard to the position of these States, and their right to have their Senators and Representatives admitted unrestricted, into Congress.

Mr. President, it seems in bad taste to use language like that employed by my colleague, the other day. He said: "Let slavery, compensation—everything else go, until we find that our children have a land to live in." Proclaim to the world your readiness to give up "everything" but the right to occupy a homestead in Mississippi! Proclaim yourselves in a yielding mood, and where will demands upon you cease? Are you prepared to grant free suffrage; prepared to accept universal equality? It is all covered by the language used by my colleague in the debate on Saturday. Give up slavery—give up compensation—give up everything else! Why, sir, what is not included in those words? I ask, is this house in the yielding mood, to give up "everything?" No, gentlemen, no! It is manifest to all, that there must be a time to pause—a time when this people must assert that they are a people, and as such have rights. We are bound to take position on Constitutional ground, and call upon conservative men, everywhere, to rally around us and maintain that position. In my judgment that time is *now*, when we should take that stand, asserting what the President asserts, for us, that as a State we have rights—that the Government owes duties to us as a people. And I do not think we can offend any man, whose support we can ever hope to have, by a firm assertion of these fundamental truths.

Again: I think there are errors in regard to the scope and effect of the emancipation proclamation. We have heard a great deal sir, about the abolition of slavery here in the South. It has been asserted, over and over again, that slavery is dead here. But while gentlemen are free to admit that slavery was destroyed by the act of the Government, they will not say so upon the record. My friend from Rankin [Mr. Cooper] thought it necessary to explain why he would vote for the Constitutional amendment, although he would permit no explanation in the form of a preamble to it. He thought, perhaps, to place himself on record in another way, and show to his constituents that he so voted because slavery was dead already. Why not come to the point and declare to the world how it is you vote for this thing? Why not vote for preambles which assert what you declare to be true?

My friend from Hinds [Mr. Johnston] declared that slavery was not only dead, but dead and killed four times over;—killed by the proclamation, by the acts of Congress, by the might of the sword, by the opinion of the Christian world. He therefore considered it very dead. But sir, is it true that President Lincoln attempted to declare *the institution* of slavery abolished in the State of Mississippi in the sense in which gentlemen speak of it? In other words, did he attempt to overturn the fundamental law on which slavery rested in Mississippi? Was he dealing with the institution, and the laws made in support of it; or was he dealing with individual slaves? You might take out of the State every individual held here as a slave on the first day of January 1863, remove them, carry them to Liberia, by every sort of laws and ordinances declare them free; but in so doing you would not abolish slavery as an institution in Mississippi. What did the President do? I give his words from his proclamation of the first of January, 1863:—"I do order and declare that all *persons* held as slaves, within said States and part of States, are and henceforth shall be free." That proclamation excepts from its operation certain parishes in Louisiana, certain specified counties in Virginia, and the whole of Western Virginia. It does not include the State of Kentucky. Beyond question, slavery exists in Kentucky to-day, notwithstanding the proclamation; I have a full legal right to go to Kentucky, buy slaves there as property, and bring them here and hold them as slaves in Mississippi. Do gentlemen deny this as a legal proposition? Do they claim that the President in declaring that *persons* held as slaves, were free, overthrew our laws and the provisions of the Constitution of the State? No, sir! There is a distinction, broad and palpable, between the act of freeing certain persons, and an act overthrowing or annulling the fundamental law and policy of the State in which those persons may happen at the time to be.

I say then, that gentlemen are talking and acting here, under a grave error, in regard to the scope and effect of that Proclamation; and for that reason, are also acting under an error in regard to the scope, purpose and effect of this proposed amendment to the Constitution. What, sir, is that amendment? In times past, we heard much of the Wilmot Proviso; and that thing was denounced throughout the whole South. But, here to-day, we have, in this amendment, that very proviso. I say, sir, it goes beyond the proclamation; it proposes to abolish, utterly and forever—to prohibit forever hereafter, the holding of slaves, as property in Mississippi.—Under the proclamation, one might go to Kentucky, and purchase, bring here, and hold slaves as property. Under the proposed amendment, this would be impossible. I wish gentlemen, to consider the difference between these two things, when they come to vote upon the proviso, proposed by my friend from Yazoo, (Mr. Hudson.)

Gentlemen have said this amendment is but a repetition of the proclamation, But they are different things; and if we propose this amendment, on certain conditions, to the people of the North, they must see that we offer them something real—something more than the mere repetition of the proclamation. I hope, sir, that gentlemen will reflect on this view of the subject, and especially that those who regard themselves as bound by the amnesty oath, to vote for the amendment, will pause and consider, in view of these things, if they are so bound. If I take a right view of that proclamation, it declared free only the persons, held as slaves, in certain parts of the South, on the first of January, 1863. If I take a right view of the amendment, it declares that slavery shall not exist here in any form; that our citizens shall not bring slaves into the State, and hold them here. Gentlemen hold that we are sworn to do all this, when the amnesty oath, in this particular, only requires us to abide by and faithfully support the proclamation and acts of Congress, which declare the freedom of certain persons, and have no further relation to the policy of the State, in regard to slavery. My friend, from Lawrence, (Mr. Goode,) thinks the word "support," as used in the oath, imports very much; and therefore he feels bound not only to maintain the freedom of those persons, but also to support every sort of proposition intended to destroy the slave policy of the State. He even asserts that he would be bound to support the proclamation and acts of Congress, although the Supreme Court of the United States should declare them void. Let us see in what sort of predicament my friend would be, if called upon to renew the oath after that Court had so decided. The first part of it binds him to support, protect and defend the Constitution and the Union of the States thereunder; and then would come an obligation something after this wise, "and in like manner, I solemnly swear to abide by and faithfully to support the proclamation and acts of Congress, for the emancipation of slaves; although by the decision of the Supreme Court of the United States, an authority which I cannot gainsay, that proclamation and those acts have been declared to be in violation of the Constitution of my country! The thing stands apparent, as I urged the other day, that the controlling part of the oath is that which regards the Constitution and the Union. There is nothing in the oath to constrain him. All that he is bound to do, is to treat those as free, who were held, on the first of January, 1863, in certain localities, as slaves.

What objection can be urged to the proviso offered by my friend from Yazoo, (Mr. Hudson?) We are told of certain promises to admit our members into Congress, if we adopt the proposed amendment, and my colleague, refering to those promises, spoke of the adoption of this amendment as a condition precedent. We all know that the advocates of this amendment are acting upon the idea, that if we adopt it, we may possibly secure the admission of our members into Congress. If there is one such advocate, who is not acting upon this hope, I desire to hear from him. Now, sir, what do these gentlemen understand the President to promise? It is this, sir: "adopt an anti-slavery Constitution, and you may secure the admission of your members. Do this, and it may be well with you as a people. You may enjoy the blessing of civil government, and a representation in Congress," Such are the terms assumed by gentleman, as having been proposed by the President. Now what does the gentleman from Yazoo propose—how does he respond to this reported policy of the President? In effect, he says: "Mr. President you propose upon condition, that we do these things, to stand by us, to give us the powerful aid of executive influence, and the aid of friends, to secure what we earnestly desire—the blessings of civil Government, and a representation in Congress. Now, sir, upon condition that you secure to us these things, we will do what you desire." And this is a proper response to the reported offer of the President. It meets him upon his own ground. "But," say gentlemen, "this is dictatorial, and not becoming to foreigners and traitors." Why, sir, the President asserts these rights for us, and may we not deal with him, as parties entitled to enjoy them? It is not dictation. It cannot offend, but will encourage our friends, and uphold and strengthen the arm of the Executive. Upon the proposition of the gentleman from Yazoo, we say to those who demand all, and offer nothing: "We grant your wish upon condition that you accord to us our right." But if we grant unconditionally, what they demand, we encourage further aggression. My colleague fears that if we adopt this proviso to the amendment, the President will regard us as still in the bitterness of rebellion. But, sir, when we adopt the amendment, we will have adopted the Wilmot Proviso; and that deed will abide, and be to the most suspicious, our conclusive proof of loyalty—that test will stand against all cavils. As urged by the gentleman from Yazoo, by adopting this proviso to the amendment, we shall aid the President and cast the responsility upon those lawless men who deny us our Constitutional rights. He can then say to those Radicals: "Mississippi has done all that can be required of her. She has adopted the Wilmot Proviso, subject to a fair and proper condition. And now it remains for you to determine whether she shall take her place as one of the free States." By anexing the proviso to the amendment, we place the Radicals in a political predicament. We offer them the Wilmot Proviso upon condition that they do us justice. Dare they reject that proviso, and meet their constituents?

There is another matter to be considered in connection with this subject. During the last four years, an unconstitutional test oath has been adopted with a view to exclude Congressional delegations from these States, and this presents another and stronger reason why we should not adopt this amendment, unconditionally, but should annex the proviso to it. If we adopt the amendment without the condition, those Radicals will approve the deed, and send back our own members until we yield up more; and after their exactions should all be granted, even to black suffrage, they will still have in reserve that test vote for members to Congress. If then, gentlemen will adopt the Wilmot Proviso, shall it not be upon condition that this test oath be annulled, and our people admitted freely to the benefits of civil Government, and to a representation in Congress? Every consideration of policy looking to an early restoration of civil government, and to immediate representation in Congress, every consideration of duty and honor that can influence us as a people, should constrain us to insist on this proposed condition to the amendment.

I cannot perceive the slightest objection to the adoption of the proviso to the amendment. I therefore give it my hearty support.

Mr. Martin, of Adams.—Mr. President: I am a member of the Committee that reported this ordinance. I took occasion to reflect what might be the result of the passage of the ordinance, and I came to the conclusion that the proposition of the delegate from Yazoo might very well be engrafted on the amendment proposed, and so suggested to the chairman of the Committee. I am willing to vote for the proposition as it stands in the report of the Committee, without the proviso. I am willing to vote for it in that condition, if it shall be found that such a proviso, or one similar to it, cannot be passed by this Convention. I have looked carefully to see whether any hope was held out to us by the appointment of a Provisional Governor, and by the partial restoration, as it was supposed, of law and order by the appointment of certain county officers in this State. I have looked anxiously to see whether we had sufficient assurance given us, that the State laws would have full force and effect, and that the rights of this State would be recognized. I have looked to see what course was pursued by the Federal Government in the States which never passed the ordinance of secession, towards the people of these States, as to those rights which are clear and unquestioned—not those doubtful rights about which there has been much controversy; and whether these rights were respected by the Federal Government. I have looked to see whether these things we see around us every day, reminding us that we are in a state of subjugation, would be removed, and that fraternal feeling manifested that we were led to believe might be shown; and I had hoped that in forming a new Constitution, or in amending the old one, we might feel safe in trusting, exclusively, to the guarantees of the Constitution of the United States, and that we might not be called upon to insist upon anything farther.

I am sorry to say I have seen very much that has led me to distrust the future. I have seen very little to encourage me in the expectation that we would very speedily be restored to our rights as a State, or that very speedily, unless we looked well to it, we would be restored to our right of representation in the Congress of the United States. You remember, Mr. President, that already a certain amendment has been proposed in the Congress of the United States, and long since agreed to by a large number of the States that compose the Federal Union, and may be engrafted in the Constitution during the next session of Congress.

One section of the amendment abolishes slavery throughout the Union. The second section confers extraordinary power upon Congress. That section gives to Congress broad, and almost, I may say, unlimited power, and at a time when throughout this country, constitutional restrictions are not regarded as they once were. I fear excessively, that there is hid away in that section, something which may be destructive to the welfare of the South. I am not willing to trust to men who know nothing of slavery, the power to frame a code for the freedmen of the State of Mississippi. I am not willing to trust to these men, who have been educated from youth upward; taught in their schools; taught from the pulpit; taught by their public speakers, and taught by their writers, that the white population of the South is a degraded race, as compared with our more favored brethren, who live in a Northern climate; who have been taught, also, that slavery is odious; that the master is not restrained by feelings of humanity—that it is only interest that guides him in his conduct towards the slave; who by exciting books, periodicals and speeches, have been led to look upon us as a race of monsters, and by whom the negro, in his ignorance and vice, is esteemed a being far superior to what we know him to be.

They have painted the good qualities of the negro as our novelists have painted those of the Indian. Our imaginative writers have so depicted the Indian, that in future years, how much of the truth will be known of the true character of the Indian? He has been described as brave, and generous, and noble, and so in an equal degree has the character and capacity of the negro been exalted.

Now, I say, I am not willing to trust to men so educated, and so taught—exasperated as they are now, on account of the resistance that has been made to the Federal authority in these Southern States—hating us and our institutions, our customs and manners, and disregarding our rights, I am not willing, I say, to trust to the fanatics of the North to frame for us a code that is to govern the freedmen of the State of Mississippi, which may, or may not, render residence in this State, to the white man, impossible.

It would be but fair to presume that if left to them to perfect this code, and direct us how we shall act in our conduct toward this people, and how the freedmen shall act in his conduct towards us—thus fixing the political status of the freedmen—they will put them upon an equality with us, giving to them the right to vote and take control of the State from us, and give it into the hands of fanatics and ignorant freedmen. The time may possibly come when this will be the result of leaving the condition of the freedmen to be decided by legislation in Congress, in the absence of representation from the Southern States. The time may come when it will be no longer a question with us whether we can remain here; it may be a question with us what country, what asylum we can find, where we may be once more secure in our lives and liberties. Inasmuch as there is a possibility that at the next session of Congress an amendment to the Constitution may be engrafted on that instrument securing to Congress the broad power given by the second section, and the whole question of the management of the freedmen in this State, and their relations to the white men of the State may be legislated upon without our being heard, I propose, sir, to vote for this proviso—not by way of a threat. I do not threaten others, and am not disposed to submit to threats myself. I put it there simply as a proviso. I propose to say, "we are willing, having fought for this great institution, and been conquered, to amend the Constitution in such a way as shall be of most service to the country. Believing, as we did, that the proper place of the negro was in slavery, we have fought for that institution. We have been overcome by those who now have it in their power to legislate upon questions which belong more properly, I believe, to the several States. We are perfectly willing to give up this institution of slavery. The result of the war has been such that the slave cannot properly be held in that capacity, but we leave you the right of fixing the moment when every slave in Mississippi shall be emancipated. We present you a free Constitution, and only ask what we are entitled to. We ask to be heard—to have a day in court, that our representatives shall be there when you undertake to legislate on the subject of the freedmen in the State of Mississippi, if you undertake to do it at all. It is a question that affects us so vitally, that all that we possess is involved in the decision.

It has been contended, I believe, until recently, by a large majority of the people of the North, that the act of secession of the State of Mississippi, is utterly null and void—that there is no Constitutional right of secession. I believed that myself, and opposed the act until the war began. I believe so yet; I think yet there is no such thing as this constitutional right. The case was well argued by the delegate from Yazoo. If we have not been out of the Union and have come back and pledged ourselves by an oath of allegiance, what reason is there for keeping us out of the Congress of the United States, when every delay is a matter of vital importance, and the condition of affairs growing worse and worse. We are much more directly interested in the question than those in the North, who are disposed to take the settlement of the question out of our hands. It is nothing but just that we should be heard—have some advocate on the floor of Congress; and if this proviso is adopted, at all events, we may be heard. I can conceive of no reasonable opposition to the passage of the ordinance with the proviso. We leave it optional with the Congress of the United States at once to get rid of every doubtful question touching the emancipation of the slaves by accepting our delegates. Upon that body will rest the blame, if evil shall arise out of the failure to allow us what we claim to be our just rights. We attempted to break up the Union, and failed. Whatever may have been thought of the right to secede, we at all events did not maintain it, and we are still in the Union.

I shall vote for the proviso, and hope in so doing there may be something approaching unanimity. You must remember that we stand first among the States called upon to reconstruct. The other States will not hold their Conventions for weeks to come; an example will be set by Mississippi, and she will play an important part in the course pursued by the other States. If in solid phalanx a large body of intelligent men go to Congress from these States, and present their claim to the right of representation, with free Constitutions, I believe to those who have never yielded to extreme fanaticism, the moderate Republicans of the North, our claim will present itself in such shape, and commend itself so strongly, that our representatives, as a body, will be received in Congress.

I may be mistaken, yet I would take every means in my power to secure representation there, and with the large number of delegates that we would send to Congress, united with the Conservatives and moderate men there, we may still hope that something may be done to relieve us of the doubt in which we are now living—from the apprehensions which make life anything but pleasant to us, and we may go to work once more and restore our State to the position she once occupied, as a peaceful, law-abiding State. We may, however, without passing this proviso, yield—yield all—in vain. We may deprive ourselves of the opportunity of standing shoulder to shoulder with those Representatives in Congress from the North who believe that this country was made for the white man—who believe that it was intended that the Caucasian should be the dominant race. We may combine with them, and probably be able to restore the reign of respect for the Constitution and the laws. We may be able to stop the tide of fanaticism, and there may be a reunion, if we all act as I think we ought; and we may again become a prosperous State, in a prosperous Union.

MR. YERGER, of Hinds, said:

Mr. President: I dislike to tresspass upon the time of the Convention; but the course of this debate has been of such a character as to render it proper in me to place before the Convention and the people whom I represent, the reasons which induce me to support the proposition originally intro duced by the committee, and to vote against the substitute offered by the gentleman from Yazoo, [Mr. Hudson.] The substitute is, in my judgment, more obnoxious (and though seemingly plausible,) will be more fatal, if adopted, to the great object for which this Convention has been called, than any of those which have heretofore been acted upon and rejected. The course of argument of those who advocate this substitute, strikes me with astonishment. They seem actually to ignore the events of the past five years—to ignore the present condition of the people and of the State; and in some dreamy, abstract revery, to indulge in visions and fancies of Constitutional law and Constitutional Government, which they think ought to prevail, but which men of practical common-sense, viewing facts—stubborn facts, as they are—well know are not attainable at this time by the people of this country. I purpose to briefly recall the events of the past four years—to present to the consideration of the Convention our actual condition, and leave it to determine for itself the proper course to adopt.

Five years ago we were blessed with as much prosperity as the Almighty ever granted to any people on the globe. We had a Constitution which guaranteed to all equal civil and political rights; we had material prosperity such as had seldom before been reached by the most favored nations; but there was one cause of discord and disquiet, which cast a gloom over the future. It had for years proved a source of discontent and agitation, and to a great extent of apprehension and alarm to the whole people of this country. Soon after the formation of the Government, two parties were organized in reference to slavery, and its abolition. Those parties had from day to day waged war upon each other in the halls of Congress, and upon the hustings, until in November, 1860, it was transferred from the forum to the camp, and produced results that have astonished the civilized world; while at the same time it has entailed upon us the most fatal and ruinous consequences.

Mr. Lincoln was elected in November, 1860, and the people of the Southern States, with a great degree of unanimity, came to the conclusion that his election imperilled, if it was not actually subversive of the institution of slavery.

Acting upon a preconceived idea, the Senators of South Carolina, within two or three days from that election, withdrew from Congress.

The Governors of the several extreme Southern States convened the Legislatures of these States in extraordinary session, for the purpose of advice and council, and of adopting such measures as they might deem necessary to protect the people of their States from the evil consequences it was supposed would follow. Mississippi assembled her Convention in this capital, on the 7th day of January, 1861, and on the 9th day of that month, an act styled "An Ordinance to dissolve the Union between the State of Mississippi and other States united with her under the compact entitled, The Constitution of the United States of America," was passed and ordained, and Mississippi declared herself thereafter a free, sovereign, and independent State. Our members of Congress and Senators, were ordered to withdraw, and did withdraw from the Congress of the United States.

Similar acts and a similar course took place in nearly all of the Southern States, and in a very short period, after the election, there was left in Congress but a small minority to battle against the Republican party in adopting any measures they might see fit to take against the institution of slavery and the rights of the Southern States.

In the month of December, 1860, before the delegates from Louisiana had withdrawn, a proposition was introduced and passed in the House of Representatives, guaranteeing perpetually the rights of the States in the institution of slavery, and protecting them thenceforward from any action or interference on the part of the General Government. This proposed amendment to the Constitution came before the Senate, and but for the withdrawal of the Southern Senators, would then have passed. In my humble judgment, but for the extraordinary disposition which then and still seems to exist in the breasts of some gentlemen to protect what they are pleased to call the dignity of the South and the manhood of the Southern people, at the expense of the peace and practical well-being of the State, an amendment to the Constitution would have been adopted, which would have secured forever the institution of slavery, until each State of its own free will, saw fit to abolish it. But our people, under the excitement which existed, and in the madness of the hour, disregarded and rejected the proposed amendment. The Senators from the Southern States had nearly all withdrawn or refused to vote, and the amendment thus proposed was lost. A few months passed, and seven of the Southern States met together in Convention, and adopted what is known as a "Provisional Constitution for the Confederate States of America." Troops were organized, arms were prepared, and places in possession of the United States were seized and held, and every where in these States the officers of the Government of the United States, of every grade, were ousted from their places, and those places filled by persons holding under the Constitution of the Confederate States of America. Mr. Lincoln, on the 4th of March, was inaugurated as President of the United States. In his inaugural address, he proclaimed that he did not intend to interfere with the institution of slavery in the States, and urged the people to return to their allegiance to the Federal Government. But exercising what they believed to be a right belonging to them, and which they supposed necessary under the circumstances, for their safety, the people disregarded this counsel, remained and continude as they were, severed and withdrawn from their allegiance, and placed themselves in hostile array against the authority and Government of the Union. After a few more months had passed, the attack on Fort Sumter was made; and this was immediately followed by a proclamation of the President of the United States, declaring that an insurrection had taken place, which it was necessary to suppress by arms. Following that, a civil war of magnitude, which has astonished the world, in which both sections of this country arrayed themselves in full panoply, with all the power they possessed, raged for nearly five years. After two years of this war had passed, with varied success, in the month of September, 1862, Mr. Lincoln again published a proclamation, in which he announced to the people of the Southern States if they would lay down their arms, return to their allegiance, and submit to the laws, they would be received, with their rights in slavery untouched, but if they persisted in rebellion, and refused to accept the proposition to return, he would, on the 1st day of January, 1863, declare all the slaves held in the States which he would then designate as in insurrection, to be free. This proclamation of warning was disregarded by the Southern people. They had assumed an attitude before the world as an independent nation, (which attitude they intended to maintain by force of arms.) They defied the proclamation, disregarded the warning, and continued the war. On the 1st of Janurry, 1863, the emancipation proclamation was issued, in which the President declared that by virtue of the war-making power, and for the purpose of putting down the insurrection, all slaves in the possession of parties in the States in rebellion, (in which number the State of Mississippi was included,) were then, thenceforward and forever, free. The shock of arms continued—two more years of desolating war passed by—the armies of the Southern people, by battle, by sickness, by desertion, and by other causes over which they had no control, were almost destroyed. The armies of the United States penetrated into the interior of every State; they invaded and took possession of the States of Mississippi, of Louisiana, of Georgia, of South Carolina, and of Alabama; everywhere the armies of the Federal Government were triumphant; the flag of the Union was carried forward, and the banners of the Confederate States was lowered before it. Things were in this attitude when the assault was made upon Petersburg by General Grant. At that time General Lee, the bravest, most cautious, prudent and skillful commander that the Southern States had produced, was entrenched within the walls of Petersburg and Richmond, with a handful of men, not exceeding 30,000 in all. Opposed to him were the mighty hosts under Gen. Grant, of from 150,-

000 to 175,000 men. A few days of contest ensued, and the brave and gallant, but weak band under Lee, was obliged to yield, and did yield, as prisoners of war, to the United States.

The armies of the United States took possession of the State of Virginia, from which they had been held by the opposing army of Gen. Lee. About the same time, General Johnston, with an army not exceeding 25,000, encountered the hosts under Sherman, 75,000 to 100,000 strong; and unable to resist this force, the gallant and sagacious Johnston, pronouncing it to be murder to continue the struggle any longer, proposed an armistice, in which could be settled the terms of a general peace. That armistice was agreed upon, and a Convention made between the parties. Among other articles, was a stipulation leaving in abeyance the questions arising under the emancipation proclamations, until they could be decided by the Supreme Court of the United States. When that Convention, thus agreed upon, was presented to the Government of the United States, it was rejected in scorn —rejected in such a manner as to cast an imputation for the time upon the integrity of the commander who had negotiated it on the part of the United States. Among the principal reasous given for the rejection, was that it contained a clause which to some extent intimated a recognition of the existence of slavery, and left, as a future cause of contest and discussion, that question before the courts, which the Government insisted had been settled by the war. The chief cause of its rejection, was the clause to have adjudicated, (as my colleague proposes,) by the Supreme Court of the United States, the question of the legality and constitutionality of the President's proclamations.

A few weeks after the surrender of Johnston, the army of the Mississippi, under the command of General Taylor, some 15,000 or 20,000 men, yielded to about five times the number under Gen. Canby. The arms of the United States were everywhere triumphant; no armed force any where this side of the Mississippi river, was then opposed to them, and unresisted; the Government of the United States enforced the proclamations and the laws of Congress declaring the slaves free. Does any sane man suppose that, after such a war; after an expenditure of three thousand millions of dollars, and a sacrifice of nearly 500,000 men, the United States will recede from a position, deliberately taken before the world, and again put in issue the very question which produced the war? Immediately after the surrender of Gen. Taylor, the Legislature of Mississippi was assembled upon the call of the Governor, and among other things, passed an act calling a Convention to take into consideration the proper manner of restoring the relations which formerly existed between the State and the United States. It also provided for the appointment of Commissioners to Washington for the purpose of conferring with the President touching the existing relations between them. At the very time Mississippi was attempting to act through a Legislature, elected after the ordinance of secession, an order passed over the wires from Washington, directing Gen. Canby to disperse the Legislature, and if any resistance was made, to arrest and imprison the members who might resist. But before the order was received, the Legislature had adjourned. On the next day, Gov. Clarke was notified that the President of the United States did not recognize the organization of the State government made since 1861; that he did not recognize the validity of any official acts, nor the rightful authority of any party pretending to hold and exercise an office under such pretended government; and a demand was made upon him to surrender the public archives and property of every kind belonging to the State. That surrender took place in this Capital, in the presence of a number of gentlemen, and was made to the armies of the United States, and Mississippi was left without an Executive—without a Judiciary—without civil government of any kind—governed alone by martial law, entirely prostrate and powerless, if willing to resist. Before this surrender, Gov. Clarke had appointed commissioners to proceed to Washington to confer with the President. After the surrender, and on the notification that all official acts of the authorities of the State would be disregarded, the Governor wrote a private letter requesting the gentlemen he had appointed, to proceed to Washington, and if not received in an official capacity, as he supposed they would not be, to represent, as citizens of the State of Mississippi, having the confidence of the Executive and Legislature, as it existed before the surrender, the condition of the people; their wants and requirements; and to urge upon the President the adoption of such measures as might restore civil order, and give peace, harmony and repose to our distracted country. In connection with the present distinguished Provisional Governor of this State, I had the honor to be appointed one of those commissioners. We proceeded to Washington, notified the President of our arrival, and the purpose for which we were there, and solicited an interview. It was readily given. The next day was appointed for our audience, and we met the President. We were met by him, I may state to this Convention, with great cordiality. We were met kindly; we were met in that spirit of kindness and courtesy which we felt and believed the Executive of the United States, notwithstanding the four years of war which had passed, entertained and felt towards the people of the Southern States. We represented to him the condition of our country—that civil law had been abolished—that anarchy reigned throughout our land—that martial law, administered by Provost Marshals, throughout the country was dominant—that our people were worn out—that our land had been desolated, and our homes destroyed, and many of our people in actual destitution—that our civil rights were gone—and we asked that such steps might be taken as would again restore us to our original relations with the Federal Gevernment—as would give peace and repose to our people, and restore the reign of civil law. The President desired to know by what scheme we proposed to obtain these blessings. It was suggested to him if we were allowed to designate the plan, we would prefer that the Convention which the Legislature had called to assemble in the month of June, might be permitted to assemble and proceed to the reorganization of the State, and to restore the relations which existed between it and the Federal Government. Upon this suggestion being made, the President remarked that that matter had been fully considered and finally decided, and under no circumstances could the Executive of the Government of the United States recognize, in any way, or for any purpose, the acts or the officers of the States during the period they were in rebellion to the United States. He then desired to know if we had read his proclamation in reference to the State of North Carolina, and the proposition which he there made for restoring civil government and constitutional law in that State. We had done so; we anticipated that a proposition of that kind would be tendered to our people, and we informed him that we had read and considered it, and that next to the course proposed by our own Legislature, we believed it would be more acceptable to the people than any other scheme that could be devised. We assured him, as I believed then, and as I believe the fact is now, that our people were desirous of being speedily restored to their constitutional rights under the government, and that in good faith they acquiesced in the result produced by the shock of arms—that in good faith they intended to abide by and support the Constitution and laws of the United States, and in the future conduct themselves as loyal citizens. The President then stated there was one thing which the Southern people must understand: that they must accept the condition of things produced by the war—that they must look upon and consider the institution of slavery as ended forever—that this would be a *sine qua non* in the establishment of civil government. He then said: "In the proposed Convention to alter and change the Constitution, so as to restore your State to its relations with the Federal Government, there ought to be incorporated an amendment abolishing the institution of slavery." There was no order—there was no dictation, that we should do this, but there was a distinct admonition that unless it was so done, so far as the Executive was concerned, he would not consent to the restoration of our members in Congress, and that we could not obtain the strength of the administration in support of our restoration; and we well knew that without the strength of that right arm, we would be totally powerless to resist the overwhelming tide of radical fanaticism which at that time was clamoring, not for the abolition of slavery, but for universal suffrage and the social equality of the negro. At a subsequent period, the President of the United States, in conference with the delegates from South Carolina, used this language, which I beg to present for the consideration of this Convention:

"Slavery is gone as an institution; the people of South Carolina could not be admitted into the Senate, or House of Representatives until they have afforded evidence by their conduct of this truth. They must have a Convention, and amend the Constitution, by abolishing slavery, and this must be done in good faith." Similar announcements seem to have been made to every delegation, and every Provisional Governor, in the proclamations they have issued—have announced, distinctly and emphatically, the fact, that slavery, as an institution, has been ended; that slavery as an institution, cannot exist within these States; that the Conventions, which would assemble for the purpose of amending the Constitution, must incorporate, within them, a clause to that effect, if they desired restoration to their original rights under the Constitution of the United States. It has thus been proclaimed by the Governors' of the States of Alabama, Georgia, Texas, South Carolina and North Carolina. Now, what does all this mean? It is suggested by my colleague, that the President has no fixed policy on the subject, or does not speak plainly and distinctly, what that policy is. Surely, such an idea, under such circumstances, cannot be entertained for an instant, by any man who will look the facts in the face, and not shut his eyes to the light of the sun. If it be not the fixed purpose of the President, to insist upon a change in our Constitution and laws, recognizing existing facts, and declaring that slavery shall not hereafter exist, why assemble a Convention at all? Unless such was his purpose—instead of a Convention, to alter or amend the Constitution, it would have been far more simple and easy—to have ordered the Provisional Governor, forthwith to hold an election, under the Constitution, as it existed, before secession—to fill all the offices of the State under that Constitution, and to elect delegates to Congress by the laws, as they then stood. Why did he not take that course. It would have been an easier, simpler, quieter and speedier way of obtaining admission into Congress, and the restoration of the State authorities. unless there was something, which in the opinion of the President, rendered imperative, and demanded on his part, the adoption of the present plan? If it was not intended by him that we should alter and amend the Constitution, so as to secure freedom—not to the white man—for he has always had it; but freedom for the black, he would have provided for the restoration of the State Government, by directing that the Provisional Governor should issue writs of election, and organize the State, under the old Constitution, without delay. But the President did not take that course—he could not take it —if he had desired to do so. He was powerless to take it. Everywhere—from the time I reached Cairo, until my return—and I made it my business, to ascertain as far as I could, public sentiment on that question—and found a fixed, universal, and without an exception, the mind of every man, determined upon one thing: that the abolition of slavery had been settled by the result of the war—in the language of the President, "it had been rubbed out by the friction of war."—There were no two parties on that question—there was not a single utterance, adverse to that view; but I did find, Mr. President, that there were two parties at the North, parties organized, not in reference to the institution of slavery. but in reference the position which the Southern States should have under the Government of the United States, and in reference to the peace which the negro should hold under the Constitution and laws. Upon this question, two parties were arrayed, and were preparing for the struggle, which is now imminent. Upon one side, the Chief Justice of the United States—supported by all the ultra Radicals—though I do not believe anything like a majority of the people—but strong in numbers—powerful in intellect—and vigorous in prosecuting every plan which their fanaticism, or their opinions of right and Constitutional law suggest to their fertile and scheming brains. That party insists that the Southern people, having withdrawn from the Government of the United States, by an act of secession—which although unconstitutional and void as to the Government, have estopped themselves, from insisting upon a return to the Government as States, except upon such terms as may be accorded to them by the parties who have triumphed in this contest. They insist, that for a period of time, indefinite in its length, the Southern States shall be kept in territorial organization—that they shall remain under martial law—that they shall remain under the control of the Federal Government and Federal bayonets, until the scheme of universal suffrage, which those gentlemen have sprung upon the country, shall have ripened into perfection: then having thus carried into effect the scheme, they will permit a Convention in the States, to be assembled—an organization of State authority take place, and a return as States into the Union; but not as President Johnson proposes we shall now return; but with members of Congress, composed of white and black delegates, with equal suffrage—with equal civil rights—with equal political rights—with equal social standing on the part of the negro. That is their platform, and their fixed determination is—if they have power, to carry it into effect. On the other hand, the President, has taken ground in behalf of the rights of the people. not only of the South, but of all of the States, on this question. In the proclamation organizing this Convention, he has distinctly announced what are the views which he entertains on this vital subject.

He says that, this Convention, when convened, or the Legislature that may hereafter assemble, will prescribe the qualifications of electors, and the eligibility of persons, who hold office under the Constitution and laws of the State—a power the people of the several States, composing the Federal Union have rightfully exercised from the orgin of the Government to the present time." There is the States Rights doctrine of the President—there is the proposition he has made to us—and it is under that proposition and for the purpose of carrying it into effect, we are here assembled—to amend our Constitution, in such a manner as will evince that we accept the policy of the Government, on the question of slavery—but at the same time, we may, for ourselves, determine who shall be electors, and their qualifications, and who shall be eligible to hold offices in this State, and under the Federal Government, Standing by and supporting the President, in this view, is a large Conservative party at the North, composed both of Democrats and Republicans. This party is sustained by the principal leaders of the armies of the United States. Gen. Sherman has distinctly announced, that he sustains the President; Gen. Blair has made the same announcement; and Gen. Logan, probably the only civilian who has taken high rank as a commander in the army, has announced the same. Gen. Cox, nominated by the Republicans for Governor of Ohio, has declared himself in favor of the same policy. Everywhere on that proposition, we have friends, that may be counted by hundreds, and by thousands, and I firmly believe there is a a large majority, sustaining the President, in the views and policy which he has inaugurated. But we have no friends—we have no partizan—we have no individual, who can raise his voice, or will raise his voice in our favor, unless we yield to the inevitable result which the last four years has produced

—unless we accord with the President, and give him sympathy, support and assistance, in the policy which he has shaped out for the Government, and restoration of the Southern States.

But gentlemen shut their eyes to the actual facts. I listened with astonishment—I might almost say, with amazement, to the remarks of my worthy and intelligent colleague, (Mr. Potter,) this morning, on the question before the Convention. Really, if I had not known the circumstances under which we are assembled, I would have forgotten that we had passed through four years of war; would have forgotten that we had been compelled to yield, after a contest of a gigantic character, every position, which we had taken, and that we were not now —as the fact is—under the absolute military control of the Government of the United States. It is not worth while to disguise this fact. It stares us in the face wherever we go, and is palpable to the vision of every man; we see it, we feel it—we cannot close our eyes if we would, to the positive, unquestioned, and though it may be, unpalatable, still overwhelming fact, that we are under the control of the Government of the United States. But, says the gentleman: "slavery has not been abolished practically, and the President knows that, when he calls upon us for a change in our Constitution,"

Mr. Potter.—I said slavery had not been abolished by the Proclamation."

Mr. Yerger.—Well, "slavery has not been abolished by the proclamation,"—though that was not the expression used.—But has it not been abolished by the proclamation or something else? Does it now, in fact, exist here? When we entered this Capitol, for the purpose of carrying on this discussion, we entered the gates, before which armed sentinels were pacing their daily march; and unless the President of the United States, had accorded to us the privilege of entering, we could not have done so. Where have we civil courts and civil laws, throughout the length and breadth of this State? Where is the right of trial by jury? Where the writ of habeas corpus? In the organization of the Freedmen's Bureau, to which the gentlemen has referred, it has been declared that in any controversy which takes place between the negro and the white man, so long as by the laws of the State, the testimony of the negro is not admitted, that controversy shall be determined—not by the laws of the State of Mississippi—not by the civil law of the land—not by trial by jury—but by a military commission, proceeding according to military law, if a criminal case, and by the officers of the freedmen's bureau, a question of civil right. A few weeks ago, a citizen of the State of Mississippi, was arrested in Washington county, and brought to Vicksburg, charged with having killed a negro. Judge Sharkey, Provisional Governor of the State, issued a writ of habeas corpus, against the officer having him in charge. The officer refused to surrender him; he did more—he arrested the Judge who issued the writ, for doing so. An appeal was made to the President of the United States, and the response was that the Government of the State at present, is provisional only; that the arms of the United States cannot be withdrawn—military law could not cease, until the State of Mississippi establisbed a form of Government, restoring her to the Federal Union, in a manner approved by Congress.

In the month of Septembeı, 1862, the President of the United States proclaimed that an insurrection existed—that it existed in the State of Mississippi, and he declared martial law throughout the length and breadth of the United States; and that all persons engaged in aiding, maintaining or carrying on that rebellion, should be tried by military tribunals. That proclamation of martial law has never been revoked; the declaration that the States were in insurrection, has never yet been recalled; and so far as the political power of the Government of the United States is concerned, they hold that the States are still in insurrection. They are so treated—and held; not only in theory, but held practically as States in insurrection. It is true, the armies of the Southern States were overcome—the capacity of the Southern States, to resist was crushed—so far as physical power and resistance were concerned; but it is also true, that the proclamation, that they were in insurrection, has never yet been recalled. It is true we have not yet been restored to our former relations to the Federal Government, and it is also true, that we will not be restored, until, in the language of President Johnson to the South Carolina delegation, "we have given evidence, by incorporating in our Constitution, an amendment, abolishing the institution of slavery, and which amendment we must make in good faith." Why has the President so declared? Not that he needed our ageney in abolishing the institution of slavery. That institution has been destroyed—whether by the President's proclamation, by the friction of war, or in consequence of the acts of the Southern people—it is needless and unnecessary to inquire. It has been destroyed.

The gentlemen say that the slaves which are in the State of Mississippi, have been set free—that as to them, slavery has been abolished—but that we have a right to go to Kentucky, and buy, and bring' slaves into the State of Mississippii, and hold them here as slaves. It is precisely because the President of the United States believed those opinions were entertained by many of the Southern people, perhaps by the majority of the Southern people—because he feared there was no cordial acquiescence in the result which had been produced by arms —because he apprehended there would be a demand further to discuss an dagitate the question of slavery—because he believed the National Councils would be hereafter vexed on this question, notwithstanding the result of the war—that he said · Before I can consent to withdraw the proclamation of insurrection—before I can consent that you shall be restored to your former relations with the Federal Government, you shall place in your organic law, evidence that in good faith, you accept and intend to abide by and maintain the result which you are powerless to resist—a result brought about, against your will it is true, but which you all admit as a fact, has been produced. The President has been assailed and denounced by the Radicals, because he has accorded to us, the privilege of assembling here, and amending the Constitution, with a view to the restoration of civil Government, and the re-admission of our members into Congress. They contend that the people of the South are not in good faith acquiescing—that they do not in good faith, intend to give up the institution of slavery; and that if he withdraws from them the armies of the United States, and releases them from the dominion of martial law, and the control of the Federal Government, they will attempt to re-establish the institution of slavery, and insist upon its maintenance. It is exactly such arguments as have been made here by some gentlemen, that give countenance, plausibility and color to the objection urged against our re-organization on the plan of the President.

It is exactly such arguments as my colleague has urged, that paralyze and strike down, the arm of the Executive, which in friendly clemency, has been held out to the people of the State, with the cordial wish and desire to withdraw them from the terrible state of destitution and misery in which they have been placed. Why fold our arms, and shut our eyes, and ignore facts, and contend for Constitutional rights and Constitutional guarantees, that we have no more power to grasp, than we have to grasp the rays of the moon? Why do this—knowing at the time we do it, we paralyze and weaken the only power, that can aid us in the struggle we have yet to maintain. Why do this, knowing that we place an argument in the mouth, and a weapon in the hands of those who wish not only to strike down the institution of slavery; but to strike down the social and political superiority of the whites? The gentleman does not deny the slaves are free—he cannot shut his eyes to the palpable fact; but I take it, there still lingers in his mind, and the minds of those who coincide with him, the idea, that perhaps in the chapter of accidents which may yet intervene; there may be found some scheme, or mode, or chance, by which the dead institution may be galvanized into a few years of feeble, flickering existence; and this idea which still haunts their minds, has induced them to put forth schemes mpracticable in their nature, and calculated only to do mis-i chief; and which must, if carried into effect, keep this State as it now is, in insurrection against the Government of the United States—keep this State as it now is, under the dominion and control of the Federal bayonet, in the hands of the negro—keep this State, as it now is, deprived of the writ of habeas corpus—keep this State, as it now is, deprived of the trial by jury, in all controversies between the white man and the negro, with our people, subject to military tribunals, proceeding by different forms, and on different principles, than they have been accustomed to in the past.

If the institution of slavery is ended practically, why not so declare it? Is there any want of dignity in making the declaration when the fact exists? Is there any want of manhood in yielding to an inevitable necessity, which we have no power to resist? When Gen. Lee surrendered the army that had confronted the forces of the United States for four years, and yielded it at last as prisoners of war, think you there was any want of manhood in acknowledging the fact that he had been overcome by force—that he yielded to arms and to uncontrolable power, which had prostrated him and his soldiers? Gentlemen who are so tender of the dignity of the State; tender of the manhood of the State, have walked up quietly for the purpose of protecting either their persons or property, and have taken the amnesty oath prescribed by the President of the United States, which oath requires that they shall not only uphold and maintain the Constitution of the United States, but uphold and defend the proclamations of the President of the United States relative to the abolition of slavery. They have taken that oath, at the same time declaring that they believe those proclamations and the oath to uphold them, to be unconstitutional. I conceive that there is as little dignity and manhood in taking an oath to support a proclamation which is believed to be unconstitutional, and which is taken to protect our person and property, as there can possibly be in endeavoring to shape the course of the government and legislation in this country in a direction that would tend to relieve our people from some of the ills which unwise counsels and untoward fate have brought upon them. In reference to this question of insurrection, and our position under it, I will read a General Order which was made on the 25th of July, at Washington, and issued at Vicksburg on the 15th of this month. Certain citizens of Mississippi had committed alleged acts of violence against negroes, and were arrested by the Federal military authorities. They claimed the privilege of being tried by the laws of the State, and it was referred to Washington to determine what should be done. The order reads as follows:

GENERAL ORDERS, No. 18.

HEADQUARTERS
DEPARTMENT OF MISSISSIPPI,
Vicksburg, Miss., Aug. 15, 1865.

The following endorsement on a communication, regarding jurisdiction of Military Courts in certain cases, which was addressed to the Assistant Judge Advocate General, and by him referred to the Judge Advocate General of the Army, and which is approved by the Secretary of War, is published for the information of all concerned:

WAR DEPARTMENT,
BUREAU OF MILITARY JUSTICE,
July 25*th*, 1865.

Respectfully returned to Colonel W. M. Dunn, Assistant Judge Advocate General.

The trials by Military Commission of the within named citizens of Mississippi, (Cooper, Downing, and Saunders,) charged with capital and other gross assaults upon colored soldiers of our army, (and in one instance of similar treatment of a colored female,) should be at once proceeded with; and all like cases of crime in that locality should be promptly and vigorously prosecuted. That the President has accorded a provisional government to the State of Mississippi, is a fact which should not be allowed to abridge or injudiciously affect the jurisdiction heretofore properly assumed by military courts in that region during the war. And especially is the continued exercise of that jurisdiction called for, in cases—1st, of wrong or injury done by citizens to soldiers, (whether white or black;) and, 2d, of assault or abuse of colored citizens generally; where, indeed, the local tribunals are either unwilling (by reason of the defective machinery, or because of some State law declaring colored persons incompetent as witnesses,) to do full justice, or properly punish the offenders.

The State of Mississippi, in common with other insurgent States, is still in the occupation of our forces, and—embraced as it is in a military department—is still to a very considerable extent, under the control of the military authorities. Moreover, the rebellion, though physically crushed, has not been officially announced or treated either directly or indirectly, as a thing of the past: the suspension of the *habeas corpus* has not been terminated, nor has military law ceased to be enforced, in proper cases, through the agency of military courts and military commanders, in all parts of the country.

It is to be added that the charges against the within named parties have been examined, and found to be generally substantially correct in form. A few changes only in the allegations have been voted as proper to be made before these charges are served upon the accused.

[Signed] A. A. HOSMER,
Major and Judge Advocate,
(*in the absence of the Judge Advocate General.*)

Approved:
[Signed] E. M. STANTON,
Secretary of War.

July 27th, 1865.
By Order of Major General Slocum:
J. WARREN MILLER,
Assistant Adjutant General.

It will thus be seen, Mr. President, that although we are here assembled for the purpose of reorganizing our State government, with a view of restoration to our position as members of the government of the United States, we are still looked upon and treated as States in insurrection, and with military law over us, and that condition of things is as certain to remain and continue as we continue and remain determined to refuse the proposition made to us by the President, so to change and alter our organic law as to accord with existing facts. But, say gentlemen, we admit that the proclamation of the President declaring the emancipation of slaves as a war measure, was constitutional, and the delegate from Yazoo, (Mr. Hudson,) remarked that as to the slaves actually captured after this proclamation, they were actually and legally free; but as to the slaves not captured, they were not free. If the first proposition is true that the emancipation proclamation as a war measure is valid, that the slaves captured became free, then I tell him that they are all free, for all have been captured by the arms of the United States. When General Lee, General Johnston, and General Taylor, surrendered; when Kirby Smith surrendered, the armies of the United States took absolute possession of the insurrectionary States, and now hold that possession, with no force to oppose them. Though they may not have taken the actual, they have obtained potential possession of all the slaves; though they may not have tangible possession, they have capacity and power to take them whenever they please. If, therefore, the proposition be true that the slaves were emancipated when captured, all are emancipated, because all are in the actual or potential possession of the government. But as I remarked before, the question whether they were set free by the proclamation, whether emancipated by capture, or set free by the result of war, as the President of the United States has said, need not be discussed; because all admit that they are free in fact. Can you institute an action of replevin for the recovery of your slave? Let any gentleman undertake it who wish to try conclusions of power with the United States. Can you maintain a writ of *habeas corpus* for the return of your slave? Make the attempt, and see how futile it would be. Have you any control or dominion over your slaves, except as is accorded to you by free contract, either expressed or implied under the laws of the United States? Do they not go where they please untrammelled and unfettered? Do they not, if they desire it, take an appeal to the military tribunals of the United States for redress against their former master or owner, if he assaults, strikes or maltreats them? Have you any power to resist this? Have they not every right of person in this State which belongs to any citizen of this country? Are they not free to go, and free to come? Have you dominion or control over them? If so, how will you assert it? I know of but one way in which it can be asserted. If you possess the physical power and the will, you may recapture and restore the dominion you once had; but unless gentlemen are ready and willing to try the conclusion of arms again—unless they say to the people of this State: "We are ready to place ourselves at the head of armed bands in this State, and do battle in behalf of the institution of slavery"—unless they are prepared for this alternative to-day, they counsel unwisely when they do not counsel acquiescence and submission to a force they have no power and are unwilling to resist. No good can be obtained by the further agitation of this question. What the people want is quiet and repose; what they need, is the re-establishment of a practical and just system of labor—just both to the white man and the black—which will insure to capital a fair remuneration, and to labor a just reward. They want peace and quiet; they want such an organization of the State government as will enable them to control the labor which is still in the country, and by wise and prudent counsels; by honestly and fairly dealing with the government of the United States, and with the negro, they can obtain this direction and control.

Mr. President, although the institution of slavery has been abolished, although as a system giving the right to control property in man, it has ceased to exist, the labor is still here upon our soil, and by just legislation and fair dealing, may be so directed as to enable the people of the South to regain a great degree of their former prosperity. Although this war has produced many and great evils, and in my humble judgment, the abolition of slavery, and particularly its abolition so suddenly, has worked great injury and brought unnecessary suffering upon our country, yet to a reflecting and right thinking mind, the state of things is not without some compensation. The results of the last four years have demonstrated beyond all question, that in a military point of view, and as a political institution, slavery is a source of positive weakness. When the Southern States were invaded by an army proclaiming freedom to the slaves, that army obtained not merely negative, but positive power, with which to enforce the declaration and conduct the war. It has thus been shown that the institution was a source of weakness to the State, and placed the country, when invaded, in a great degree, at the mercy of the invader. This fact was recognized by the Congress of the Confederate States, which at the last session were prepared to declare, and probably did pass laws declaring the emancipation of slaves upon condition of service in the army. What did this say to the civilized world? That this institution, to which we have heretofore clung so tenaciously, has failed in the hour of trial. It was also a declaration that in the opinion of the Confederate Congress, there were some things better than slavery; that in the opinion of that Congress, the independence of the Southern States was better. So, too, I think, there are things better than the institution of slavery; though, as a slave-holder in the past, and having invested in it the earnings of twenty-eight years of toil, I would have done all I could to uphold and maintain it when attacked. Still there are some things of far greater value: civil liberty is better than the institution of slavery; political liberty is better; the right of trial by jury; the writ of *habeas corpus;* the political supremacy of the white man over the negro; all these are better than the institution of slavery. There are many things which we could not sacrifice for it; and yet, these things, dear to all of us, important as they are in their character, and essential to our peace and prosperity, gentlemen who uphold and sustain this substitute, and the different amendments made to the proposition introduced by the Committee, are ready to yield—not for the institution of slavery, because they say that is gone, dead, a thing of the past, and cannot be revived—but they are ready and willing to give them all up; to jeopardize them all; in the *ignis fatuus* pursuit of a chimerical right under the Constitution of the United States, to test the validity of the President's Proclamation, and the laws Congress passed abolishing the institution of slavery in accordance with it. Are these men practical? Do they present practical issues, by whose success the people can hope to live hereafter in peace and prosperity, occupying their former position as members of the Federal Government? Certainly such things are not believed by any one who looks at facts as they are—who does not shut himself up in what ought to be and forget what actually is.

But again: As I said before, though slavery is gone, the

negro is here, with his capacity for labor unimpaired. Wise legislation may organize that labor; wise legislation can organize that labor, and organize it upon a basis fair and just to the white man and the negro. The white man owns the land, the negro owns the labor; such an organization may be made as will compensate the negro for his labor, and yield to the white man a proper return for the use of the land. The State thus organized will not probably, as a State, be in a worse financial condition than before. In the year 1859 the State of Mississippi, by slave labor, produced 1,300,000 bales of cotton, which brought in the market $45,000,000. I know that under any system of labor we will hereafter organize for many years such product cannot be returned. But as a diminution of the product will increase the value of the article produced, the amount of money brought into the country will be as great. Where we heretofore received ten cents per pound for cotton, we may receive 20, 30, or 40 cents, and thus be remunerated in price what we lose in product.

If the State of Mississippi raised only 300,000 bales, we could realize to-day $60,000,000—one third more than for the large crop of 1859.

There is another point of view at which this subject may be looked, which to some extent may modify the opinion of absolute ruin in which we are too prone to indulge. By the organization of slave labor, the largest possible product of cotton was always made; and as a consequence of over-production the price was depressed in the markets of the world; and thus the poor man who raised cotton with his own hands, could only realize for the products of his labor, the depressed price caused by a glut in the markets—the consequence of over-production. But when the quantity is reduced, a different result follows. The man who produces cotton by his own labor, obtains an increased price, according to the diminished product. As we see is the case at this time, the poor man who has raised by his own hands, four bales of cotton in the year, instead of getting only ten cents per pound, as formerly, can realize to-day 35 or 40 cents; and thus the yearly value of his toil, instead of $150 to $200, reaches $850 to $1000, nearly five times as much. Here, then, is some compensation; for while the whole amount of money brought into the State in consequence of the increased price will not be diminished by the lessened production, the industrious poor man who raises cotton by his own hands will find in the increased price an increased reward for his toil and labor.

But again: while we held negroes in slavery, we were not permitted representation on the floor of Congress for more than three-fifths; now we get the representation of the remaining two-fifths, and our political consideration and capacity is increased by that amount; and on the present ratio of representation, will be increased by fifteen to twenty additional members. Thus it will be seen, that there is no evil so great but it has some compensating advantage. Although the destruction of this social institution at this time, so suddenly and rudely, has worked great hardship upon many individuals, and resulted in great pecuniary destitution, now that the loss has been sustained and cannot be helped, let us not sit down and repine over the inevitable past which we cannot control, but look in hope to the future, and to those things which may in some degree give compensation for what we have lost. As men of sense, let us endeavor to remedy what we cannot alter, and gather together whatever may tend to palliate our misfortunes. Of all the industrial systems, that of slave labor was probably the most costly. The man who owned land in this country, could not cultivate it unless he owned or actually bought for life the the labor which was necessary for the purpose of cultivation. If he wished to cultivate one hundred acres of land, he had to buy the labor necessary to do it, at a cost of $1090 to $1500 for each laborer. The interest upon this money was never less than ten to twelve per cent; equal to an annual hire of $150 per year. Besides, he had to feed and clothe, employ the physician, and lose the time in sickness; and if the slave died, he lost in actual capital the value of the slave. He was in fact an insurer of the life and health of the slave. Now, every man who has a hundred acres of land to cultivate, can go into the market for labor, and for an annual hire can cultivate his land without insuring the life or health of the laborer. He simply pays for the use of the labor during the year; and thus, by a small annual outlay, the land is cultivated, and the surplus over that sum he puts into his pocket. Instead of using it as capital to buy hands, it is at his disposal to invest in railroads, internal improvements, insurance offices, banks, &c.

It is precisely this which has enabled the North to make such progress in these things. They do not buy their labor in fee, but simply pay an annual hire for it. We purchased it; put our capital into labor, and had no money for any other purpose. Looking at it in this way, there is some compensation in these things for what we have lost. But while I thus look at the compensating facts in our condition, I never would have been willing, if it could have been avoided, to see so great an interference with our social relations as has taken place. For one, so far as the unfortunate negro is concerned, I believe his situation was better in the past than it will be in the future. It protected him in sickness, sheltered him in his old age, and gave him a protector always interested in seeing that he was fed and clothed and sheltered. Therefore, to him it was unquestionably an institution that ought not to have been rudely broken. If done at all, it should have been gradual, that both he and his owner might have been prepared for it. But it has been done, and there is no alternative. And being done, it is the part of wisdom to accept without repining at the inevitable destiny, and so to manage the labor system hereafter as to produce the best return possible for the land owner, and to give the best security possible to the laborer for the protection of his person and a fair reward for his labor.

The events of the past four years have demonstrated that slavery, as an institution, was generally of a character benignant to the negro, and not calculated to create the fiendish passions which malignant fanaticism represented, in his breast against his master; on the contrary, it cultivated the kindly sentiments of humanity and affection for the household aud hearth of the man who sheltered and protected him. All over the country, wherever the armies of the United States have penetrated; when the men of the South were on the field of battle; when the sons and fathers were withdrawn from home, our people relied confidently on the loyalty and fidelity and kindness of their slaves. History does not show in any wars which have taken place for what is termed "the freedom of mankind," a people who, while accepting the freedom offered to them, have remained more true and loyal to their masters than our slaves have been to us.

Is is a tribute, just to them—it is a tribute, just to us, because it has proved, what we heretofore declared to the civilized world—that although our system of labor was called slavery—it was an institution, which cultivated kindly affections between the master and slave; and which—while on the one part, it exacted obedience; at the same time, upon the other—demanded and gave protection.

It has demonstrated to the world, that though there may have been wrongs perpetrated under it, as there have been wrongs perpetrated under every industrial regulation, which imperfect man has made; yet, in its moral and social influences, it tended to cultivate kind feelings on the part of the white man and the slave.

It has shown that the charges made against our people of unkindness and inhumanity were not founded in justice, and had no basis in truth.

I think at this time, there can be in the minds of the Convention no doubt, as to the policy we should adopt. If we go to Washington with the substitute offered by the gentleman from Yazoo, and announce that we have declared the institution of slavery abolished, on the conditions contained in that substitute, we will certainly be told, "you assert that slavery is still an existing legal institution, in your State—you thus show that you do not acquiese in the result of the war—but intend to wait, and see if you cannot obtain some opportunity, by which that may be restored practically, which you say is not legally and constitutionally destroyed." The gentleman from Marshall, it seems to me has put the question, in a shape, hat is logically irresistible to the mind of any man.—The Government of the United States has not begged us to come back, and be restored as co-equal members of the Government. They are not soliciting our return; in fact there is a large party who do not wish it at this time, and will if possible, prevent it—do what we may. But from the proposition of the gentleman from Yazoo, it would seem that the Government is a suppliant for our return—and not we asking to be restored to our ancient political position.

If this substitute is adopted—a hue and cry will be immediately raised by the whole Northern press, that the Southern States are attempting to dictate the terms of their restoration to Congress—that the proud Southern people, who, for four years carried on a war at the cost of many millions of money and hundreds of thousands lives, are not yet subdued, but come with the language and air of conquerors, to dictate terms and conditions to the Government, whose protection they forfeited, and which they still defy. As a matter of course there will be found no one having the hardihood to sustain us in this course.

The President cannot do it, for he has now to stand up against a clamor that is threatening to overwhelm him. The conservative people of the North cannot do it; they have as much as they can do to withstand the tide of fanaticism, which is seeking to overwhelm us by giving social equality and suffrage to the negro.

In what way, then, are we to be benefitted by this substitute? If, with the amendment to the Constitution proposed by the Committee, we are not admitted to representation in Congress, it is positively certain we will not be if this substitute is adopted. Suppose admission is refused, when our members present the Constitution as amended by the Committee, we will at least have done all we can do for the restoration of peace and civil order; we will have shown to the conservative people of the North that we seek a restoration of the fraternal relations which were severed by the war, and we will thus make friends who will come to our relief; the rejection of our members will be followed by an immediate reaction, that will force the party in power to grant us those rights under the Constitution to which we are entitled. But if we present the substitute and are rejected, as we most assuredly will be, our friends will be powerless to aid a defeated people who, it will be said, still defy the Government, and undertake to dictate the terms of restoration to political rights they have forfeited by rebellion. This substitute is, in fact, an attempt to dictate to Congress, and if adopted, will betray a want of wisdom, which no people so situated, have ever before exhibited. We are at this time, utterly powerless. We meet here to-day, by the clemency of the President. Martial law exists, and is in enforced throughout the State. No civil courts are open—the right of trial by jury does not exist —the writ of habeas corpus is suspended—our former slaves are practically free—and so far from being under the control of their former masters—are hardly subject to the control of the law; and yet, with these facts staring us in the face, gentlemen talk of the dignity of the State—and introduce propositions—dictating terms to the Government, which we resisted four years with arms—and so defying it, give color to the clamor raised against the President, of acting with too much haste in his efforts to relieve us. It does seem to me, that there can be no doubt in the mind of any one, that the substitute should be rejected.

But gentlemen talk about compensation for the slave. Who is to get compensation? How is compensation to be had?—We cannot sue the United States in any Court; we can bring no action against it, for any lost property, or other claim; all that can be done, if a man is loyal, and has a claim of any kind against the Government—is to petition Congress to allow it, or bring it before what is called the Court of Claims, and if an adjudication is made in its favor. he can then ask Congress for an appropriation. And this it may refuse, or not, as it pleases. We have no right that can be executed by force, or process of law.

If we have any right to compensation at all, that fact now exists as a fixed, distinct, positive right at this time, and the proposition introduced by the committee, in no way, shape or form, affects it.

The proposed amendment simply declares, that in the future, the institution of slavery shall not exist. But if it be destroyed as the gentlemen say it has been, by the act of the United States—if the emancipation proclamation has takan it away—if the armies rubbed it out—if it has been taken by force, from the people of the State, and they have a right to compensation, that right now exists, in full force. A man to-day, can urge his claim, and make it with equal success, after as before the amendment is adopted, because the right is a present existing one, and no action we can take, can impair it.

I deem it proper to say however, that so far as the question of compensation is concerned, I do not believe the Government of the United States will entertain it. I would not delude the people with the idea, that I believe that the Government will make general compensation for the slaves which have been taken or emancipated. Mr. Lincoln, in his proclamation of December, 1863, declared to the people of the Southern States, if they would return to their allegiance, and lay down their arms, he would ask Congress to make compensation.

It is also said that when the Commissioners from the Confederate Government met him and Mr. Seward, at Hampton Roads, he was then willing that compensation should be made. But these offers were rejected, and the war was carried on, at a cost of two thousand millions of dollars, and the lives of 250,000 or 300,000 soldiers. Does any man suppose that those who thus carried on this war, regardless of the offer of amnesty, who refused to accept payment when it was tendered, will meet with any favor in preferring a claim to compensation.

There is a class, who probably in the future, may receive some compensation. The orphan, whose slave was taken from him, without any hostile action on his part—the widow, whose property was destroyed, without any participation on her part in the war—the lunatic, who was ignorant of what was being done; and those persons whom the United States may deem loyal, if there be any such—there is a possibility, that in the future, some compensation may be made to these. But when will that compensation be made? It will not be until the asperities of the war have been smoothed down—until the passions, which four years of contest produced have been quieted—until the malignant feelings, excited by it have been subdued—until an "era of good feeling" shall return, in which the Northern and Southern gentlemen can stand together in the halls of Congress, legislating for a common country, and a common destiny; and then an appeal may be made. "Now that this war is past—now that we are again united—now that we are in union, moving forward, and shoulder to shoulder, battling for the same Constitutional rights, united against the world, we appeal in the name of humanity—we appeal in the name of brotherly love—we appeal in the name of our common ancestors, to make some compensation to these innocent parties, for losses sustained in a war which they had no agency in bringing on; losses entailed upon them, by the misguided zeal of brothers and friends, who have paid a terrible penalty, for their action; and who claim no compensation at our hands, for losses arising from their deliberate but misguided conduct."

I have thus attempted to present my views, in support of the amendment, offered by the Committee. I have wearied the Convention longer than I ought, and have not presented them in the clear and perspicious manner that they appear to my mind; but before I had the honor to be elected a member of this Convention, I considered, as I do now, that the true policy for the State, is to adopt a course, which wisdom, patriotism and manly dignity require at our hands; is to turn our back, without repining, upon the inevitable past; and looking towards the future, to determine, if possible, to rescue the State from the destitution, into which it has been dragged —to restore our people, if possible, to the Constitutional rights which they once had, under the Federal Constitution— to give peace and quiet, and repose to a distracted country, which has been desolated by four years of war—a war, in which the property of our people; their homesteads and their fields—all have been destroyed: and their political and civil liberties almost crushed.

On motion of Mr. Harrison, of Lowndes, the substitute was laid upon the table.

Mr. Harrison offered the following amendment to the second section:

"Strike out the word "that," and insert the words: 'The institution of slavery having been destroyed in the State of Mississippi."

Upon which Mr. Harrison moved the previous question.

Which, being sustained, the question was taken upon the amendment, and decided in the affirmative.

Mr. Marshall, of Warren, offered the following amendment:

Amend by striking out the word "property," in the fourth line, and insert: The regulation of the labor and wages.

On motion of Mr. Harrison,

The amendment was laid upon the table.

Mr. Cooper, of Rankin, offered the following amendment:

Amend by inserting the word "personal," before the word "property," in the fourth line of the amendment proposed.

On motion of Mr. Yerger, of Hinds,

The amendment was laid on the table.

Mr. Martin, of Adams, offered the following amendment:

Amend by inserting after the word "property," the words: "and regulation of the labor and wages."

On motion of Mr. Yerger, of Hinds,

The amendment was laid upon the table.

Mr. Harrison, of Lowndes, moved the previous question upon the second section, as amended—

Which being sustained—

The main question was then put, and the section adopted by yeas and nays, called for by Messrs. Marshall, of Warren, Franklin, of Neshoba, and Johnson, of Smith, as follows, to-wit:

YEAS—Mr. President, Messrs. Barr, Bailey, Billups, Binford, Blackwell, Bond, Brandon, Brown, Byars, Carter, Cason,

Compton, Cooper, of Rankin, Cooper, of Panola, Crawford, Crum, Cummings, Davis, Dorris, Dowd, Duncan, Farley, Gaither, Gowan, Goode, Griffin, Gully, Hall, Hamm, Harrison, Heard, Hemingway, Hill, Horne, Houston, Hurst, Jarnagin, Johnson, of Choctaw, Johnson, of Smith, Jones, Kennedy, King, Lambdin, Lewers, Lewis, Lindsey, Loper, Martin, of Adams, Martin, of Sunflower, Matthews, Montgomery, Mayson, McBride, Morphis, Niles, Owen, of Tunica, Owens, of Scott, Peyton, Phipps, Pressley, Quin, Rives, Rushing, Sanders, of Attala, Simonton, Slover, Sparkman, Stanley, Stone, Stricklin, Tate, Trotter, Wade, Wallace, Wall, Watson, Webb, White, Wier, Wooley, Woodward, Wylie, and Yerger, Johnston, of Hinds, Johnson, of Marshall.—87.

Nays.—Messrs. Franklin, Hudson, Malone, Marshall, Maury, Potter, Reid, Reynolds, Sanders, of DeSoto, Swett, and Wilson—11.

The following is the section as adopted:

The institution of slavery having been destroyed in the State of Mississippi, neither slavery nor involuntary servitude, otherwise than in the punishment of crimes, whereof the party shall have been duly convicted, shall hereafter exist in this State; and the Legislature, at its next session, and thereafter, as the public welfare may require, shall provide by law for the protection and security of the person and property of the freedmen of the State, and guard them and the State against any evils that may arise from their sudden emancipation.

on motion of Mr. McBride,

The Convention adjourned until 4 o'clock, P. M.

FOUR O'CLOCK, P. M.

The Convention met pursuant to adjournment, and proceeded to the consideration of the regular order, to-wit:

The third section of the majority report of the committe on State Constitution, which is as follows:

Third—That the twelfth section of the Declaration of Rights, be amended by the insertion of the following proviso, to-wit:

Provided, That the Legislature in cases not capital, and of misdemeanors, may dispense with an inquest by a grand jury, and may authorize proceedings by information or otherwise, and the proceedings, in such cases, shall be regulated by law, and be had in such courts as the Legislature may direct.

Mr. Harrison, of Lowndes, offered the following substitute for the proviso:

Provided, That the Legislature, in cases of petit larceny, assault, assault and battery, affray, riot, unlawful assembly, drunkeness, vagrancy, and other misdemeanors of like character, may dispense with an inquest of a grand jury, and may authorize prosecutions before justices of the peace, or such other inferior court, or courts, as may be established by the Legislature; and the proceedings in such cases shall be regulated by law.

On motion of Mr. Yerger, of Hinds,

The substitute was adopted.

On motion of Mr. Harrison, of Lowndes,

The fourth section of the report of the committee was stricken out.

The Convention then proceeded to the consideration of the ordinance reported by said Committee, providing for an election for State officers, representatives in Congress, members of the Legislature, and all county, district, judicial and ministerial officers, according to the Constitution and election laws of the State as they existed on the first day of January, 1861.

The ordinance having been read,

Mr. Hudson, of Yazoo, called up an amendment to the same, which was submitted by him on Thursday last, providing that certain judicial and other officers be reinstated and restored to their several offices and positions for the unexpired terms for which they were elected, as follows, to-wit:

Be it ordained by the loyal people of the State of Mississippi in Convention assembled,

1st. That the High Court of Errors and Appeals of this State, the several Circuit and Chancery Courts of this State, the Criminal Court of Warren county, the office of Attorney General of this State, the office of District Attorney of the several judicial districts and criminal courts of this State, the office of clerk of the several Circuit and Criminal Courts of this State, and all county officers known to the Constitution and laws of this State on and before the 6th day of January, 1861, be, and the same are hereby revived, re-established and declared to be in existence, full force and operation, and that the several persons elected to said offices by the people at the last election therefor, in this State, and holding said offices at the time of the suspension of their functions and powers, in May, 1861, be, and they are hereby reinstated, restored and elected to their said several offices and positions, upon their respectively taking the amnesty oath, if not already taken, and the proper oath of office, and giving new bond and security, to be taken conditioned and approved according to law, in the case of bonded officers, for and until the end of the unexpired term for which they were severally elected: *Provided,* That any such office now filled and held by any oppointee of Governor W. L. Sharkey, shall be held and filled by such appointee for the unexpired term of said office; and in case any of said offices are or may become vacant by the death, removal, resignation, refusal to qualify or act, or other legal cause, such vacancy shall be filled, in cases of district and State offices, by executive appointment, and in case of county officers, by election according to existing laws in such cases, for the unexpired term thereof.

Mr. Hudson, of Yazoo—Mr. President:—The condition of the country demands that the officers specified should be restored to their offices. In order that the ground I take in this matter, may not be considered improper on my part, I desire to say, that in the event of the passage of this act, I shall certainly resign the position which I have heretofore held. The condition of the country is such that the exercise of Judicial power, is now indispensably necessary, at the earliest moment that it can be brought into operation. An election is proposed to be held, on the first Monday in October next, and that is but a short time, it is true, but I think it is amenable and objectionable in another sense. It will be almost impossible for the action of this Convention, as gentlemen know, owing to the want of mail facilities, and other things, to reach them, so they may know, what has actually been done; and place it before the people, and the various candidates, who may aspire to such positions; as to enable them to act judiciously and wisely, in the selection of their officers. This is more particularly true with reference to the district officers. They cannot canvass, or make themselves known to the people, before the election will transpire; and in many cases the people will be obliged to select, without having any very intelligent means of determining. It would be impossible, in some instances, to hold elections.

There are many parties now confined in the jails of the counties, and the military authorities are taking cognizance of these cases, on the express ground, that there is no civil authority that can take cognizance and jurisdiction in the State. I have a letter from Gen. Slocum, Commander of the Department, proposing to intervene, in a case, where a party is confined in the jail of Yazoo county, on the ground that there is no civil authority. There are many complaints against the action of the military authorities, for intervening in questions of this sort, that properly belong to the civil authorities, when in fact, they place their action in many of the cases, on the ground that there is no other tribunal; and as an act of humanity and mercy, they assume power, whether legally or constitutionally, it belongs to them or not. I propose to reinstate the officers, who can take cognizance of these questions. Those officers who are known to our Constitution and laws, whether in a State of rebellion or not, have been elected by our own people, who will pass again on this question, whenever it is presented. They hold positions wholly judicial and ministerial in their character, and have been selected for their own fitness, in such cases, and so far as I know, there has been no disposition on the part of the people to make any changes in these things.

I would remark further, that it has been intimated to me, that the old officers being elected during a state of rebellion, and that it might be improper to re-instate them ; or in other words, notwithstanding their fitness—notwithstanding, that in all probability they will be immediately returned to their respective offices—that going from this Convention, it might operate unfavorably upon us, in regard to our relations with the Federal Government. Gov. Sharkey has set a precedent, on this subject, with the approval—at least the recognition—and to the satisfaction of the Federal Government; for I have heard no complaint, and so far as he has thought it his duty, or proper to the State, or the Federal Government, to make changes—it has been done. I propose by this amendment, to recognize what has been done on that subject; confirm the appointments he has made, and continue his appointments until the expiration of the unexpired term of the officers.

Mr. Yerger, of Hinds—Mr. President :—I object to the substitute offered by the gentleman from Yazoo, (Mr. Hudson,) and to my mind, my objections are of such a serious character, that I am constrained to present them to the Convention.

In the first place, the amendment starts out with the idea that the present incumbents, have unexpired terms to fill.—According to the theory, on which this Convention is proceeding—according to the theory on which the Government of the United States is proceeding, the parties who fill these offices, though elected by the people, were merely officers, *de facto;* elected under a Constitution established by insurrectionary parties—not under the Constitution of the State of Mississippi, as an organized State, and part of the United States; therefor there is no unexpired terms to be filled by the gentlemen, who were incumbents at the time the State of Mississippi yielded to the forces of the United States.

Again, it is true, that Gov. Sharkey, filled minor places—such as, Justices of the Peace, and as high as the office of Probate Judge ; and he did it with the approval of the President of the United States, for he stated to him, that for the purpose of speedy organization, and in order to obtain a Convention at an early day, we would have to take that course with the minor officers; but he did not fill, and could not fill the higher grade of offices, with incumbents who had filled them, and only the minor offices were attempted, until the Convention should meet. He only did it, in order to have an immediate organization. Although Gov. Sharkey, thus filled these minor offices, for that purpose; yet his course has been subjected to severe criticism on the part of the Northern press, who hold that the idea was to whitewash what has been done under the Ordinance of Secession.

But a still more satisfactory objection to it, in my mind, is this: the offices were filled at a period of time, when a large and very important portion of the citizens of this State, were absent from home, and they had no voice, no word, in filling the offices, or in choosing the incumbents. They have come back after years of absence, spent in privation and toil, and I think their views, and their wishes, should be consulted, if these offices are vacant now, for they have a right to choose the parties who will fill them. For these objections, I shall be constrained to vote against the gentleman from Yazoo, believing as I do, that it will militate seriously against the action of this Convention, and also exclude from a fair chance to express their wishes and opinions, those who were absent; and deprive them also, as it will, of the opportunity of calling on their fellow-citizens, to place them in these same positions, should they be entitled to fill them.

Mr. Crawford, of Jones—Mr. President:—The people of one of the counties, being dissatisfied with the officers, who held the offices, at the time the Provisional Government was established, petitioned Gov. Sharkey for their removal. Upon that petition, he removed two of the officers of the county, in which the petition originated, which created disturbance and ill-feeling there. I only bring this to show the difficulties which may arise from the adoption of the substitute, in lieu of the original amendment; consequently I oppose it.

Mr. Martin, of Adams—Mr. President:—I think we will save very little by attempting to continue, or put into office, those who have held these offices, under the State Government, while in rebellion, because a large proportion of the judicial officers will resign, if restored to office.

Mr. Hudson.—Mr. President:—I simply desire to suggest this; so far as the objection of the gentleman from Hinds is concerned, that the action of Gov. Sharkey, in the restoration of a few unimportant officers to their positions, has been the subject matter of severe criticism in the North, it does not for one moment, affect my action as a delegate in this House! It is not a political question; it is one that certainly does not rightfully concern the North. Are we to submit everything from A to Z, for their approbation, before we are permitted to act upon it? If so, I say, let us sit here and await orders. If, in these matters, which affect us alone—which affect mere communities, and of a mere judicial character—which affect the regulation of right and wrong, as between us, and not as between us and them—is to be subject matter of criticism, and we are appalled by that criticism from discharging our duty to ourselves, I say, let us sit down, and await orders. I do not understand that the Government of the United States criticises this subject. If criticism from any other source is to deter us from discharging what we concede to be our duty, we shall do nothing. The only question it seems to me is this : whether or not, the exigencies of the country require that this should be done—whether or not, public good and private interest would be best subserved, by re-instating or putting into position, officers, who can take cognizance of these things, and relieve the military authorities from intervening, as they do from necessity—a necessity which will exist, until these civil officials are placed in their proper positions.

So far as the question of unexpired term is concerned, the amendment to the ordinance proposed, does not mean to say, they have been legally or constitutionally in office; but it means, by law as existing in this State, prior to 1861, and prior to the passage of the Ordinance of Secession; that there is now an unexpired term, so far as the tenure of office is concerned, and that this Convention may place the present incumbents in position, for that unexpired tenure of office. That is all that it means to assert—all it means to accomplish. In case of the resignations spoken of by the gentleman from Adams, (Mr. Martin,) that can be promptly remedied by the provision here.

Mr. Harrison, of Lowndes—Mr. President :—I would suggest another difficulty to the gentleman from Yazoo. The ordinance of the Committee is general in its character; it provides for the election of officers of the State generally, and members of Congress. That is, a general election is to be held. It also provides for a special election of all county and ministerial officers. This ordinance, offered as a substitute, touches none of the offices in the first section of the original bill, but the Attorney General, and unless it is modified in some way, it is not an amendment. In order to test the sense of the house, I propose to lay the amendment on the table.

The motion to lay on the table prevailed.

Mr. Potter, of Hinds, offered the following, as an additional clause to the ordinance under consideration:

First. That the High Court of Errors and Appeals of this State, the several Circuit and Chancery Courts of this State, the Criminal Court of Warren county, the office of Attorney General of this State, the office of District Attorney of the several Judicial Districts and Criminal Courts of this State, the offices of clerk of the several Circuit and Criminal Courts of this State, and all county offices known to the Constitution and laws of this State on and before the 9th day of January, 1861, be, and the same are hereby revived, re-established and declared to be in existence, full force and operation, and that the several persons elected to said offices by the people at the last election therefor, in this State, and holding said offices at the time of the suspension of their functions and powers in May, 1865, be, and they are hereby reinstated, restored and elected to their said several offices and positions, upon their respectively taking the amnesty oath, if not already taken, and the proper oath of office, and giving new bonds and security, to be taken, conditioned and approved according to law in the case of bonded officers, to hold said offices until the first Monday in November, A. D. 1865: *Provided*, that any such office now filled and held by any appointee of Governor W. L. Sharkey, shall be held and filled by such appointee until said first Monday in November, and in case any of said officers are or may become vacant by the death, removal, resignation, refusal to qualify or act, or other legal cause; such vacancy shall be filled in cases of District and State officers, by Executive appointment; and in case of county officers, by election, according to existing laws in such cases; and the terms of office of all such officers shall expire on said first Monday in November, 1865.

Mr. Potter, of Hinds—Mr. President:—The object of the amendment is simply to secure judicial and other officers, to perform these duties until the officers to be appointed under the ordinance reported by the Committee, shall assume their offices. If this be adopted, we will have re-established civil law, so far as it can be reached by the appointment of State and county officers. It seems to me the objection can be regarded of very little force, seeing that the purpose of their re-appointment is merely to meet a present emergency. It is a matter of great necessity, and the time of their continuance in office very short, as they will go out on the first Monday in November.

Mr. Harrison.—I had proposed to move to alter the report in relation to the time of the assembling of the Legislature, to the second Monday in October; also the term of the ministerial officers to commence on the second Monday in October. In moving to lay this amendment on the table, I think it is due to say that I propose so to amend, at the request of several gentlemen, as to bring the meeting of the Legislature, on the second Monday in October.

12

On motion of Mr. Harrison,

The amendment was laid upon the table.

Mr. Cooper, of Rankin, offered the following amendment:

Amend first section by inserting after the words "shall be held," in the first line, the words, "on the first Monday of October next."

Which was adopted.

Mr. Simonton, of Itawamba, offered the following amendment to the first section:

Strike out all after the word "same," in the fourth line, to the word "as," in the fifth line.

On motion of Mr. Cooper, of Rankin,

The amendment was laid upon the table.

Mr. Harrison moved to amend the first section by striking out the word "first," in the sixth line, and insert the word "third," in lieu thereof, and by striking out in the same line, the word "November," and inserting in lieu thereof the word "October."

Which amendments were adopted.

The first section, as amended, was then adopted, and is as follows, to-wit:

"That a general election shall be held on the first Monday of October next, according to the Constitution, and the election laws of the State as they existed on the first day of January, 1861, for Representatives in Congress, and all State officers and members of the Legislature. The several Congressional Districts shall be the same, and the time of holding the election for Representatives in Congress the same, as fixed and established by the Legislature in the year A. D., 1857. The Legislature shall convene on the third Monday in October, 1865, and be organized and classified as the Constitution directs.

The second section was then taken up.

Mr. Johnson, of Smith, offered the following amendment, which was adopted:

Strike out the words "until the next regular election thereafter," in the third line, and insert after the words "successors," in the fourth line, and before the words "qualified," the words "elected and."

Mr. Harrison moved to amend by striking out from seventh line the word "first," and insert in lieu thereof the word "third," and by striking out in same line the word "November," and insert in lieu thereof the word "October."

Which was adopted.

The second section as amended was then adopted, and is as follows:

A special election shall also be held at the time of said general election, the first Monday in October, A. D., 1865, for all county, district, judicial and ministerial officers, and the officers so elected shall hold their offices until their successors are elected and qualified, and enter upon the duties of their respective offices, according to the Constitution and laws—and the term of office of all such State, county, district, judicial and ministerial officers so elected, shall commence on the third Monday in October, A. D., 1865.

The third section was then taken up.

Mr. Harrison offered the following amendment, which was adopted:

Strike out the word "take," in third line, and insert the words "have taken" in lieu thereof.

No other amendment being offered to the third section, it was adopted, as follows:

"No person shall be qualified as an elector, or be eligible to any office at said elections, unless in addition to the qualifications required by the Constitution and election laws aforesaid, he shall have taken the amnesty oath prescribed in the proclamation of the President of the United States, on the 29th day of May, A. D. 1865.

The fourth section being taken up,

Mr. Maury, of Claiborne, offered the following amendment:

Amend fourth section of the ordinance by striking out the whole thereof, and inserting as follows, viz:

"No person shall be qualified as an elector at said election, unless, in addition to other qualifications required by law, he shall take an oath to support the Constitution of the United States, and the State of Mississippi."

On motion of Mr. Harrison,

The amendment was laid upon the table.

The fourth section was then adopted as follows:

"And immediately after the adjournment of the Convention, the President thereof shall issue writs of election directed to the Sheriffs of the several counties in the State, requiring them to cause said elections to be held according to the election laws in force, and existing on said first day of January, A. D., 1861."

The question was then taken on the ordinance as amended, and decided in the affirmative.

On motion of Mr. Yerger, of Hinds,

The Convention adjoured, until to-morrow morning, nine o'clock.

EIGHTH DAY.

TUESDAY, AUGUST, 22D., 1865.

The Convention met pursuant to adjournment.

Prayer by the Rev. C. Johnson.

Journal of yesterday read and approved.

Mr. Reynolds, of Tishomingo, asked leave of absence for Mr. Wade, of Issaquena.

Which was granted.

Mr. Sessions, of Holmes, who was absent yesterday on account of illness, asked leave to have his name placed in the affirmative on the final vote adopting the second section of the report of the majority of the Committee on State Constitution.

Which was granted.

Mr. Wier offered the following resolution—

Which was adopted:

Resolved, That the Committee on State Constitution be instructed to take into consideration the propriety and expediency of submitting the amendments of the Constitution, together with the ordinances adopted by this Convention, to the qualified electors of this State for their ratification or rejection, and report to this Convention as early as practicable, what action they recommend this Convention to take thereon.

On motion of Mr. Hudson, of Yazoo—

The Convention proceeded to the consideration of an ordinance to be entitled "An ordinance in relation to the Ordinance of Secession, and other ordinances and resolutions adopted by a former Convention of Mississippi, held at Jackson on 7th January, 1861, and on the 25th March, 1861,"— said ordinance having been reported by a majority of the Committee on Ordinances and Laws.

Mr. Johnson, of Marshall, moved that said ordinance be considered section by section, which being agreed to—

Mr. Johnson further moved that the ordinance reported by the minority committee, and submitted by Mr. Trotter, of Marshall, be substituted for the same, which ordinanee is as follows:

Be it ordained, That the Ordinance of Secession, adopted by a Convention of the people of this State, on the 9th day of January, 1861, be and the same is hereby repealed and abrogated.

Mr. Trotter, of Marshall, said:

Mr. President: The question which concerns the proper disposition to be made of the ordinance under consideration, is one which has interested every member of this body. It is the general opinion, that it must be settled in some form by the action of the Convention, and a majority of the Committee, to whom the subject was referred, have thought it sufficient to declare by the "ordinance" reported by them, that it is simply "*null and void*." This eonclusion is based upon the ground that the Convention which ordained it had no authority to do so. A minority of the same Committee, however, believe that, whether the Ordinance of Secession was lawful or unlawful, or in other words, whether the State of Mississippi, acting in her sovereign capacity, as a State, had a right to dissolve her connection with the other States of the Union, and resume the powers delegated by her by the terms of the compact, that the action condemned was nevertheless an exertion of power by a sovereign State, which, regarded merely as a revolutionary measure, was sufficient to command the obedience of her citizens, and to excuse and justify them. The ordinance created a government in fact, if not in law, and according to the well settled principles of public law, and the decisions of the courts of every civilized nation, the citizens of that government were not only excusable for obeying its authority, but were bound to do so. They had no option. Possession in this case, as in questions concerning the right of property, is *prima facie* evidence of good title. The community at large are not supposed to be capable of deciding grave and complicated questions of this sort, and are therefore bound, in determining the course of action to be pursued, to look no further than to the fact of actual possession. This was the rule adopted in England during the civil wars between the rival houses of York and Lancaster, which found one claimant in possession this year, and his antagonist the next. The people were of course kept in a continued state of alarm and perplexity. They knew not which to obey. Hence the importance and absolute necessity of the rule mentioned, which decides the duty of the citizen by the safe criterion of present possession. Any other principle would, in times of civil commotion, place them in a predicament of such peril as cannot be imagined without the most serious alarm. It would place them where they can neither do wrong without ruin, or right without affliction. "Wretched indeed, above all forms of wretchedness, must be their condition, if the rightful government might punish them for obedience to the powers in being, as the powers in being certainly would do for *disobedience.*" In view of these conservative doctrines, as applicable to the action of the State in the instance under consideration, this body should, in my humble opinion, be very cautious and considerate in their final disposition of this question. It has been decidedly the arbitrament of arms against the validity of the ordinance. The State has been compelled to yield her pretensions and recede from the stand she assumed. The forces of the Union have triumphed over those of the State as well as of the Confederacy. The "ordinance" can no longer be maintained, and the people of the State desire to see it formally *repealed and annulled* by the action of this body. This can be done without the use of such phraseology as will unnecessarily place the seal of censure and condemnation upon our proceedings. The "ordinance" has been crushed by the physical power of the United States, and I am of opinion that they will give themselves no concern about the reasoning of this body or its action in reference thereto. Hence I do insist, that whatever may be the differences of opinion here as to the power of the Convention of 1861, we should not so shape our action as to reflect discredit upon the intelligence and patriotism of that body. For though they may have erred, they acted in the discharge of what they conceived to be a concientious duty; and their error was shared by a large majority of the people of this State, as well as by those of eleven of their sister States. To adopt the language of the ordinance, reported by the Committee, would not only tend to discredit the Convention of 1861, by a reflection upon their intelligence and patriotism, but would have the effect of imputing to every member of that body, as well as every citizen of the State who yielded obedience to its authority, the grave crime of treason. For that which is simply *null and void* can justify the obedience of no one. And whilst we may acquiesce in the decision of the United States, and yield a ready and cheerful obedience to their authority, as our duty requires, yet it is certainly not necessary nor proper that we should go further, and by our voluntary resolution, cast any odium upon our predecessors. We all now regret the step that was taken, and sincerely desire to retrace it, and as soon as possible repair the mischief which have flowed from it. This it is believed can be best accomplished by a simple *repeal* of the original "ordinance," which puts it at rest, in a manner which meets the general wish, and will wound no sensibilities and compromit no rights. In this shape it can unite the conflicting views of those who believe it to have been void *ab initio*, as well as of those who believe otherwise, since it is a common practice with legislative bodies to repeal an act, whose constitutionality has been seriously questioned, or ascertained by a determination of the proper judicial tribunal. By the course recommended by the minority report, the end desired by all can be accomplished in a manner which will secure general acquiescence and that harmony of feeling which should be cultivated by every means in our power, and which is so essential to our welfare.

Mr. Harrison, of Lowndes, offered the following amendment:

"Strike out the word 'abrogated' in the second line, and insert in lieu thereof the words: declared to be of no force and effect."

Mr. Martin, of Adams, offered the following, as a substitute for the ordinance reported by the Minority, with the amendment thereto, offered by Mr. Harrison, of Lowndes :

That the Ordinance of Secession, passed by a Convention of the people of the State of Mississippi, on the 9th. day of January 1861 : not having been passed in the exercise of Constitutional right, or of a right reserved to the State; and being in violation of the Constitution of the United States, is hereby declared to be null void, and of no effect.

Pending which,

Mr. Morphis, of Pontotoc, moved to adjourn until 4 o'clock, P. M.

Which was lost.

On motion of Mr. Houston, of Monroe, the Convention adjourned until 3 o'clock, P. M.

THREE O'CLOCK, P. M.

The Convention met pursuant to adjournment.

On motion of Mr. Compton, of Marshall, the regular order of business was suspended, to enable him to introduce the following resolution:

Resolved, That a Committee of three be appointed to take into consideration the pay of the officers and members of this Convention, and report thereon.

On motion of Mr. Compton,

The resolution was adopted.

The President announced as the Committee, provided for in said resolution: Messrs. Compton, of Marshall; Matthews, of Panola; Horne of Wayne.

The regular order of business was resumed, to-wit:

The substitute offered by Mr. Martin, of Adams, for the ordinance, reported by the Minority Committee, with the amendment thereto, by Mr. Harrison, of Lowndes.

Mr. Martin, of Adams. moved the previous question,

Which was not sustained.

On motion, of Mr. Yerger, of Hinds, the substitute offered by Mr. Martin, was laid upon the table, by yeas and nays, called for by Messrs. Martin, of Adams; Wier and Morphis, as follows, to-wit:

YEAS.—Mr. President, Messrs. Barr, Bailey, Binford, Blackwell, Bond, Brown, Byars, Carter, Cason, Compton, Cooper, of Panola, Crum, Cummings, Davis, Franklin, Gaither, Goode, Griffin, Gully, Hamm, Harrison, Heard, Hill, Horne, Hurst, Jarnagin, Johnson, of Marshall, Jones, Kennedy, King, Lewers, Lindsey, Loper, Marshall, Martin, of Sunflower, Matthews, Maury, Montgomery, Mayson, Owens, of Tunica, Owen, of Scott, Phipps, Potter, Reid, Reynolds, Rives, Rushing, Sessions, Simonton, Slover, Stanley, Stone, Stricklin, Swett, Tate, Trotter, Wallace, Wall, Watson, White, Wilson, Woodward, Yerger.—64.

NAYS.—Messrs. Cooper, of Rankin, Crawford, Dowd, Gowan, Hall, Houston, Johnston, of Hinds, Johnson, of Smith, Lambdin, Lewis, Martin, of Adams, McBride, Morphis, Niles, Peyton, Pressley, Quin, Sanders, of Attala, Sparkman, Webb, Wier, Wylie.—22.

The question recurring on the ordinance of the Minority Committee,

Mr, Yerger, of Hinds, offerred the following, as a substitute for said ordinance:

Be it ordained by the Delegates of the people of Mississippi in Convention assembled, That an act entitled "An ordinance to dissolve the Union between the State of Mississippi, and other States, united with her under the compact, entitled, the "Constitution of the United States of America," passed and adopted on the 9th day of January, 1861, by a Convention of delegates of the people of Mississippi, assembled at Jackson, and all other acts, resolutions and ordinances, and all alterations, amendments and changes, and proposed amendments, alterations and changes of the Constitution of the State of Mississippi, adopted by said Convention, at said session, and the adjourned and called session thereof, in the year 1861, were without Constitutional validity or force, and the same are hereby repealed, and declared of no effect.

Mr. Matthews, of Panola, moved to lay the substitute upon the table,

Which was decided in the affirmative, by yeas and nays, called for by Messrs. Bond, of Pontotoc; Matthews, of Panola; and Yerger, of Hinds; as follows, to-wit:

YEAS.—Messrs. Barr, Bailey, Binford, Blackwell, Brown, Byars, Carter, Compton, Cooper, of Rankin, Cooper, of Panola, Crawford, Davis, Dorris, Duncan, Franklin, Gaither, Goode, Gully, Hamm, Harrison, Heard, Hill, Hudson, Hurst, Johnson, of Marshall, Johnson, of Smith, Lewers, Malone, Marshall, Matthews, Mayson, McBride, Morphis, Niles, Phipps, Potter, Reid, Reynolds, Sanders, of DeSoto, Sessions, Stone, Stricklin, Swett, Tate, Trotter, Wall, Watson, Wilson, Woodward and Wylie.—50.

NAYS.—Mr. President, Messrs. Bond, Cason, Crum, Cummings, Dowd, Gowan, Griffin, Hall, Hemingway, Horne, Houston, Jarnagin, Johnston, of Hinds, Johnson, of Choctaw, Jones, Kennedy, King, Lambdin, Lewers, Lindsey, Loper, Martin, of Adams, Martin, of Sunflower, Maury, Montgomery, Owens, of Tunica, Owen, of Scott, Peyton, Pressley, Quin, Rives, Rushing, Sanders, of Attala, Simonton, Slover, Sparkman, Stanley, Wallace, Webb, Wier, Wooley, White, Yerger.—45.

The question recurring on the ordinance, reported by Mr. Trotter, of Minority Committee,

Mr. Yerger, of Hinds, moved to lay the same upon the table—

Which was decided in the affirmative, by yeas and nays, called for by Messrs. Johnson, of Marshall; Trotter and Compton, as follows, to-wit:

YEAS.—Mr. President, Messrs. Blackwell, Bond, Byars, Cason, Crawford, Cummings, Dorris, Duncan, Gowan, Goode, Griffin, Hall, Hemingway, Hill, Houston, Jarnagin, Johnston, of Hinds, Johnson, of Choctaw, Johnson, of Smith, Jones, Kennedy, Lambdin, Lewis, Lindsey, Loper, Martin, of Adams, Martin, of Sunflower, Maury, Montgomery, McBride, Morphis, Owens, of Tunica, Peyton, Pressley, Quinn, Reynolds, Rives, Sanders, of Attala, Simonton, Sparkman, Wallace, Webb, White, Wier, Wooley, Wylie, Yerger.—48.

NAYS.—Messrs. Barr, Bailey, Binford, Brown, Carter, Compton, Cooper, of Rankin, Cooper, of Panola, Crum, Davis, Dowd, Franklin, Gaither, Gully, Hamm, Harrison, Heard, Horne, Hudson, Hurst, Johnson, of Marshall, King, Lewers, Malone, Marshall, Matthews, Mayson, Niles, Owen of Scott, Phipps, Potter, Reid, Rushing, Sanders, of DeSoto, Sessions, Slover, Stanley, Stone, Stricklin, Swett, Tate, Trotter, Wall, Watson, Wilson, Woodward.—46.

Mr. Goode offered as a substitute, the following Minority report:

WHEREAS, A Convention of the people of the State of Mississippi, assembled at the Capitol, on the 9th day of January, 1861, adopted an Ordinance of Secession, of the State, from the United States Government, and declared that the State resumed her sovereignty; and in a war resulting therefrom with the United States Government, which refused to recognize the legality or validity of that ordinance, the State failed to maintain her asserted sovereignty, and is now willing and ready to resume her status in the Union, as before the passage of that ordinance; Therefore,

Be it ordained by this Convention, That said Ordinance of Secession be, and the same is, declared to be henceforward null, and of no binding force.

Mr. Brown, of Yalobusha, offered the following amendment, which was accepted by Mr. Goode:

Strike out of the last line, the words: "henceforward null and"—

On motion of Mr. Jarnagin,

The substitute, as amended, was laid upon the table.

The question then recurred on the first section of the ordinance, as reported by the majority of Committee.

Mr. Potter offered the following amendment:

Strike out all after the word "hereby," in the 5th line, and insert the words, "vacated and annulled."

Which was lost.

Mr. Johnston, of Hinds, moved the adoption of the first section; and upon that motion, called the previous question—

Which being sustained—

The question was taken upon the first section, and decided in the affirmative, by yeas and nays, called for by Messrs. Barr, Slover and Crum, as follows, to-wit:

YEAS.—Mr. President, Messrs, Bailey, Billups, Binford, Blackwell, Bond, Brown, Byars, Carter, Cason, Cooper, of Rankin, Compton, Cooper, of Panola, Crawford, Cummings, Dorris, Dowd, Duncan, Gaither, Gowan, Griffin, Gully, Hall, Harrison, Heard, Hemingway, Hill, Horne, Houston, Hudson, Jarnagin, Johnston, of Hinds, Johnson, of Choctaw, Johnson, of Smith, Jones, Kennedy, King, Lambdin, Lewis, Lindsey, Loper, Malone, Marshall, Martin, of Adams, Martin, of Sunflower, Maury, Montgomery, McBride, Morphis, Niles, Owens, of Tunica, Owen, of Scott, Peyton, Potter; Pressley, Quinn, Reynolds, Rives, Rushing, Sanders, of Attala, Sanders, of DeSoto, Sessions, Simonton, Slover, Sparkman, Stanley, Stricklin, Swett, Tate, Wallace, Wall, Watson, Webb, White, Wier, Wilson, Woodward, Wooley, Wylie, Yerger.—81.

NAYS.—Messrs. Barr, Crum, Davis, Franklin, Goode, Hamm, Hurst, Johnson, of Marshall, Mayson, Phipps, Reid, Stone, Trotter.—14.

The first section, as adopted, is as follows:

SECTION 1. *Be it ordained by the people of the State of Mississippi in Convention assembled,* That an ordinance passed by a former Convention of the State of Mississippi, on the 9th day of January, A. D. 1861, entitled "An ordinance to dissolve the Union between the State of Mississippi and other States, united with her, under the compact entitled the "Constitution of the United States of America," is hereby declared to be null and void.

The second section being taken up,

Mr. Wier, of Yalobusha, offered the following amendment:

Amend the second section by striking out the 4th line, and inserting in lieu thereof, the words, "are hereby delared null and void."

On motion of Mr. Franklin, of Neshoba,

The amendment was laid upon the table.

Mr. McBride, of Madison, offered the following as a substitute, for the second section:

Be it further ordained, That all ordinances and resolutions amending, altering or changing, or proposing to amend, alter or change the Constitution and laws of the State, passed by said Convention of the State of Mississippi, which assembled at Jackson, the 7th day of January, A. D. 1861, and on the 25th March 1861, be and the same are hereby declared null and void.

On motion of Mr. Potter, of Hinds,

The substitute was laid upon the table.

Mr. Johnston, of Hinds, offered the following amendment:

Amend by striking out, after the 4th line, the words, "to raise means for the defense of the State;" and also, by striking out at the end of the section, the words: "supplemental to an ordinance, entitled an ordinance, to raise means for the defense of the State, passed March 29th, 1861.

Mr. Sanders, of Attala, moved to lay the amendment upon the table,

Which was decided in the negative, by yeas and nays, called for by Messrs. Sanders, of Attala, Bond and Potter, as follows, to-wit:

YEAS.—Messrs. Bailey, Crum, Dorris, Hall, Hemingway, Hurst, Johnson, of Marshall, Johnson, of Choctaw, Kennedy, Rives, Sanders, of Attala, Webb, Wooley.—13.

NAYS.—Mr. President, Messrs. Barr, Billups, Binford, Blackwell, Bond, Brown, Carter, Cason, Compton, Cooper, of Panola, Crawford, Cummings, Dowd, Duncan, Gaither, Gowan, Griffin, Gulley, Harrison, Heard, Hill, Horne, Houston, Hudson, Jarnigan, Johnston, of Hinds, Johnson, of Smith, Jones, King, Lambdin, Lewers, Lewis, Lindsey, Loper, Malone, Marshall, Martin, of Adams, Martin, of Sunflower, Matthews, Maury, Montgomery, Mayson, McBride, Morphis, Niles, Owen, of Tunica, Owens, of Scott, Peyton, Phipps, Potter, Pressley, Quin, Reid, Reynolds, Rushing, Sanders, of DeSoto, Sessions, Simonton, Slover, Sparkman, Stanley, Stone, Stricklin, Swett, Tate, Trotter, Wallace, Wall, Watson, White, Wier, Wilson, Woodward, Wylie, Yerger.—76.

Mr. Yerger, of Hinds, offered the following as a proviso to the amendment, offered by Mr. Johnson, which was accepted by the latter:

Amend by proviso to second section:

Provided, That an ordinance, (bearing no date,) entitled "An ordinance to raise means for the defense of the State," and an ordinance passed March, 29th, 1861, entitle an ordinance, supplemental to an ordinance, entitled an ordinance, to raise means for the defense of the State, are intended to be left by this Convention, for such action on the same, as the people of the State, by their Legislature, may deem it right and proper to take—having in view the honor and prosperity of the State.

Mr. Marshall, of Warren, moved to strike out the proviso—

Which was decided in the negative by yeas and nays, called for by Messrs. Potter, Marshall and Crum, as follows, to-wit:

YEAS.—Messrs. Crum, Franklin, Lambdin, Lewers, Marshall, Martin, of Adams, Potter, Swett, Woodward.—9.

NAYS.—Mr. President, Messrs. Barr, Bailey, Billups, Binford, Blackwell, Bond, Brown, Byars, Carter, Cason, Compton, Cooper, of Rankin, Cooper, of Panola, Crawford, Cummings, Dorris, Dewd, Gaither, Gowan, Goode, Griffin, Gully, Hall, Hamm, Harrison, Heard, Hemingway, Hill, Horne, Houston, Hudson, Hurst, Jarnagin, Johnston, of Hinds, Johnson, of Marshall, Johnson, of Choctaw, Johnson, of Smith, Jones, Kennedy, King, Lewis, Lindsey, Loper, Malone, Martin, of Sunflower, Matthews, Maury, Montgomery, Mayson, McBride, Morphis, Niles, Owens, of Tunica, Owen, of Scott, Peyton, Phipps, Pressley, Quin, Reynolds, Rives, Rushing, Sanders, of Attala, Sanders, of DeSoto, Sessions, Simonton, Slover. Sparkman, Stanley, Stone, Stricklin, Tate, Trotter, Wallace, Wall, Watson, Webb, White, Wier, Wilson, Wooley, Wylie, Yerger.—83.

The question was then taken on the amendment, with proviso, and adopted.

On motion of Mr. Johnson, of Hinds, the second section, as amended, was adopted:

On motion of Mr. Cooper, of Panola,

The third section was adopted.

MR. BARR, of Lafayette.—Mr. President: I desire, before the vote is taken on this subject, to say one word.

It seems to me, sir, that in no sense is the language true—I mean the language in which the ordinance passed by the Convention of 1861, is declared "null and void." There have been, and there are yet—so far as my information goes—but two parties in the State on that subject. There has been, and I doubt not there is to-day, a large and respectable party in this State, who hold that the right of secession is a reserved right. There is also a party who hold that there is no such reserved right as that of secession, but that the right of revolution exists. Now, sir, these being the two doctrines held by the people of this State. (and so far as my information goes, the only two positions held by them,) I submit that, in the opinion of both these parties, the language of the ordinance reported by the Committee is incorrect.

If the right of secession is a reserved right, then the ordinance passed on the 9th day of January, 1861, is not annulled, for the right of revolution exists. Then, the ordinance passed in the Convention on the 8th of January, 1861, is but a solemn declaration of the people of this State, whereby a revolution was inaugurated, and it is not null and void, unless the rtght of revolution is null and void; but I do not suppose the Committee who reported this ordinance, undertake to say that the right of revolution is annulled.

Again, sir: This body is representative in its character. We pass ordinances, we adopt amendments to the laws: we may make a Constitution; and what are these ordinances and amendments but law? We are here as a legislative body, enacting laws which become the highest law—the controlling law of the State of Mississippi. Well, now sir, I ask what is the language of legislative bodies? What is the peculiar, the proper, the technical word to be used by a legislative body, when it desires to set aside or abrogate an obnoxious or unconstitutional law? Who ever heard that the legislature used the words "null and void" in repealing an obnoxious and unconstitutional amendment? The words "null and void," are peculiar to courts. Courts can declare laws and ordinances "null and void," because the words are peculiar to them and proper to be used by them; but it is and has been customary—time out of mind—for a Legislature in repealing, setting aside and abrogating unconstitutional enactments, to use the word "repeal." It by no means follows that because we say that the ordinance passed on the 9th day of January, 1861, is "repealed," we mean by the use of the word "repeal" to declare that the State of Mtssissippi exercised a reserved right not inconsistent with the Constitution of the United States. No such inference can arise from that use of the word, because it is a word peculiar to legislative bodies, and the only proper word to be used by them in setting aside and abrogating an unconstitutional law or ordinance.

I submit, then, whether it would not be most respectful to that large body of our citizens who did believe—unless the question has been finally settled by the late war—that the right of secession was a reserved right not inconsistent with the Constitution of the United States, to reject the form of words used in the majority report of the Committee? I submit whether it would not be treating that large body of our citizens who believe in that right, with disrespect, and whether it would not be an attempt to set the seal of condemnation upon them, to come here now and use a word not peculiar to legislative bodies, and attempt, instead, to use words peculiar to courts—the words "null and void?"

Here, in the first section of this report, the ordinance passed on the 9th day of January, 1861, is declared by the Committee to be "null and void." Well, sir, they then proceed to say further: "Be it further ordained, That the following ordinances and resolutions passed by said former Convention of the State ef Mississippi, which assembled in the city of Jackson on Monday, the 7th day of January, A. D. 1861, and on the 25th day of March, 1861, be and the same are hereby repealed." Now, what are those enactments that are declared to be "repealed?" "To raise means for the defence of the State," is one of the ordinances referred to, passed manifestly against the Government of the United States, and in anticipation that war might follow upon the adoption of that ordinance passed on the 9th of January, 1861. Then follows: "To regulate the military system of the State of Mississippi;" "Concerning the jurisdiction and property of the United States of America, in the State of Mississippi," and other ordinances. Now, sir, these things are all consistent with the idea of that ordinance of secession passed by that Convention—breathe the same spirit—emanate from the same supposed right—and if the one is "null and void," why are not all the rest? Why have not the Committee, after pronouncing the ordinance of the 9th of January a nullity, gone on and pronounced everything in support of that ordinance, and to carry it into effect, "hereby repealed?" It does seem to me, Mr. President, and gentlemen, that the Committee set out with a determination to declare the ordinance of the 9th of January a nullity, and then, upon sober, second thought, have come back and made use of the proper word, "repeal"—to the use of the word that would give no offence to any portion of our citizens—to the use of the word that would not set the seal of condemnation upon a large portion of our citizens.

I submit, then, to the Committee, that the word "repeal," as used by them in regard to all the ordinances subsequent to that of January 9th, 1861, is the proper word to be applied to the ordinance of secession.

Mr. Johnson, of Hinds.—Mr. President: Not intending to consume much of the time of this Convention, knowing we ought to expedite our business as fast as possible. I would, nevertheless, submit a few remarks in reply to the gentleman from Lafayette, explanatory of the views and sentiments of the Committee, of which I had the honor to be Chairman, and that reported this ordinance.

The words "null and void," as applied to the ordinance of secession, were not words employed without due deliberation on the part of the Committee. They have a meaning, a significance, and an object. It is proper to remark, that in that Committee this point was the subject matter of extended discussion, which finally resulted in instructions to myselt as Chairman, to report the ordinance in the words in which it is now before the House. I admit that with myself, (and I believe with the rest of the Committee,) the motive in employing the words "null and void," sprung out of our peculiar notions as to the right of secession. As I remarked the other day, in connection with another subject, I never have admitted the right, on the part of a sovereign State, to secede from the Union; but if we had used the word "repeal," in reference to the ordinance under discussion, it would have been a confession upon our part that the ordinance of secession had some original validity—that the right existed, and that it was exercised under the Constitution. "Repealing" it would have given this construction by irresistible implication, if not by particular terms; and believing, as we did, the majority of the committee, at least, that the right of secession nowhere existed under the Constitution of the United States; we necessarily took the view, that the ordinance was "null and void," *ab initio*, and never had any binding effect and legal force.—My view of it then is now and always will be—other gentlemen of course, can think as they please—that no such right, I say, ever existed. I admit, that this ordinance, as reported, brings up the direct question as between us of the right of secession; and I do not suppose of course, that those gentlemen of this Convention, who were secessionists, and recognized the right of secession and I have no doubt they did, so very honestly—would support the ordinance, with the words, "null and void" in it; because, being inconsistent with their principles, they would be constrained to oppose it—while for me, and the majority of the Convention, to be consistent in our principles, we were bound to report it in that shape. Now I do not intend to enter in a discussion as to the right of secession, as I remarked heretofore; the argument has been exhausted upon that subject, and I should not be guilty of reviving it.

The gentleman himself has not attempted to revive it, but has yet taken a position, I think he is very much mistaken in—that by insisting on the words, "null and void," we are acting disrepectful to those members of the Convention, whe recognize the right of secession. Such was not the intention of the committee, and it was certainly very far from my intention; for with regard to those gentlemen, who have advocated that doctrine sincerely and honestly—as I believe almost all of them have—I yield the same right to them, to exercise their opinions on that subject, as I certainly have to exercise mine in opposition to them. There is nothing disrespectful in it; but if the gentleman's argument be good, and the opposite side insists upon the word "repeal," in opposition to our sentiments, it is acting disrespectfully towards us, I think; the truth is. there, is no disrespect in it, one way or the other—opinions being different, and each one entitled to his own. "I would not vote," says a member of the committee, for the repeal of the ordinance of secession, because thereby, I would stultify my past political life and principles, and yield the point that I believed the right existed. I don't care particularly, how the members of this Convention may choose to settle the verbage of the report; but I want the report and record to show that I, and the rest of the Committee, have not been guilty of inconsistency in our sentiments. But there was no design to offer the slightest disrepect to the gentleman who addressed the Chair this morning, or to any other member of the Convention; or to arraign their principles, or hold them responsible—but it was a mere assertion of the views and sentiments of a majority of the Convention, which they had a right to assert—which, if this Convention carries out, it is well and good; but in regard to which, if it chooses to ignore it, we have no right to say a word. This is not a mere verbal criticism, but an important matter, having a direct bearing upon our great object here; because when it is seen that we acknowledge the original validity of the ordinance of secession, by simply repealing it, and that we concede its original validity, it will be said that we are holding on to the right of secession, in our Convention, and that the majority believe in the existence of a right, to be exercised hereafter, if occasion requires. Therefore, I think the adoption of the remarks of the gentleman, by the Convention, will prove a serious obstacle to the representation of Mississippi in the National Council. I accordingly believe it important to adhere to the phraseology of the report. Those gentlemen who differ from us in sentiment, of course can record their votes in favor of the substitute, which has been offered; whilst I claim for myself the right of thinking upon these great questions, and freely recognize the right of other gentlemen, to differ from the view which I take. I have no feeling of disrespect for any man who differs from me, on any question; but a sincere respect for the opinions of any one's political, religious, and other views, where they are entertained in good faith. Having fought ultra States Rights opinions so many long years, I yet can but have a sincere repect for those holding the political views involved in that doctrine, and concede the same honesty to the advocates thereof, as I claim for myself and those associated with me.

The gentleman seems to think, Mr. President, that we are denying the great right of revolution—not at all. The committee have not been guilty of that—for every gentleman knows that whatever may be the right in regard to secession, the right of revolution exists here and everywhere, the world over. There is not a people so oppressed and down-trodden, that have not within themselves, the glorious right of revolution. It is a right over and above all written Constitutions. It can be asserted by tbe down-trodden serfs of Russia; and any people on the globe, can revolt against their Government —raise up the standard of revolution and rally around it. If they succeed, they become founders of great empires—but otherwise, the consequences fall upon themselves. We are not denying the right of revolution, but acknowledge it; and the very terms employed in the ordinance, tend to recognize that we were engaged in a revolution—because we say that the ordinance of secession was "null and void." It certainly was so when the war terminated disastrously, and in my view, it was *ab initio*.

Lastly: the gentleman has said that the terms, "null and void" are unusual in legislative bodies—that we are traveling out of the ordinary verbage, to bring in these words. I admit, that when a mere legislative body attempts to do away with a law, they do use the word "repeal;" but I do not look upon this Convention, in the attitude of a mere legislature. We are dealing with fundamental principles; and this body is infinitely above a mere legislative body—for, in fact, we have the power to sweep away every vestige of the Constitution, and establish a new one, different in all its features. While I admit, that whereas legislatures use the word "repeal," when destroying a law they wish to do away with—yet we may unquestionably use the words, "null and void." I am no great stickler for for mere words, except when those words are the representatives of substantial things, and I conceive this language rises above the dignity of any verbal criticism, and raises the question between ultra States Rights men, and those of opposing doctrines, who must settle that question according to their different opinions. I hope the substitute will not prevail, but the ordinance reported by the Committee will be adopted.

Mr. Johnson, of Marshall—Mr. President:—All wise legislation must proceed on principles of mutual concession and forbearance. The highest statesmanship is distinguished by a spirit of compromise. The adoption of this particular language is moved upon such a principle. That this may be more manifest, I will call the attention of the Convention, to the fact, that they have three reports from this Committee before them. The Majority Report, which uses the language "declared null and void"—a Minority Report, by Goode and Cooper, which says, "declared to be henceforth null and of no binding force," and this, by my colleague, Judge Trotter, which simply "repeals and abrogates" the ordinance of secesion. Here all can meet. If the ordinance was really null and void, so much the greater reason to repeal and abrogate it.—If there are any here, who consider that it was originally valid and binding—then there exists a necessity now to repeal and abrogate it. All concur, it seems, in the opinion that it is now dead. For the strongest of reasons, it is now inoperative. In this respect, it is something like the discussion on a former day, on the subject of slavery—all agreed that it was dead.—

Some gentlemen were very vehement in their asseverations, that it was *dead, dead, dead*—and the only question seemed to be—who had *killed Cock Robin?* Some insisting, as in the old rhyme, that it was the sparrow, with his bow and arrow—others, that it was the fly, because he *saw* him die—and others, again, that it was the mute and harmless fish, with his little dish. A plan was hit upon then, and I hope will be now, to give or permit due weight to all these important means, so that all may be satisfied—so that those influenced by the arguments of the mighty sparrow, the discerning fly, and even of the loaves and fishes, may all concur in their vote.

A great deal has been said, Mr. President, on the old question of the right of secession, which I cannot but consider mis-timed, entirely irrelevalant. No one, sir, ever contended, that I am aware, that secession was provided for in the Constitution of the United States. That would have been to provide for its own destruction. And as to the language used by others—that it was a revolutionary right, this surely is a contradiction in terms. To say that it was a violation—violation, mark you, of the Constitution, and yet a revolutionary right, is like contending for the right to commit treason, arson and murder. If it was not a right reserved to States, or to the people thereof, outside of, and above all Constitutions and compacts, whether leading to revolution or not, it was no right at all, and ought never to be spoken of as such, either to affirm or deny. But as I said, this is all irrelevant to the question before us. Whether a revolutionary right or a right leading to revolution—matters little now. There never will be another attempt to exercise it; we only now want to get the ordinance off the statute books, and give it a decent burial. Decency, aye, sir, respect, in this proceeding, is due our State—due the distinguished citizens, who, whether right or wrong, believed they were right, and are entitled to the meed of sincerity—is due our devoted people—due the gallant dead, and due to ourselves.

Give us a little breathing time, gentlemen!—"some mollification for your giant, over the way there!" In the late proposition, (the Constitutional amendment,) passed on yesterday, it was manifest, what unanimity a little concession could produce. Ancient Pistoe never devoured his "leek" with more gusto, than we were prepared to swallow that measure. We only wanted you to "silence the cudgel" awhile, and give reasonable time for mastication. So now, we ask you to yield a little to the prejudices and feelings of this people. I respectfully submit, the words here used, "repealed and abrogated," are the most comprehensive and conciliatory that could be employed.

I object to the language of the majority on another ground: it does not repeal or destroy the ordinance, but is merely declaratory of opinion; not that I think it incompetent, or entirely irregular for a body of this kind to use such a form; and in this, I differ slightly with the gentleman from Lafayette, (with whose general views upon this subject, I most fully concur,) that such a style is peculiar to the Courts, and that this body has no judical powers. If I understand it, sir, this is a Convention of the people of Mississippi, and contains in embryo, in idea, all the powers of Government, Legislative, Judicial and Executive; yet it is neither, and is above them all. It is the State. Still, it is a Convention of limited powers, because it consists not of the people actually, but of their delegates, called together for specific purposes. The majority of the Committee, have also been inconsistent with themselves—for in the same report, they reccommend the repeal of other ordinances, passed by the Convention of 1861—which were corollary to the ordinanee of secession, and dependent upon it for validity and vitality. Yet, I have not risen to censure or criticise, but to endeavor to promote harmony. The gentleman from Hinds, (Mr. Johnston,) deprecated the idea of unkindness, or disrepect to any delegate of this Convention. I did not so receive anything he said—nor do I consider there is any unkindness couched in the words of his ordinance to us. It is not for ourselves, but for the people, I am asking consideration; for the people of this State, who with unanimity, rarely equalled, ratified and unheld for four years, this ordinance, which is now sought to be declared a nullity. Sir, these remarks might be extended to any length, were I disposed to trespass upon the precious time of the Convention. I will only conclude as I began, with entreating them to harmony, and not to forget the dignity of the State of Mississippi, or their own; and that for these purposes, no words are more suitable, than repealed and abrogated.

Mr. Brown, of Yalobusha—Mr. President:—I never have believed that a State has the peaceable or reserved right to secede; and I am prepared on all proper occasions so to declare; and if, in disposing of the ordinance, now under consideration, I have to meet the direct proposition, whether a State has or has not the right to secede, I shall give my vote in the negative. But I hope we will not be required in Convention form, to express an opinion on the subject, because we are not required to do so from a sense of duty to the country. It will only be our collective opinion as individuals. It will not settle the matter, and can do no possible good. If this right does exist, or if it has been surrendered, it was done long years before Mississippi had an existence as a State, done by the people in the formation of the Union; and it is only for the highest tribunal of the people to *decide* whether that right was reserved or surrendered. I hope we may dispose of this ordinance, without expressing any opinion in regard to what we conceive its validity to have been at the time of its passage. I think we should forbear this, in consideration of circumstances that have so lately transpired. In consideration of our conduct for the past four years, I should forbear in respect to the feelings and opinions of a respectable number of our fellow citizens, who honestly differ with the majority of the Convention on this subject. The distinguished gentleman from Adams, thinks we should pass severe condemnation upon this ordinance. He said, "yesterday we burried slavery, to-day, let us burry its twin brother, secession." Mr. President, I too, was at the burial of slavery, and participated in the imposing ceremonies of that occasion, and I there demanded that the authors and perpetrators of that outrage and crime should be inscribed upon the tombstone. But "no!" said distinguished gentlemen, and the majority of this Convention. They were unwilling to wound the feelings—unwilling to reflect upon the tender sensibilities of those who are our enemies—and have never been our friends! Mr. President, secession is no more. To-day, we lay it in the grave—and here at the funeral, I only ask that forbearance for our friends that was manifested on yesterday, for our enemies. I was there taught a lession of forbearance and charity towards my enemies; may I not observe it now that I am dealing with our friends? Secession is dead—let it sleep in peace—and let our opinions unexpressed, sleep in the grave with the dead.

Five years ago, Mississippi called a Convention—in this hall it assembled—its authority was as potent as ours—it declared the allegiance of Mississippi absolved from the Federal Union—the Government scorned its validity, and demanded back the allegiance. Mississippi as boldly denied that she owed it—and pointing at the dome of Montgomery, said: "Yonder is my allegiance, and here, (*hand on his breast,*) is my sovereignty!" The clash of arms, and the din of war was the sequel! For four years, an astonished world, in breathless anxiety, watched the doubtful struggle! It is over now, and fallen are the fortunes of Mississippi. But I, who have followed her flag so long—who was her companion in her majesty, and in the honors of her triumph—am unwilling to stultify Mississippi, now that she has fallen, and is in chains! Let secession sleep in peace, in the grave where we lay it. It was a child of our section—born perhaps in error—but reared, I have no douht, with integrity of purpose. Let it sleep in peace—and let us cast no reflections upon the opinions of those who cherish its memory. It has been so lately, that we treated with feigned and slavish difference, the sensibilities of our enemies; let us have some little respect now, for the feelings of our friends. While we are attempting to conciliate

Federal favor—let us also try and conciliate the feelings of our people at home. Let us seek now for unity of purpose, and unity of effort in the great work of reconstruction and recuperation.

Mr. Johnson, of Smith—Mr. President:—I thought that if any one question had been settled by the war of the four years past, that of the reserved and Constitutional right of the secession had been. It appears, however, that other gentlemen do not so regard it, but desire to leave it as an open question for the consideration of the Supreme Court of the United States; but how it is to get before it, I am not able to determine, and do not believe it will come up there.

One gentleman insists that if the Ordinance of Secession is a nullity, and not binding, because the State had no right to secede, it yet had some vitality, as a revolutionary measure. But it was not passed as such; but as a measure which the State of Mississippi had a right to pass—it being insisted that the State of Mississippi had a Constitutional, reserved right to pass the ordinance, dissolving her relations and connections with the United States Government—and it is in this sense we have to treat this Ordinance of Secession—and not as a revolutionary measure. I take the position that the Ordinance of Secession is a nullity, and if it is, there is no reason why this Convention should not treat it as such. There is nothing undisguised in our adopting an ordinance, declaring the fact; nor is it any discourtesy to any gentleman, who formerly entertained, or may now entertain different views on this subject, from those who occupy seats in this Convention.

Is the Ordinance of Secession a nullity? I do not understand that the report declares it a nullity *ab initio*—though I believe such was the fact—but simply declares that it is "null and void." According to the amendments adopted by the Convention, to the Constitution, which passed the Ordinance of Secession, certain officers in the State of Mississippi, were bound to take an oath to support the Constitution of the Confederate States and of the State of Mississippi. Is there any vitality in that provision? If this ordinance, abrogating and nullifying the Ordinance of Secession, should not be adopted by this Convention, would the officers specified be required to take this oath? I say not, because this was done in support of the Ordinance of Secession, and therefore this ordinance has no binding force.

Suppose this Convention should *not* nullify or repeal this Ordinance of Secession—what effect would that have upon our future—would it at all change our relations to the United States Government? If this body should dissolve without having taken any action of this character, and our delegates be elected—would this want of action be any objection to their being admitted? I say "no,"—because the Ordinance of Secession is a nullity, with no binding force whatever. And I see no reason to declare that which is certainly the fact, that it has no binding force or effect.

Mr. Yerger, of Hinds—Mr. President:—A sense of duty impels me to object to the report of the Minority. If I could so, consistently with principles which I always entertain, and consistent with the oath which I have taken to support the Constitution of the United States, if by so doing, I could save the feelings of any member, while at the same time, doing no harm to the State or country, of which I am a citizen, It would afford me pleasure; but having fixed and defined opinions on the subject—opinions long entertained, and which the events of the past four years have graven indellibly upon my mind, I cannot, without self-stultification, adhere to the proposition contained in the Minority Report. The repeal and abrogation of a law, by necessary implication, admits its prior validity; otherwise there would be no occasion for repealing and abrogating a law; when therefore, I should undertake to vote for a proposition to repeal and abrogate the Ordinance of Secession, I would necessarily imply, according to all legal construction, that there had been a period of time, at which, in my judgement, there was validity and force in the ordinance, which we seek to repeal and abrogate I cannot, sir, consistently with the principles which I have long entertained and which have been established beyond question—it seems, to me, by the past four years of war—support the Minority Report.

How do we sit here—under what circumstances are we convened? The President of the United States, acting in the name of the people of the United States, and under the Constitution of the United States, has declared that all the official acts of all the officers, appointed by the State of Mississippi, under the Ordinance of Secession, were null and void, and they have all been set aside and treated as nullities, by the Government of the United States. So treating them, the President of the United States, for the purpose of restoring the relations which have formerly existed between the State of Mississippi, and the Federal Government, appointed a Provisional Governor, for the purpose of convening an assemblage of the people of the State of Mississippi; and in doing so, he proceeded upon the idea, that the acts which had taken place under the Ordinance of Secession, were nullities—and, if they were not, we have no business here. When we came here, we took an oath, to support and maintain the Constitution of the United States. Under that vote, I am constrained to vote, according to the opinions which I entertain, in reference to it—that the Ordinance of Secession was null and void. I cannot do otherwise, and not violate the oath which I have taken —because I am satisfied that there was no power existing in the State of Mississippi, in the year 1861, or at any other period of time after she was a member of the Federal Union, to secede and withdraw from that compact, and that the act, being done, was under the Constitution and Laws of the United States, "null and void."

It is said by gentlemen, that there is a right of revolution; that there is a revolutionary right; and that when we speak of the rights of revolution, we do not speak of Constitutional rights. When we speak of "revolutionary rights" we speak of the natural right, which a people retain, outside and above the Constitution, to relieve themselves from an oppressive Government, whether it is a Government operating under Constitutional forms or not; and that the party who undertakes to exercise that natural right, exercises it at his peril.—If successful, the Government which is established by revolution, becomes a member of the States of the world; if unsuccessful, the parties who attempt it, are rebels, according to the Constitution and laws of the country, from which they sought to separate themselves. When, therefore, men say there is a right of revolution, they don't mean to say by that, that there is a right recognized by the laws of the country to secede from it, and withdraw from it; but there is an inherent right, which you can exercise in withdrawing from any Government. I have now, as a citizen of the State of Mississippi, if I believe her laws are oppressive, injurious and tyrannical, and that I am unable to withstand them, and maintain my dignity, self-respect, character and liberty, under those laws, I have now a natural right, and if I had the power, I could assert that right, and establish a revolutionary Government here; but I do not derive it under the Constitution and laws of the State; and if I was to persist, and set up a revolution, it would simply be "null and void," so far as the Constitution and laws of this State were concerned.

We do not, in the slightest degree, impeach the integrity of the gentlemen who voted for the Ordinance of Secession; for they took their action, I believe, upon their conscience, holding themselves responsible to God and the country, for the act they did, I accord to them, sincere purposes—that sincerity of purpose, and integrity of conduct, which I caim for myself, in the opinions and acts which I express and entertain. I do not seek, in the slightest degree, to cast imputations upon the motives of men, for their conduct and practice. I know that many, if not all of them, were sincere in the opinions which they entertained. I differed from them then; I differ from them now; but in that difference, I reflect upon the motives of no man. I do not even reflect upon the conduct of any man, believing that the last four years, have shown that those gentlemen were earnest and sincere—that their opinions were the honest opinions of their hearts; and that as far as they have been enabled to so, by arms, they have carried out their convictions. I do not reproach them—no man should, The sufferings and privations though which this country has passed, in the last four years, should serve the purpose of wiping out forever, all past differences, and past animosities, upon this question of secession. Let us begin anew! Let us start anew! If any of us were wrong in the past, let there be thrown over that the same amnesty, the same act of oblivion, which the President of the United States professes and gives for acts done against the Government of the United States. But while we do not hold them responsible in a political character, for the past, nor load them with the results of their conduct, and the consequences which have followed from their acts—let us not at the same time, go forward and stultify our own opinions, by yielding on a question of courtesy, a matter of Constitutional law—a matter of absolute principle, without an assertion of which, we have no business here to-day, and should retire home. On yesterday, we voted that the Ordinance of Secession was a nullity, so far as the effect was concerned, when we ordered an election, for the purpose of filling offices in the State of Mississippi; for if it had not been "null and void," the officers elected under it, were officers of this State; but their offices have been vacated. Now, there is no reason for any sensibility upon the part of gentlemen on this floor. There is no reason for sensibility on the part of any citizen of this State. After the act of secession took place, almost with one accord, the people of the State acceded to the act, which was done; and if the gentlemen, who passed the Ordinance of Secession, were wrong in passing it, all the citizens of the State who upheld or sustained them in their action, have been guilty of an equal crime; and if there is any man here, who is not guilty, let him throw the first stone at the gentlemen who passed that Ordinance of Secession. We do not blame them now for what they did in the past, acting under their oaths and consciences; although we believe that act without Constitutional law, and void; we accord to them, a belief of sincerity and truth, in the opinions they expressed, and the act undertook to perform. So believing, let that not, for an instant, be imputed to the gentlemen who fought against them, or to any portion of the people of the State, a desire to reproach them for their acts, in the past.

The President has offered amnesty—an act of oblivion, for that which has been done; and we, as fellow-citizens, although we may have differed from them—can do no less than in our political, private and social conduct, to give the same amnesty, the same forgetfulness of the past; but, as I said before, unite with them; and as good citizens, determine in future, disregarding the errors, heart-burnings and animosities of the past, to work together with one accord, to restore civil Government; to restore peace and order; to restore permanent prosperity and happiness to the people of the State.

Mr. Brown, of Yallobusha—Mr. President:—I merely wish to state, that if the direct proposition before the House was—whether the State has a right to secede, I should be compelled to vote it down; but, that if possible, it is very desirable that we should so act, as not to reflect upon our Government and people.

Mr. Hudson, of Yazoo—Mr. President:—I am free to say, that, in my opinion, there never was more humbuggery contained in two words, than in those of "peaceable secession;" and in so saying, I represent merely my individual convictions upon the question.

It has been said, that secession, like slavery, is dead—very dead. That may be true, and it may be the disposition of this House, to go further, and bury it like slavery, with its face downward; with the inscription on its back:—"no resurrection;"—but, the question presents itself to my mind, whether it is judicious or politic to do that. In the county which I have the honor to represent, this question was not discussed at all, and while I, as an individual, shrink not from an assertion of my opinions, or the maintenance of those opinions, when called upon to do so. I do not feel that I have been sent here, as a representative to assert whether the Constitutional right of secession, did or did not exist. As has been said of Billy Pringle's pig—so it may be of secession—when it lived, it lived in clover, and when it died, it died all over—or rather, I would say—when it lived, it lived, and when it died, it died a bubble. We have been sent here to harmonize our relations with the Federal Government—would it not also be politic to harmonize our own people, when we have an opportunity? The action advocated by some gentlemen, is, as has been said—putting the seal of condemnation on the action of honest and respectable men, declaring that they were revolutionists, transcending their power. I do not see the necessity of doing this; nor do I believe that we have been convened here for the purpose of passing upon that question.

This Ordinance of Secession, is regarded in the eye of all, as mere rubbish upon the statute book, and the only question is—in what manner shall we dispose of it—shall we notice it at all? I want it distinctly understood, that, although I believe there never did, and does not exist, a Constitutional right of secession—any vote, I may cast here on this subject, will be a mere expression of individual opinion. If, however, we are to dispose of this ordinance, let us do it in such a manner, as to cause the greatest good feeling, and harmony among ourselves.

In 1851, a Convention of the delegates of the people of Mississippi, declared that no such right existed; while in 1861, another Convention of delegates, chosen by the people, and with expressed reference to this one point, declared the opposite doctrine to be the true principle. It is then the right of the people, through their delegates, sent to assert at various times, the opinion of the people; but now there is no necessity of this Convention, announcing an opinion, one way or the other. That being the case, can we not harmonize our own people, and bring ourselves into one common brotherhood, by pronouncing the Ordinance of Secession, repealed and abrogated. I beg that in the name of common brotherhood and humanity, nothing shall be done by this Convention, to reflect, even inferentially, pain upon the honesty, wisdom and integrity of those who have preceded us, in action on this question.

Mr. Harrison, of Lowndes,—Mr. President: I move to strike out the word "abrogated," and insert instead the words, "declared to be of no force and effect."

I hold the word "repeal," to be proper, for it is unquestionably the word always used by the law books in questions of this kind, and is used in both the Minority and Majority Reports.

I do not agree entirely with the report of the majority of that committee. They don't propose to repeal the Ordinance of Secession at all, but simply express the opinion that it was null and void. As I understand, the Government is divided into three grand departments,—the legislative, executive and judicial. It is the part of the legislative branch —whether assembled in convention or mere legislature—to pass laws; it is the part of the courts to pronounce upon the legality of those laws; but what is done here? In the report of the Majority of the Committee, they simply, in relation to the great question of Secession, declare that in their opinion it is "*null and void*," and then recite twenty-six different articles passed by that Convention, and *repeal* them every one, *except* the Ordinance of Secession.

It is stated in the proclamation of Governor Sharkey, our Provisional Governor, that the Proclamation of the President of the United States and the laws of Congress passed upon the subject of emancipation and slavery, are assumed to be legal—and for why? Until they are adjudicated and proved to be otherwise; and so every enactment standing upon your statute book is *presumed* to be the laws of the land. In what a dilema do we place ourselves! We leave this Ordinance to stand, merely declaring that, in our opinion, the matter is "null and void." We will not undertake to repeal it. I hold that of all the laws in the world, we ought to repeal this unconstitutional ordinance, and not allow it to stand upon our statute book as, *presumably* the law of the land; but insist that the language which I have just used, is the appro. priate mode of expression. I hold, therefore, that it is necessary, and becoming, and proper in us to repeal this Ordinance, and not allow it longer to remain, for good or evil; and I think that gentlemen who cannot stand by the language which I have suggested for the disposition of the Ordinance, must be exceedingly technical upon the words "null and void." This language does not import that that was the case, but the expression is so general as to offend no one—giving no definite opinion at all. I do not hold that because we say the Ordinance is repealed, and then say it is of no legal force and effect, that it is Constitutional and has legal force as such; but I hold that the word "repeal" is the proper one for the abrogation of both constitutional and unconstitutional enactments. I think, then, that we could all fairly stand upon that.

In the case of the proposed amendment "to amend the Constitution of the State of Mississippi, in certain particulars," the Committee proposes merely to repeal it, and not consider it null and void. Several other amendments are then proposed, to be effected through the use of the same language. I ask, then, why these distinctions are drawn, and why the Ordinance of Secession is declared "null and void," when the word "repeal," is used in connection with the abrogation of other acts? Most unquestionably these last were intended to carry out the end, object and aim the parties passing the Ordinance of the ninth day of January, had in view; and so in regard to certain other ordinances which follow those I have referred to. I hold it to be clear that if these ordinances are bad in part, they are so as a whole, and that they must all stand or fall together. I shall, therefore move, at the proper time instead of adopting either of these reports, to repeal all these Ordinances, and state in general terms, that not only is the Ordinance of Secession repealed, but to include all the rest, because, if the original Ordinance is void, I cannot see how the others are to be sustained, and I am not willing to declare the principal one "null and void," while *repealing* the others: when we say they are *repealed*, we do not commit ourselves as to whether they were constitutional or unconstitutional, but say that reasons exist to satisfy this Convention of the propriety of striking them from the statute book.

To avoid any difficulty, I propose to insert words declaring *all* these Ordinances to be of no force or effect. I desire harmony, and that in relation to every subject coming before this Convention, we may act together.

MR. JOHNSON, of Marshall : So far as I am concerned, Mr. President, I accept the proposed amendment with a great deal of pleasure, and thank the gentleman for his suggestion.

MR. MARTIN, of Adams—Mr. President:—If anything has been settled by the war, from which we have just emerged, it seems to me, that the doctrine of secession certainly has been. I opposed it, with all my energy, in 1851; and in 1860, opposed it with such pertinacity, that I was accused of being unfaithful to the South, and not fit to be trusted. I was sincere, for I believed, that a Government of States, held together only by such a "rope of sand," as many of our politicians represented the Constitution of the United States to be, would not be worth preserving.

The right of secession is antagonistic to the true theory of our Government. It does not—it ought not to exist. It was disputed in argument—and if it ever had an existence, it perished in the clash of arms. There is, however, a remedy left us, against oppression and wrong—in those who hold the reins of power. It rests in the exercise of that right which Constitutions do not give, and cannot take away—the right of *Revolution.* I would have nothing to do with that kind of revolution, called secession. Sir: in the future, if secession should again be proposed, as a *peaceable* and *Constitutional* remedy, as it was in 1860, let no sad mistake be made, but let us all understand that it means revolution, war, exposure, disease and death; that it means destitution and want; half rations, and no rations at all; that it means long, weary marches, by day and by night; all the hazards and privations of the camp and field; that it means the risk of property and health, and the exposure of all that we hold dear, to the chances of war. Such risks have no terrors to appal the man, who is determined to be free. Never again, may it happen, that any of our people, shall rise in armed resistance to the Government, till, as one man—knowing all, daring all—they sternly resolve, that war, with all its dread concomitants, is better than submission to the wrongs they suffer! Then, when all who engage in the struggle, offer upon the altar of patriotism, ease, comfort, wealth and life itself—resistance will be crowned with success, and tyranny be rebuked.

The Ordinance of Secession, was an act of revolution. As such alone, I was willing to fight, to sustain it. When the war of sections began, all my sympathies were with the South. Here I was born, of parents of Southern birth. There is no blood in my viens derived from a Northern source. Four generations of my fathers lived and died slaveholders. I believed the negro was intended to be a slave. I did not hesitate to join my people in arms; but I did it, knowing that I was aiding an attempted revolution; and was risking all I had, and making me and mine liable to all the evils that war could inflict.

I trust that the Government may be so administered that rebellion may never again be necessary. But if its exactions, its insults or tyranny, should demand of us, to take our lives in our hands, and risk them, and all else besides, rather than submit to wrongs that freemen cannot bear, I do earnestly hope, that none of those who would persuade me to resistance, may fail me in the hour of need; or may attack me in rear, by discord, by dissention, by unmanly complaints, by speculation, and by acts and words of selfishness and discouragement, while I am fighting the enemy in front.

It is dangerous to entertain the idea, that in one Government, there can be such a thing as peaceable secession. It is as dangerous in Government, as in marriage relations. It would invite dissolution, and cherish discord. It is dangerous, because men were deceived by it, in the fearful ordeal though which we have passed. If I had ever entertained it, this war would have eradicated it. When, after four years of active service, in the field; after our depleted armies, had performed prodigies of valor; and call after call was made in vain, for men to fill the thinned and exhausted ranks; in the saddest hour of my life, I, with others, was called to surrender. That which stung me most, was the reflection, that I had risked and lost all, save honor, in a contest, not inaugurated by my assistance, from which so many thousands were absent, who had recommended the *peaceable* right of secession. If we had been wise, we might have forseen the consequences of representing that any dissolution could be peaceful. When the war actually began, and the stern reality was felt, it was seen, that the people were not prepared for it. Then we heard it said: "we were told that secession was a *peaceable* remedy, and that all would be well, if we would but assert one of our *reserved rights*." Let us, sir, look to it, that no such mistake be made in future; mistakes to be atoned for in want, humiliation and sorrow.

In the midst of our late conflicts; even when victory perched upon the Confederate banner—for we had our days of triumph—there were many among the most sanguine, to whom these questions presented themselves: "what is it at last, that we fight for?" If, after so much sacrifice of treasure and of life, we are successful in maintaining our independence, will our Government be one to protect us permanently in the enjoyment of life, liberty and property? Or will it soon be wrecked, since its Constitution, by affirming the right of secession, provides for its dissolution?" We can now only speculate upon what would have been the result. As for myself, I never could reflect upon that clause in the Confederate Constitution without disquietude.

I did not intend to enter into an argument upon the question. If recent events have not argued and settled it, I may well be silent.

The questions growing out of slavery, are now passed beyond discussion in this assembly. In my estimation, the matter now before us, far transcends in importance, all others we may properly consider. If we sincerely desire to restore, fully and completely, our relations with the Federal Government, and to make our Union peaceful and permanent, there is no act by which we can so well manifest that sincerity—or that will go so far in convincing all men that we are in earnest in what we are doing—and that there is no lurking intention, to violate our pledges, as by solemnly declaring our conviction, that there is no such Constitutional right—no such reserved right, as that of Secession.

Mr. Barr, of Lafayette,—Mr. President:—I desire to offer a word of explanation.

I did not state that I, myself, believed secession to be a reserved right under the Constitution of the United States, or that I did *not* believe it to be. As I made no such question, I do not now deem it important that this body should know my views upon that subject. I merely spoke to the propriety of using the words "null and void," in this Ordinance, under all the circumstances: I intended, Sir, to say, that by the use of those words in that document, the direct question *was* raised as to whether it was a reserved right or not. I meant to say, that in no sense did I believe the Ordinance to be a "nullity." Manifestly, if it is a reserved right, the Ordinance is not a nullity; if it it is not a reserved right—why, then, what is the Ordinance of Secession? What was the object and purpose of that Ordinance? It was to divorce the State of Mississippi from the Government of the United States, and assume her independent, sovereign position—the same as she occupied—and the same as the old States occupied, before they entered into the compact called the Constitution of the United States. It was, to all intents and purposes, the same, in effect as the Declaration of Independence declared by our ancestors, when they proposed to cut loose from the Government of Great Britain; and I insist that whether Secession be regarded as a reserved right or not—whether it be a truth or not—that Ordinance stands here as a solemn declaration on the part of Mississippi, to divorce herself from the Government of the United States, and assert her independence. Then, what does it amount to? It amounts to nothing more or less than a simple declaration on the part of Mississippi, whereby a revolution was inaugurated. How could the revolution have commenced, without some action on the part of the State? Can it be supposed, Sir, that we would have spontaneously got together and taken up arms against the Government of the United States, without any Convention, without any consultation, or without any solemn declaration, like that contained in the Ordinance of the ninth of January, 1861? No such thing ever *did* occur in the history of a civilized people. There must have been some form of proceeding by which the revolution was inaugurated; and if gentlemen deny the right of Secession, here stands a Convention of the people of Mississippi—a consultation of the people together—the result of which is a solemn declaration by which they undertook to divorce themselves from the Government of the United States, and set up their independence. What is that but a Declaration of Independence? and what is that but a revolutionary act? and what is *that* but a solemn act by which the State undertook to inaugurate a revolution? *This* Ordinance *does* raise the direct question as to whether the right of Secession exists, which I desire to avoid. There are irreconcilable differences of opinion among our people, but I believe no man will endeavor to strive for that right—for, by the sword, the question has been decided against us. All parties know what those who believe in the right of Secession must expect, if they undertake to exercise that right, and I do not have any idea that any party will attempt to again exercise that right.

While I declare that the language used by the Committee does raise the direct question as to the right of Secession, I, at the same time, contend that the use of the word "repeal," does not do so, because that is the appropriate and peculiar phraseology of legislative bodies,—for I insist that this is a body—legislative in its character, (though not a legislature,) and that it is not to occupy any other character. It is not a judiciary body—but those words, "null and void," are peculiar to Courts.

If this Minority Ordinance is passed, no questions will arise as to whether that Ordinance of Secession is a nullity or a right, because in the history of legislation, in every country, the word "repeal" has been invariably applied to abrogating an enactment confessedly unconstitutional. It was applied to the Missouri Compromise Act, which the Supreme Court decided to be unconstitutional, and that was the reason why it was so applied. Therefore I say that no inference can arise that, by using this word, we mean to say that the Ordinance of the ninth of January, 1861, was legal and valid.

The adoption of this word "repeal," commends itself,

it seems to me, to this body, because we thereby escape all controversy between those who believe in the right of secession and those who deny that such a right exists. We should strive to avoid the raising of any asperity in the minds of the people of this State, because in our present condition we have no strength to expend—and we should act in such a manner as to ensure harmony of action in our efforts to restore ourselves to our civil privileges. It seems to me that the Ordinance reported by the minority of the committee does not raise any question, and that the adoption thereof, will have the desired effect to which I have just alluded, as being so essentially necessary in the present condition of this State.

Mr. Stone, of Copiah,—Mr. President: I regret exceedingly that the report of the Committee should not have been couched in such terms as this Convention could have unanimously accepted, and as would have avoided the possibility of the spread of crimination and recrimination throughout the land. I was in hopes that some plan might be adopted by which the Ordinance of Secession might be repealed, or stricken from the statute book, so that every man might be left to enjoy his own opinion in regard to the constitutionality or unconstitutionality of that enactment. I believe that a State can never be guilty of rebellion, and that rebellion exists in a different form of government from that of a republican one; but the fact is that a Secession took place, which I think might probably be possible.

I can well anticipate what will be the result of this debate here, and the result of the adoption of that report of the Committee which purports to be the Majority Report; for I understand the vote stood seven to seven, and that the chairman had the casting vote, so that there was but little difference of opinion. Now, I agree with the gentleman from Yazoo, [Mr. Hudson] that we should do nothing here which would have a tendency to keep alive anything of rancor in the community among which differences of opinion prevail in regard to the right of Secession; but that in regard to this matter the Convention should stand to by its action, and ensure harmony among the people of this State.

I wish to say a word upon another subject which I deem very important. Gentlemen talk about rebellion and secession. What is the difference? Whichever term we may choose to adopt, the action was inaugurated by one piece of paper first, and results in the same thing. The document was harmless up to the point that the clash of arms took place. War was the result, and the people of this State, almost unanimously, (so far as I know) went into that rebellion, secession, or war, and fought it out bravely.

I regret to hear so much said about rebellion. If I understand anything to be a principle of law, it is this: That a rebellion, although at first it may not be greater in force than is a cloud in appearance as large as one's hand, if it rises to that magnitude and becomes such in its dimensions that it requires the opposing party to acknowledge the rights and civilities of war, if that pseudo rebellion arises among one people, then it is called a civil *war*, and all those engaged are belligerents. Was our late struggle a civil war? I call it so, and one of gigantic magnitude. Holding this principle, I wish to call the attention of gentlemen to the fact that there are thousands of Mississippians now absent from this State, who have been driven from their homes into exile. Now, if we were in rebellion, whenever these put their feet upon the soil of Mississippi, or of the United States, they are to be treated as traitors and liable to the penalty of treason, which is death. I wish to avoid this dreadful consequence by declaring our late contest a civil war, and viewing it as carried on between two independent nations. According to all law writers, it was not a rebellion, but a war, conducted as if between foreign nationalities, on account of the exchange of prisoners, the cartel, and the flag of truce were acknowledged, and as can only be the case in such a war, and which, upon the establishment of this principle depends the life of Jefferson Davis, and the lives of hundreds and hundreds of Mississippians who were forced to abandon all in the State of their birth, and are now absent from it. Shall we, at home, who have had mercy extended to us, who have taken the amnesty oath, and who are assembled here to-day, adopt a proposition which will hang every one of our former citizens at present sojourning in other countries? I do not think we ought so to do. Let rebellion, secession, and everything of that kind go to the dogs, and assume the position which the Federal Government has already virtually assumed,---that we were engaged in a civil war, and it cannot assume this position for one purpose, and deny it for another; and although it does so, I suppose, in order to bring about the very thing we are here assembled to do, I do not believe that when the question comes up for trial, that even Chase himself will dare to assert that right. When Mr. Davis, and those other individuals now in prison, are tried under the laws of the land, I desire no better opportunity for the salvation of their lives, than that they be tried in the civil courts of the country. The Court will then instruct the jury that they are to be governed by the law that insists we were engaged in a civil war, and are now entitled to all the amenities and privileges of those thus engaged. I therefore hope this idea of secession and rebellion will be thrown aside, for this

Convention has nothing to do with it, and that we will take such measures as will protect our citizens in future, wherever they may be. In New Orleans, a few weeks ago, an individual was brought before a civil magistrate, charged with murder, in having shot several deserters from the Confederate service. It was proved that he had a commission from the Confederate Government, to arrest and punish the men in question, and therefore the Judge, deciding that we had established a government *de facto*, permitted the man to go scot free. When the Courts have, according to the law, thus decided the principle, shall we, by our action, consign hundreds of our fellow citizens to felon's graves? I wish to hear no such doctrine talked here!

Let us then not do any act which will again enkindle feelings of animosity and hatred among this people. Whatever action we may take in regard to this question, will not affect our relations with the Federal Government, for we have already accomplished the object for the performance of which we were assembled. I therefore hope that the amendment offered by the gentleman from Lowndes, [Mr. Harrison] will prevail, as I see nothing in it casting any imputation upon any one, while it leaves every individual, whether secessionist or anti-secessionist, to form his own opinion upon the whole matter,

Mr. Peyton, of Copiah,—Mr. President:—I did not intend to enter into the debate upon this matter, but the remarks which fell from the lips of my colleague, [Mr. Stone] make it proper that I should express my views on this subject.

One would infer from the remarks of the gentleman, that the action of this Convention would affect the condition of persons now in duress, under the authority of the United States. The question of our having had a *de facto* Government, is not that now before the Convention, but it *is*, whether the act of Secession was a valid, constitutional act, or whether it was void, without any reference to the result of the war.

Now I have long since concluded to follow my own views of right and wrong, without reference to anything my constituents may think, and I take the responsibility of saying that I do not believe that act was valid, and that there was no authority under the laws of the United States recognizing the right of the secession of a State from the Union. I shall, therefore, cast my vote against recognizing, in any shape or form, the validity of that Ordinance. If the principle of Secession was incorporated in the Constitution of the Confederate States, it would have been a misfortune for us to have succeeded, for then the Constitution contained within itself he gem of its own destruction. I cannot, therefore, but believe that in endeavoring to secure a recognition of our former political and civil rights here, we should say that that political heresy has not and never had any validity in the State of Mississippi. I wish the record of this Convention to show that we entertain the opinion that the Ordinance of Secession was void—not on account of the result of the war or revolution, but *ab initio*. I believe that the word "repeal," would intimate that it had, at some period, validity, and I think that the fact of our entertaining that idea would prejudice our cause at Washington, forming as it would a pretence on the part of the Republican party, for our exclusion from Congress.

In regard to a rebellion being a civil war,—that word "peaceable" Secession, was what took with the masses of the people, and if they had supposed that our separation was to have been followed by war, there would not have been a corporal's guard to have voted for it; but they were made to believe that it was a legal, constitutional right, and were delighted at being freed from "Yankees." But immediately afterwards, came the conscript laws, and *then* I dare say there was not a corporal's guard who,—in the county where I reside,—would have voted *for* this same *Secession*. Though believing at all times that there is a right of revolution whenever a government becomes unreasonably oppressive,—whether the Constitution recognized that doctrine or not, I have, therefore, no doubt that my vote will represent their sentiments as well as my own, although I have had no general discussion with my constituents on the subject. I believe that the people elected their delegates to this Convention, with reference to their integrity, judgment, intelligence and manly character, trusting to their wisdom, and believing that they would stand up for and maintain their rights as far as possible. I apprehend that my constituents will not complain therefore of any vote I have or may cast in this Convention.

Mr. Hall, of Covington,—Mr. President:—I only wish to state that I shall vote against the report of the Minority. I believe, and do now believe, that Secession was a nullity,—unconstitutional. I look upon it as a grievous sore which has afflicted, incalculably, the people, and I am not now in favor of applying any emoluments. I shall therefore vote for the Report of the Committee of Fifteen, and in so doing I feel that I assume no responsibility, but am willing to answer to my constituents for what I do in the premises. In 1861, they were all Secessionists,—made so by politicians, who told them that Secession was to be *peaceable*, and that it was a constitutional remedy; but the results of this war have convinced them of the error of their views, and I have no doubt that they will sustain me in my action.

Mr. Houston, of Monroe,—Mr. President:—There is a discussion, it seems, in regard to what all parties might come together on. I do not understand that the Ordinance, as proposed by the Committee, undertakes to say that the Ordinance of Secession of the ninth of January, 1861, was null and void, *at that time*, but only that *at this time*, it is so. Now, sir, if a statute passed by the Legislature was regarded as being illegal and unconstitutional, and we should apply to the courts for the purpose of establishing the fact that it was unconstitutional, and the courts should determine that such was the fact, then that would be null and void, because of that decision. In ancient times there were two modes of appeal: one was by appeal to the law of the country,—while the other was by an appeal to arms. One was by wager of law; the other was by wager of battle. Now we agree that if this Ordinance of Secession had gone before the courts, and they had declared it to have been null and void, it would so stand here to-day. In this case, however, we did not appeal to the law, but to a different arbitrator—to a different party—to adjudicate this question, and that party was the bayonet and the sword. What has been the result? What was the question at issue? If we had a legal and constitutional right to secede, then the other party, the Government of the United States, had no power and no right,—no constitutional power,—to force us back. But we appealed to a different arbitrator, as I have said, and the question was decided against us. Therefore, I contend that that Ordinance of Secession—the question at issue—has been declared, by the highest arbitrator known to man, to be null and void. The Committee says that this Ordinance "is hereby declared to be null and void." Not that it was null and void from the time it was passed or attempted to be passed, but that now, at this time, it is "null and void." It has been rendered so by the clash of arms, by the disastrous war we have just passed through, and whatever we may say to the contrary, this is the fact, and we may as well so declare it.

Gentlemen think we are attempting to stultify the Convention that met in 1861, by the action we are about to take in declaring that this Ordinance is now "null and void." There are one of two things I have to do here to-day, as a delegate to this Convention. I shall have to stultify myself and the former course which I have pursued in reference to this question, or I have to say that the action taken by the Convention of 1861, was wrong, and that its action is "null and void." The large majority of this House stand in the same position I do. From the votes heretofore given, I come to the conclusion that nearly half of this House agree, with me, that the right of Secession was not a right that could be or can be exercised under the Constitution.

Suppose we pass from the substitute offered by the gentleman from Lafayette, [Mr. Barr] to the substitute offered by the gentleman from Lowndes, [Mr. Harrison] which recognizes the fact that the Ordinance of Secession had some binding force and efficacy. What do we mean by repealing a law or act? To set aside that which had some existence, force, validity and efficacy, and not something a nullity in itself. In 1851, I withdrew from my then party, because of its views and feelings upon this subject, although I occasionally voted perhaps, for its candidates, believing them to be the best men! For ten, long years, I suffered before this Secession took place. I fought the question, which I believed to be a political heresy, and after these five years of disastrous war, shall I say that Secession was a constitutional remedy, or that the Ordinance had force and validity at the time it was passed, and afterwards? I see no sufficient ground on which to change my course.

But it said that we must seek to mollify and save the feelings of gentlemen who happened to be in that Convention. But, let me ask, where is the necessity, because I entertain different political views from gentlemen who might have been in that Convention,—where is the necessity for any ill-feeling to exist between us on that question? I should regret the existence of such ill-feeling as much as any man, but my duty is to the Constitution of the United States, and the State of Mississippi, first, and then to myself, my constituency and my own heart; and if I regard either of these considerations, I shall vote for the Report of the Majority.

The gentleman from Copiah says that if we pass this Ordinance, saying that the Ordinance of Secession is "null and void," we place those who may not wish to come under the Amnesty Proclamation of the President, in a condition of suffering. *I* do not so understand it—for two reasons. The first is one which I presume the gentleman himself will recognize, and he has in fact given it himself,—that when a revolution assumes such a proportion as this did, it is regarded as being a territorial war, rather than as a mere revolution, and men are not then regarded as traitors,—when the parties are compelled to recognize the rights of men as due to each other, (as the exchange of prisoners, and all those other courtesies which are extended by the belligerent parties of one nation to those of the opposing nation.) Whenever a revolution becomes so majestic as that, the parties engaged therein cease to be traitors to the country with which they are engaged in war.

What is the other reason? Is it to be supposed that—after the United States Government (certainly in its executive and its legislative, if not in its judicial department), has, during the whole of this war, recognized this as nothing else than a rebellion, and the Act of Secession as a mere nullity,—that they did not reflect the sentiment of their whole people, and that they will not,—when there is so much division among ourselves, unite on this subject?

Do not the courts of the country entertain the same views that the politicians and statesmen do? If they do, they are not going to regard the mere fact that we recognize this as having validity and force, or that it ever had; they will not be governed by this at all, but by their views of law, prejudiced though they may be on the one side or the other.—Therefore the passage of this Ordinance will have no effect so far as those who may be prosecuted for treason are interested, and I regard that as one of the weakest of all arguments for the purpose of trying to enforce the passage of the amendments which have been offered.

As I said before, there are but two courses for me to pursue, and I must vote conscientiously on the question, and cannot stultify myself after so many long years of settled opinion on this question, simply for the purpose of preventing asperities and feeling where there is no necessity or cause for them on the part of those gentlemen who do not agree with the vote I may cast.

Mr. Watson, of Marshall—Mr. President: I somewhat regret the debate that has occurred here, and was sorry to discover that there were so many matters upon which there seemed to be different opinions on the part of members of this body. I hope that the amendment just proposed as a substitute for both the Majority and Minority Reports, may meet with general approbation.

It asserts that the Ordinance of Secession, and the other ordinances and acts of the Convention, by which the Ordinance of Secession was passed, were without constitutional authority. Now, Sir, this was the opinion then entertained, and it is now entertained by all who do not recognize the right of secession as a constitutional right, or as a right *paramount* to the Constitution—if you please. This amendment declares that opinion in the mildest form that could be adopted, and in a form which, I hope, will be deemed by no one as intended to be offensive, and which cannot be offensive to the sensibilities of any gentleman.

It is conceded, on all hands, that no one now believes that the right of Secession is an existing, vital, living right. The decision has been made by the bayonet, and our people are acquiescing in that decision. I shall support this amendment, because I never did entertain the opinion that Secession was otherwise than in conflict with the Constitution of the United States. I am willing, therefore, to declare that it was in conflict with the Constitution of the United States, and without constitutional validity; and that, therefore, I am in favor of its repeal. That leaves, untouched, the Government, *de facto*, that was the consequence of that Ordinance of Secession, and all the various acts of that Government, so far as they may have validity or effect upon any ground or principle whatever—let them remain untouched. I think, Sir, that there is a disposition upon the part of the people at large, to exercise towards each other every possible degree of consideration and kindness. We all desire tranquility and repose, and it is to be deprecated if anything like evil grows out of the discussion of this body, or if the members of this body act otherwise than under the influence of mutual kindness and good will. We all desire that mere party feeling may not again rear its head within the limits of this State.

I hope, therefore, that the amendment may prevail.

Mr. Matthews, of Panola—Mr. President: I will only trespass upon the attention of this body for a few minutes:

It seems to me that the amendment of the gentleman from Marshall, [Mr. Trotter] expresses an opinion, if anything does, as to the constitutional power or right of the Convention here assembled, that passed the Ordinance of Secession. I see no real propriety in asserting that it had, or had not, the right. It *did* pass it, and passed it with a unanimity rarely expressed in the history of our country. Of the gentlemen of the Convention, here before me, I notice some delegates who voted for that Ordinance; a little further on, and I see the name of every solitary delegate signed to it, except one. It does, then, look to me, as if they were honest, entertaining an opinion that they had to do this thing; and there was not a man in the whole length and breadth of this country who raised a dissenting voice. It was not unusual to find a secessionist then. You could meet them on the corners of the street, on the highway, and, in short, every man one did meet, was a secessionist and revolutionist, and no one doubted the right or policy of the movement. I speak in general terms. It was a general manifestation of public sentiment; whereas, one would judge from what we hear to-day, that there was only a secessionist here and there,—that the influential men were leading the young men of the country astray, to shoulder their arms, and go into the strife of battle. Why, Sir, it was not so. I say that four out of every five of the delegates here to-day, if not in arms themselves, were stimulating their friends, and sons, and neighbors' sons to arm and go to the field! And now, when everything has failed, why does any one shoulder off the responsibility? In looking over the names of the gentlemen who passed the Ordinance of Secession, I see among them many of the brightest minds in the State—honored and trusted by the people of the State—and when, after mature deliberation, the acts of that Convention were placed before the people, scarcely a dissenting voice was raised against their adoption. I speak to men who know, and remember what took place five years ago, on this subject! Hence, I regarded the whole action as that taken by the entire State, by the people of the State, and I am now unwilling to come and cast a slur upon them by saying they had no constitutional right to do so, unless there is some necessity for so doing.

I am satisfied with the amendment proposed, and believe that it would help to harmonize the opinions of nearly all gentlemen. I shall vote for it, with a great deal of pleasure, and, I trust, that hereafter, all discussion may be short, and confined to the point equitably under consideration.

Mr. Watson, of Marshall—Mr. President: I am prepared to vote, cordially and heartily for the amendment proposed by the gentleman from Hinds, [Mr. Yerger] but had feared that perhaps there could not be found a majority who would take that ground. It would best accord with my feelings to do so, should a majority sustain me.

Mr. Reynolds, of Tishomingo—Mr. President: The majority of the Committee would have reported in favor of annexing to the amendment before us, the words, "*ab initio*," but it was thought hardly expedient, on the whole.

Whatever *may have been* the opinion of some in regard to the right of a State to secede, they must, it seems to me, have been forced to the conclusion by the result of the arbitration of arms, that the Ordinance of Secession was void. Hence there is no necessity for sensibility on the subject, for we may all agree in regard to the *fact* that, whether by the force of arms or on account of the want of constitutional sanction, it is absolutely void. The Committee have compromised, but did not express the views of the majority of it, because, I believe, the majority agreed that the Ordinance was void from the commencement, so far as the Constitution is concerned. But, to express the views of all, without offending the sensibilities of any, they agreed to insert the compromising words, "null and void." I shall, hence, vote for the original ordinance, believing those words to be the best possible to be used.

It was very properly insisted that, even unconstitutional laws are repealed, and that legislative bodies use the word "repeal," frequently, in abrogating a law which the members think unconstitutional, and that the word "repeal," is the word used for that purpose. That is true; but no legislative body would "repeal" a law that it believed it to be unconstitutional, and which the proper tribunal had *declared* to be unconstitutional. All its vitality is gone. Hence the principle, that a law must remain a law, until declared void by the proper tribunal, does not obtain here. The only tribunal which could decide whether or not it was void or constitutional, was that to which we appealed, and that against us, "null and void."

Mr. Niles, of Attala—Mr. President: I have no objection to the adoption of the amendment proposed by the gentleman from Hinds, [Mr. Yerger] so far as regards its wording; but it seems to me, that it declares, with one fell swoop, that the Convention was an illegally constituted body, and that because it passed the Ordinance of Secession, it was a nullity of itself, and all its acts were null and void. It seems to me that this is going too far—though not having examined, I cannot say how far those ordinances may be void. It appears to me that the Convention was legally called and constituted, and that so far as their action was not repugnant to the Constitution of the United States, it ought not to be pronounced null and void. It seems to me that some of their acts might very properly be regarded as valid. The gentleman from Hinds, [Mr. Yerger] proposes to include nearly all of the ordinances in one fell swoop, and I merely call attention to the fact. For instance, here is an act "to regulate the rights of citizenship in the State of Mississippi," and several others, which it seems to me there is no necessity of, or propriety in treating in this summary manner.

Mr. Goode, of Lawrence—Mr. President: I have been listening anxiously to hear some gentleman advocate the report of the Majority of the Committee, and the amendment of the substitute offered by the gentleman from Hinds, [Mr. Yerger] and to state, why it is necessary for this Convention to declare the Ordinance of Secession "null and void." We certainly were not convened for that purpose, and I do not think it is necessary, in order to resume our status in the Union, that we should take that step. I wish to ask what good is to result from declaring it "null and void." I cannot conceive any. If "null and void," it must be so declared, as I believe it has been in the Proclamation of the President of the United States, and as we have indirectly so declared, by providing for the election of State and County officers. Why adopt an Ordinance declaring it so? It has struck me as being rather undignified for a Convention representing the people of the State of Mississippi, to declare the action of a previous Convention also representing the people of Mississippi, to be "null and void."

I was very much struck with the remark that, whether it was a revolutionary movement, or claimed as a constitutional movement, it did not matter. The Ordinance simply asserts the fact that she did secede, and resume her sovereignty as a State. This might be considered here merely as such action as the State of Mexico would be—as a sort of pronunciamento of a revolutionary position that the State assumed—a declaration of an intention not longer to submit to the Constitution and laws of the United States. The Ordinance of Secession was the first step in that revolution. It is not claimed in that ordinance that a constitutional right was exercised, but merely that the power of resuming State sovereignty was exercised. No assertion that it was, or was not unconstitutional, appears on the face of the Ordinance. The United States Government, time and again, recognized the State of Mississippi as a *de facto* Government, and so in regard to the Confederate States. I will give one instance: Mr. Commissioner Browning, in an early stage of the late revolution, announced, by authority, that in regard to the confiscation of property of people in the rebel States—in the States then in a state of rebellion or revolution—that the law of nations authorized the United States Government to treat them territorially—that the States had assumed the right, and had the power to enforce the people within their respective limits; that they were treated as States, and the confiscation laws would be enforced against the people who inhabited those States, not as *individuals*, but as *inhabitants of certain territories or localities*—and a justification was claimed by public law.

Mr. Lincoln, in his two Proclamations of emancipation declared that from and after a certain date, all the slaves in certain States should be free—making certain exceptions. The slaves in Mississippi were included and were declared to be free; not the slaves of persons or individuals in the States in rebellion, that were disloyal, but all the slaves in the State.—Why was it that slaves of loyal persons who had never committed an act of treason, were declared free by a Proclamation declared to be simply a war measure? It was because he recognized the authority of the State of Mississippi over its citizens, when the State asserted its sovereignty by the action of the majority, the minority were bound to be governed by the laws of that majority, for the reason that the majority had power to enforce, and did enforee those laws. So with the amnesty proclamation. It does not state that all those who had been disloyal, and want to be members of this Convention, should take this amnesty oath, but all must—whether in the rebellion or not; whether disloyal or not. They lived in a disloyal State, declared to be so by the Ordinance of Secession. That ordinance was the act of a majority of the people of the State, who had power to enforce, and did enforce laws. There was a general acquiescence in the sovereignty of the State, and the right of the State, when its will was properly expressed through its proper authority, its representatives—a right of the State to control the minority, which it did control, it having all those attributes common to a government *de facto*.

Suppose this ordinance is adopted as reported by the committee. There were other matters before this Committee, which will come before the Convention. For instance: an ordinance legalizing legislative, executive and judicial acts. If this Ordinance of Secession was null and void; if the ordinance declaring a change in the Constitution, striking out "United States," and inserting "Confederate States," null and void, how is it possible for this Convention to legalize and validate the acts of judicial officers who took the oath to support the Confederate States, a government in armed opposition to the United States; and who did not take the oath prescribed to support the laws of the United States, which was necessary to authorize them to discharge the functions of their offices. It has been my opinion, as a lawyer, and I am still of that opinion, that its acts are null and void—they cannot be rendered valid—if they are voidable, they may be. If this ordinance is declared to be null and void; if it is asserted by this Convention, that the Convention of 1861 was not legally organized, and did not properly represent the people of Mississippi; if it is said that though it did, its acts were not legal or Constitutional, and had no virtue or force whatever—then all that has been done through the legislative, executive and judicial officers in this State, during the past war, is null and void, and this Convention cannot galvanize it into life. This Committee have undertaken to recommend an ordinance for the consideration of, and adoption by this body; that legalizes all these legislative, executive and judicial acts. I wish to draw this distinction, and think it proper. The President maintains in his proclamation, and the people of the United States have always declared that the Ordinance of Seeession was null and void, as to the United States Government. They do not declare that it is null and void as to the people of Mississippi; and they, by implication, (as I argue,) declare it to be valid and binding upon them, as a *de facto* Government; and that by the Ordinance of Secession, as an order of that Government—whether claimed as a Constitutional right or asserted as a revolutionary right—the people were bound to obey the Confederate States, and not the United States. Whether this ordinance is called an Ordinance of Secession, a pronunciamento, or an order of a *de facto* Government—in either case, it was binding upon the minority of the citizens, because the majority had the right to enforce it, and undertook to, and did enforce it.

I have been interested, having been a member of that Committee of fifteen, and believing I recall the history of this Majority and Minority Report, in the claims that have been made to both of the reports, that have been presented by them, being compromise reports. It was stated in advocacy of the Minority Report, of the gentleman from Marshall, (Mr. Trotter,) that there was a compromise between the Majority Report, and another report which I have before me. It was claimed by a gentleman, subsequently, who I believe, was also a member of the Committee, that the Majority Report was a compromise made to avoid objections that might exist in the minds of members of that Committee. My recollection is, Mr. President, that the Majority Report, just as it stands, was the first one presented; and that the Minority Report of the gentleman from Marshall, was the next one presented—though I think it had been introduced in Convention, before the appointment of that Committee. There is another Minority Report, which has not yet been presented before this Convention, in this debate; but, which I have before me, and which I suppose, I have a right to claim, is also a compromise report. I would be glad, in commenting upon the Minority Report, which has been brought before the House, and on the substitute presented by the gentleman from Hinds, (Mr. Yerger,) to read this other Minority Report for the information of the Convention, in order to make some remarks upon it, in connection with the others. It reads as follows:

WHEREAS, A Convention of the people of the State of Mississippi, assembled at the Capitol, on the 9th day of January, 1861, adopted an Ordinance of Secession, of the State, from the United States Government, and declared that the State resumed her sovereignty; and in a war resulting therefrom with the United States Government, which refused to recognize the legality or validity of that ordinance, the State failed to maintain her asserted sovereignty, and is now willing and ready to resume her status in the Union, as before the passage of that ordinance; Therefore,

Be it ordained by this Convention, That said Ordinance of Secession be, and the same is, declared to be henceforward null, and of no binding force.

This discussion arose in the Committee. It was urged by some, that the Ordinance of Secession was null and void, *ab initio.* It was suggested by others, that the words, "annulled and vacated" should be inserted, instead of "null and void," but no Minority Report urges that. The Minorty Report was presented to the Committee, and was not approved by them.—

I was requested by some members of that Committee to reduce it to writing; and present it, which has been done, in connec- with the others, and I wish to call the attention of the House to it.

It merely states what was the fact, and avoids the responsibility of deciding whether or not, this doctrine of secession was intended to be claimed as a Constitutional or revolutionary right—but simply asserts that the State did sever her connection with the Union, resumed her sovereignty, and undertook to order her citizens to obey her laws, and not those of the United States. Its preamble asserts the further fact, that the United States refused to recognize the validity or legality of that Ordinance of Secession—whether it be insisted upon as a Constitutional right or a revolutionary right—and that we went to war upon that issue—the State asserting—the United States denying. There was a wager of law, as well as of battle—and the preamble declares that the question was decided against us. Now the State of Mississippi, is ready and willing—after all that has taken place—in view of all—to resume her status in the Union. Gentlemen have expressed a great desire to bury this twin brother or sister of slavery, which was buried on yesterday, and they may be gratified, it seems to me, if they vote for this report. This declares that the issue has been finally decided against us; that the State, in view of that failing, seeking no further remedy or redress, and asserting no intention of ever asserting that right again—is ready to resume her status in the Union. This insists that the right of secession is dead—that the movement has finally failed, and does not exist as a practical measure. What is the necessity, after asserting this, and yielding this point, and declaring in substance, that it will never again be re-asserted—for us to go back and stultify the people of Mississippi, who sat here, in the persons of her delegates, in 1861, by saying that what they did then, was "*null and void.*" It does not matter whether we believed in the right of secession, at that time, or not. If we say it is dead, and gone forever, and that in view of that fact, we are ready to come back into the Union—why assert that the action of that Convention was "*null and void?*"

There were reasons urged, as having a bearing upon our action in regard to the emancipation question, as connected with our future National relations, which had their due weight with me. But I am not disposed to be so very anxious "to crook the pregnant hinges of the knee," as to do a needless act, and inflict, as I conceive, a gratuitous insult upon the Convention, that assembled on the 9th day of January, 1861. Is it necessary to enable this State to resume her status in the Union, that we should declare the Ordinance of Secession, *"null and void?"* The United States Government does not require it of us at all. This Convention was not called to annul this ordinance; and it was no where intimated, that it was expected that we should do it. There are many persons, who voted for that Ordinance of Secession, under the conviction that it was the exercise of a Constitutional and legal right.—There may be members here, who believe they had a right to adopt that ordinance as an initatory step in a revolution, and what position will such action if proposed on our part, place these persons? They may be willing to vote that the right of secession has been decided finally against us, and pledge the people of Mississippi, through this Convention, that it should never be re-asserted; and yet they would have to vote in the negative, and against declaring the Ordinance of Secession, "null and void." It has been boastingly stated, and I feel a delicacy in saying anything about it myself, because of the frequency of that boast—that I was opposed to secession, and denied, and do still deny the right; but I may simply remark that I was opposed to the secession of the State, at the time she seceded. I thought it the worst step that could have been taken; and I am now advocating a becoming conduct on the part of this Convention, towards the Convention which met in this hall, on the 9th of January, 1861, whose action was endorsed almost unanimously, by the people of the State. All of us did some act—some more, some less—in the advocacy of its acts; and I no not think that this Convention should now declare its principle act "null and void."

It might be inferred from the remarks of the gentleman from Adams, (Mr. Martin,) delivered this morning, that those who favored secession, had done nothing upon the battle-field, in support of it, and that those who opposed it—after the State had been plunged into war—had been left to "stand in the imminent, deadly breach," and fight the battles of those who brought it on. I wish to say, in vindication of those alluded to, that they backed their doctrine with a strong arm, and I know many, who believed in the right of secession who vindicated it on the battle-field. Although, I give the gentleman full credit for his personal gallantry, I must say, that there were those who opposed secession, who went as far in the battle as he did. I think this is but just and due to the secessionists of the State.

I do not understand the meaning of the amendment offered by the gentleman from Adams; or else, I must think that he used language in an ironical sense, when he intimated that the effect of its adoption would be like the pouring of oil on the troubled waters. I thought the report of the Majority of the Committee, likely to produce many heart-burnings; but the gentleman proposed to put the case in a still more undesirable and unpalatable manner yet—and hence my opinion.

I am opposed to the Minority Report, of the gentleman from Marshall, (Mr. Trotter,) because, from it, it might appear hereafter, and now perhaps, to some, that this Convention simply repealed the Ordinance of Secession, because it was not thought proper, that it should be attempted to be enforced further—and because, I see no evidence in a simple repeal of that ordinance—that this Convention does not still insist on the right to re-enact such an ordinance should occasion require. I am in favor of adopting something which will show that we abandon now and forever, the right of secession. It is gone—it is a thing of the past—and I, for one, wish it buried out of sight—never to be raised again. If repealed, it may be brought up again, and re-enacted.

Therefore, although opposed to the amendment of the gentleman from Hinds, (Mr, Yerger,) I would vote for it, rather than be forced to vote for the Majority Report of the Committee, or have my vote recorded against it, as though I was in favor of secession.

Mr. Martin, of Adams—Mr. President:—So far as I am concerned my feelings are never hurt, if my friends vote against me, and I propose to vote for the strongest possible ordinance that declares the ordinance of secession "void," and not to vote in support of the language which the gentleman has suggested, and which may possibly import as much. I propose to use languge that cannot be mistaken, and to so wipe out this ordinance that no one can understand anything else, than that there never was such a right as that of secession, that not one of us voted for such miserable doctrine as that.

The gentleman from Yazoo, (Mr. Hudson,) indicates that we are here to restore our relations with the Federal Government, and at the same time, proposes to hold on, and not give up at once, this dogma—though I believe it far more important for us to set at rest forever, this question of secession, than for us to do any other act, we could do as a Convention. Of course, I should be much gratified, if I could vote for the ordinance of secession, if somebody would call it by some other name, and persuade me that I was doing something else! I never could bring myself to say, that "the constituency I have the honor to represent" &c., &c., "desired" &c., &c. If my constituents think that what I believe to be right and proper is so, well and good—but I never have been, or will be the mouth-piece of those who hold different opinions from myself on great Constitutional questions; but have exercised, and always will, my judgment, and decide for my constituents, what I hold best for their interests. I think, and have thought for years, that we have grown too democratic as regards this matter—and that men should be selected, not as mere speaking trumpets, but rather with reference to their own thinking qualities, and manliness; their earnest feeling and proper exercise of judgment. I think that the gentleman, (Mr. Hudson,) will do nothing but right, when he votes according to what he individually believes to be right, and that in case he does, his constitutency will not consider him to have done anything wrong.

Mr. Johnston, of Hinds—Mr. President:—I do not propose to enter into an argument at all, but simply to define my position, that my action may be subject to no misconstruction. It is not necessary to go into a detailed statement of what occured in the Committee room—suffice it to say, that there was not a unanimity of opinion among the Committee, in reference to the report which was presented here. That is manifest in the Minority Reports which are before the house, in addition to the Majority Report—to say nothing of the history of our deliberation in the Committee room. But finally the proposition was made, as it is embodied in the ordinance reported—simply declaring the Ordinance of Secession, a nullity and void—without any further expression whatever. That was certainly satisfactory to me, as Chairman of the Committee, and was to the majority of its members; and in that shape it was reported. It might be supposed, therefore, that I, as Chairman of that Committee, would stand up in defense of that report, which has been made; but I consider that there is no such obligation resting upon me, and that it is entirely parliamentary and proper for the Chairman to say anything in opposition to a report which he makes by the instruction of that Committee, and although the report, as I have said—is satisfactory to me, I wish to make no further declaration in regard to the Ordinance of Secession, than is contained in the report itself; but a substitute having been offered by my colleague, (Mr. Yerger,) in lieu of all pending amendments, and the original ordinance, as reported by the Committee, I arise simply for the purpose of announcing that I favor that proposition, and shall vote for it. That substitute clearly enunciates the great facts and principles, to which I have always subscribed, and I feel bound to favor it.

Much has been said in regard to the action of the Secession Convention. I have only this to say, in regard to that matter—that the sentiment and action of Mississippi is not uniform on the right of secession—very far from it. Gentlemen certainly remember the celebrated contest in reference to the compromise measures in 1850 and 1851. Surely they have not forgotten that a Convention of the people of the State of Mississippi, assembled in this very hall, in 1851—ten years before the Secession Ordinance was passed—and although, I have not the records before me, I remember very distinctly, its action, having the honor of being a member of that Convention, as well as of this. There was adopted there—and gentlemen can examine for themseles—a broad denial of the Constitutional right of Secession, on the part of any State—passing by an overwhelming majority of that enlightened and patriotic body. Now, if a course, opposite to the one proposed, be pursued here—what could the members of that Convention say in regard to their action? Gentlemen talk a great deal about hard feeling, and bring up unpleasant matters to others, whose action has been different; but I cannot see that the action of this Convention, is an aspersion or disrepect to any gentleman who voted for the Ordinance of Secession in 1861; and if it be so, most unquestionably it would be as great an insult or aspersion to the members of the Convention of 1851, who solemnly voted that no such right of secession existed under the Constitution. I desire, Mr. President, to place myself fully upon the record, for the sake of consistency. Having, in 1861, voted in solemn Convention, that the right of secession did not exist under the Federal Government. I consider it but right and proper, and consistent again to avow those principles, by voting for the proposition which my colleague has offered. I would not have insisted upon it myself, as a proposition before this Convention, and had no agency in bringing it before this body; but being presented, and meeting my views, and enunciating what I conceive to be a great truth, springing out of the Federal Constitution, I am bound to support it, to be consistent with the action I have always maintained.

MR. MATTHEWS, of Panola—Mr. President:—In order to test the question, I move to lay the substitute on the table.

The motion was carried by the following vote:

YEAS.—Messrs. Barr, Bailey, Binford, Blackwell, Brown, Byars, Carter, Compton, Cooper, of Rankin, Cooper, of Panola, Crawford, Davis, Dorris, Duncan, Franklin, Gaither, Goode, Gully, Hamm, Harrison, Heard, Hill, Hudson, Hurst, Johnson, of Marshall, Johnson, of Smith, Lewers, Malone, Marshall, Matthews, Mayson, McBride, Morphis, Niles, Phipps, Potter, Reid, Reynolds, Sanders, of DeSoto, Sessions, Stone, Stricklin, Swett, Tate, Trotter, Wall, Watson, Wilson, Woodward.—49.

NAYS.—Mr. President, Messrs. Bond, Cason, Crum, Cummings, Dowd, Gowan, Griffin, Hall, Hemingway, Horne, Houston, Jarnagin, Johnston, of Hinds, Johnson, of Choctaw, Jones, Kennedy, King, Lambdin, Lewers, Lindsey, Loper, Martin, of Adams, Martin, of Sunflower, Maury, Montgomery, Owens, of Tunica, Owen, of Scott, Peyton, Pressley, Quin, Rives, Rushing, Sanders, of Attala, Simonton, Slover, Sparkman, Stanley, Wallace, Webb, Wier, Wooley, White, Yerger.—45.

Mr. Yerger, of Hinds,—I now move, Mr. President, to lay on the table, the amendment of the gentleman from Marshall, (Mr. Trotter.)

The motion was carried by the following vote:

Yeas.—Mr. President, Messrs. Blackwell, Bond, Byars, Cason, Crawford, Cummings, Dorris, Duncan, Gowan, Goode, Griffin, Hall, Hemingway, Hill, Houston, Jarnagin, Johnston, of Hinds, Johnson, of Choctaw, Johnson, of Smith, Jones, Kennedy, Lambdin, Lewis, Lindsey, Loper, Martin, of Adams, Martin, of Sunflower, Maury, Montgomery, McBride, Morphis, Owen, of Tunica, Peyton, Pressley, Quin, Reynolds, Rives, Sanders, of Attala, Simonton, Sparkman, Wallace, Webb, White, Wier, Wooley, Wylie, Yerger.—48.

Nays.—Messrs. Barr, Bailey, Binford, Brown, Carter, Compton, Cooper, of Rankin, Cooper, of Panola, Crum, Davis, Dowd, Franklin, Gaither, Gully, Hamm, Harrison, Heard, Horne, Hudson, Hurst, Johnson, of Marshall, King, Lewers, Malone, Marshall, Matthews, Mayson, Niles, Owens of Scott, Phipps, Potter, Reid, Rushing, Sanders, of DeSoto, Sessions, Slover, Stanley, Stone, Stricklin, Swett, Tate, Trotter, Wall, Watson, Wilson, Woodward.—46.

Mr. Goode, of Lawrence—Mr. President:—I now offer this Minority Report, as a substitute for the Majority Report of the Committee, reading as follows:—

Whereas, A Convention of the people of the State of Mississippi, assembled at the Capitol, on the 9th day of January, 1861, adopted an Ordinance of Secession of the State from the United States Government, and declared that the State resumed her sovereignty; and in a war resulting therefrom with the United States Government, which refused to recognize the legality or validity of that Ordinance, the State failed to maintain her asserted sovereignty; and is now willing and ready to resume her status in the Union, as before the passage of that Ordinance; Therefore,

Be it ordained by this Convention, That said Ordinance of Secession be, and the same is hereby declared, to be henceforward null and of no binding force.

After this and several other amendments had been offered and rejected—

On motion of Mr. Johnston, of Hinds, the first section of the Majority Report, of the Committee was adopted, by the following vote:

Yeas.—Mr. President, Messrs. Bailey, Billups, Binford, Blackwell, Bond, Brown, Byars, Carter, Cason, Cooper, of Rankin, Compton, Cooper, of Panola, Crawford, Cummings, Dorris, Dowd, Duncan, Gaither, Gowan, Griffin, Gully, Hall, Harrison, Heard, Hemingway, Hill, Horne, Houston, Hudson, Jarnagin, Johnston, of Hinds, Johnson, of Choctaw, Johnson, of Smith, Jones, Kennedy, King, Lambdin, Lewis, Lindsey, Loper, Malone, Marshall, Martin, of Adams, Martin, of Sunflower, Maury, Montgomery, McBride, Morphis, Niles, Owen, of Tunica, Owens, of Scott, Peyton, Potter; Pressley, Quinn, Reynolds, Rives, Rushing, Sanders, of Attala, Sanders, of DeSoto, Sessions, Simonton, Slover, Sparkman, Stanley, Stricklin, Swett, Tate, Wallace, Wall, Watson, Webb, White, Wier, Wilson, Woodward, Wooley, Wylie, Yerger.—81.

NAYS.—Messrs. Barr, Crum, Davis, Franklin, Goode, Hamm, Hurst, Johnson, of Marshall, Mayson, Lewers, Phipps, Reid, Stone, Trotter.—14.

MR. WILSON, of Yazoo—Mr. President :—I merely wish to say, that I do not intend, by my vote to declare that I consider the Ordinance of Secession, of any legality or binding force ; but I voted as I did, because I merely objected to the verbage.

The Convention then proceeded to the consideration of section two, of the Majority Report of the Committee, reading as follows :

SEC. 2. *Be it further ordained*, That the following ordinances and resolutions, passed by said former Convention of the State of Mississippi, which assembled in the city of Jackson, on Monday, the 7th day of January, 1861, and on the 25th day of March, 1861, be and the same are hereby repealed, viz :

"To raise means for the defense of the State," (said ordinance having no date.)

"To regulate the Military system of the State of Mississippi," passed 23d. January, 1861.

"To amend the Constitution of the State of Mississippi in certain particulars," passed January : 6th, 1861.

"Concerning the jurisdiction and property of the United States of America, in the State of Mississippi," passed January 16th, 1861.

"Supplemental to an ordinance concerning the jurisdiction and property of the United States of America, in the State of Mississippi," passed January 26th, 1862.

"To provide for postal arrangements in the State of Mississippi," passed January 12th, 1861.

"Further to provide for postal arrangements in Mississippi, passed January 26th, 1861.

"To provide for the formation of a Southern Confederacy." (No date thereto.)

"To regulate the right of citizenship, in the State of Mississippi," passed 26th January, 1861.

"To provide for the representation of the State of Mississippi in the Congress of the Southern Confederacy," passed January 26th, 1861.

"To provide for surveys and fortifications of military sites within the State of Mississippi," passed 26th of January, 1861.

"To authorize the Governor to borrow a sufficient amount of money to defray the expenses of the troops now in the field." (No date thereto.)

"To adopt and ratify the Constitution adopted by the Convention, Montgomery, Alabama, passed March 29th, 1861."

"In relation to lands in the State of Mississippi belonging to Indian orphans, passed March 29th, 1861.

"To define the power of the Legislature of this State in relation to ordinances and resolutions, adopted by this Convention, passed March 30th, 1861."

"To provide a coat of arms and flag for the State of Mississippi, passed March 28th, 1861."

"To revise and amend the law in relation to foreign insurance companies." Passed March 27th, 1861.

"To provide for the appointment of Electors of President and Vice-President of the Confederate States of America." Passed March 30th, 1861.

"To alter and modify the ordinance entitled 'An ordinance concerning the jurisdiction and property of the United States in the State of Mississippi." Passed March 30th, 1861.

"Supplemenal to an ordinance entitled 'an ordinance to raise means for the defense of the State,'" passed March 29th, 1861.

MR. WIER, of Yalobusha—Mr. President:—I move to strike out the words "be and the same are repealed" and insert "are hereby declared null and void."

MR. JOHNSTON, of Hinds—Mr. President:—I shall have to vote against that proposition. There is one of these ordinances which it is proposed to repeal, under which certain paper money was issued, by authority of the State of Mississippi—a large amount of which is yet out in circulation. I did not wish that ordinance repealed by the Committee at all, and opposed that action; but a majority of the Committee insisted on its repeal. Now, if the amendment prevails, declaring the ordinance null and void—what is the effect upon the notes and bills, issued under that ordinance? It would undoubtedly be, to destroy the value. It seems to me, that without intending it, that act would be one of repudiation, and therefore, I was opposed to the repeal, because I feared such would be the effect, and because I am opposed to repudiating anything. I was partly convinced, however, that the mere repeal of the law would not invalidate the issue of the money—though I had my doubts, and would yet prefer to have that ordinance left standing and untouched.

Mr. Weir, of Yallobusha—Mr. President;—It seems to me that the Convention might dispose of these Ordinances as it did of the Ordinance of Secession, but in order to test the question as to the form in which that section should stand, I move the adoption of the amendment.

The amendment, on motion of Mr. Franklin, was tabled.

A substitute, offered by Mr. McBride, having been laid upon the table, Mr. Johnston, of Hinds, offered an amendment:

"Amend by striking out, the word, "to raise means for the defense of the State;" and also, by striking out at the end of the section, the words: "supplemental to an ordinance, entitled an ordinance, to raise means for the defense of the State, passed March 29th, 1861."

A motion to table the above was lost, whereupon Mr. Yerger, of Hinds, offered the following proviso, by way of amendment, which was accepted by Mr. Johnson:

"*Provided*, That an ordinance, (bearing no date,) entitled "An ordinance to raise means for the defense of the State," and an ordinance aproved March, 29th, 1861, entitled supplemental to an ordinance, entitled an ordinance, to raise means for the defense of the State, are intended to be left by this Convention, for such action on the same, as the people of the State, by their Legislature, may deem is right and proper to take—having in view the honor and prosperity of the State."

Mr. Marshall, of Warren,—Mr. President: I move to strike out the proviso of the gentleman from Hinds. The State of Mississippi, by ordinances, invited her citizens to come forward and invest their money, and it has declared as an inducement to that end, that the legislature should have no power to repeal those ordinances, or to modify or alter them, that the security that was intended to be given to the people might be undisturbed: but by the adoption of that ordinance it will be taken from them, and the subject will be left under the control of the legislature. I must therefore oppose the adoption of the proviso.

Mr. Yerger, of Hinds,—I shall insist, Mr. President, as a matter of course, so far as I am concerned upon the proviso. The ordinances proposed to be struck out are ordinances providing for the raising of money which was intended to be used in carrying on and conducting the war which this State was at about that time inaugurating. In my view, all those ordinances are absolutely null and void. I know that many of the people of this State invested their money as has been stated, and I for one, as a citizen, am willing to pay my share of the taxes necessary to pay this indebtedness; but I know the fact, and I suppose that many of the members of this Convention do also—that these notes were at a great discount in the market, and were purchased by brokers for the purpose of some day or other making a speculation and profit on them. So far as the mere obligation is concerned towards these parties, we are under no more obligation no pay them than to pay the holders of Confederate bonds, or any other security which they allowed during the progress of the war. But I do not wish this State to repudiate what was entered into by that Convention. In deference however,—although I believe the Convention had no power to take the action which it did,—I would have the matter left entirely with the Legislature in the future, which, regarding the amount of actual investment made by parties, can give them such remuneration as they may deem them entitled to; but I do not wish, by our silence, to give credit and value to these ordinances at all. If we strike out and refuse to pass the proviso, we simply countenance the view that the ordinances, in the opinion of this Convention, are valid,—thus pledging the State to pay the holders the entire amount of these notes. I wish the matter to be left to the Legislature, which can take into consideration the condition of the people in reference to financial affairs and the amount paid therefor by the holders of the obligations I do not wish, in any way, to tie the hands of the Legislature, and make it obligatory upon them to provide for the payment of these notes whether or not they are rightfully and validly received.

The motion to strike out the proviso was lost, by the following vote:

YEAS.—Messrs. Crum, Franklin, Lambdin, Lewers, Marshall, Martin, of Adams, Potter, Swett—8.

NAYS.—Mr. President, Messrs. Barr, Bailey, Billups, Binford, Blackwell, Bond, Brown, Byars, Carter, Cason, Compton, Cooper, of Rankin, Cooper, of Panola, Crawford, Cummings, Dorris, Dowd, Gaither, Gowan, Goode, Griffin, Gulley, Hall, Hamm, Harrison, Heard, Hemingway, Hill, Horne, Houston, Hudson, Hurst, Jarnagin, Johnston, of Hinds, Johnson, of Marshall, Johnson, of Choctaw, Johnson, of Smith, Jones, Kennedy, King, Lewis, Lindsey, Loper, Malone, Martin, of Sunflower, Matthews, Maury, Montgomery, Mayson, McBride, Morphis, Niles, Owen, of Tunica, Owens, of Scott, Peyton, Phipps, Pressley, Quin, Reynolds, Rives, Rushing, Sanders, of Attala, Sanders, of DeSoto, Sessions, Simonton, Slover. Sparkman. Stanley, Stone, Stricklin. Tate, Trotter, Wallace,

Wall, Watson, Webb, White, Wier, Wilson, Woodward, Wooley, Wylie and Yerger.—83.

The question was then taken on the amendment with proviso and adopted.

On motion of Mr. Johnston, of Hinds, the second section as amended was adopted.

On motion of Mr. Cooper, of Panola, the third section was adopted.

On motion of Mr. Jonnston, of Hinds, the ordinance as amended, was then adopted.

Mr. Harrison, of Lowndes, made the following report:

Mr. President:—

The Commttiee on the State Constitution to whom was referred the resolution to enquire into the propriety and expediency of submitting the amendments of the Constitution, together with the ordinances adopted by this Convention, to the qualfied electors of this State for their ratification or rejection, rereport that they have duly considered said resolution, and they are of the opinion that it is not practical or expedient to submit said several amendments and ordinances, to the people, under existing circumstances, and accordingly they recommend that the said resolution do not pass.

Mr. Johnson, of Smith,—Mr. President:—I hope that report will not be agreed to, at least as far as the submission to the people of the free clause of the Constitution is concerned.

The shortness of time intervening between now and the general election cannot be urged against such a step, for that article might be submitted separately.

It has been said that if the Ordinance of Secession had been fairly submitted to the people, they would have refused to ratify it. I do not wish to have it said in future that the abolition of slavery was forced upon the people of this State, through not allowing them the opportunity of expressing their opinions in regard to it at the ballot box.

With the purpose of making an amendment to this report by which that amendment may be passed upon by our constituents (which I will present myself and vote for, if no one else will) I move that this Convention now adjourn until 9 o'clock to-morrow morning.

On motion of Mr. Harrison, the report was received.

Pending the question of agreeing to the report—

Mr. Barr, of Lafayette, moved that the Convention adjourn until to-morrow morning, 9 o'clock.

Mr. Johnson, of Smith, moved to amend by striking out the word "nine, and inserting the word eight."

The question being taken on the motion of Mr. Barr, of Lafayette, it was decided in the negative.

The amendment offered by Mr. Johnson, of Smith, was then adopted, when—

The Convention adjourned until to-morrow morning, eight o'clock.

[NOTE.—The following speech forms a part of the debate of the previous day, on the proposition to abolish slavery. It was enclosed, by Reporters, with the proceedings of Tuesday, and thus failed to be inserted at its proper place.]

MR. MARSHALL, of Warren—Mr. President: Before the yeas and nays are taken, I desire to state the reasons which control my action on the question under consideration. I have voted gainst laying several of the proposed amendments on the table, not because I framed either of them; but, simply, to allow their friends an opportunity of discussing them asfully as they wished. As a general rule, I do not approve of that mode of cutting of debate. But if we are to insert in the Constitution an anti-slavery clause I prefer the form reported by the Committee. I would rather feel, and have the people of the country now and hereafter believe, that our action is free and voluntary; and that we are not here merely to register the edicts of Federal power. We all wish to attain the same result. All desire to see the soldiery removed from our midst; or, at least, that the military should again become, as the Constitution intended it always should be, except in extraordinary emergencies, subordinate to the civil power. We want law and order restored—that our people may feel once more secure in their persons and property, and enjoy the blessings of peace and quiet; that they have an opportunity of recuperating, if possible, their wasted resources and wealth. How are we to accomplish this, is the question? It is urged by some that we have no discretion left us—that we are bound by the oath we have taken, to support this amendment; and others tell us the President demands it as a condition precedent to the admission of our representatives in the next Congress; while a large majority of this body seem to regard it as affording our only hope of getting rid of Federal bayonets.—Is it true that we are bound by our oath to support this amendment? I do not so understand it. In my view, it was an act of tyranny to require it of us. The innocent and guilty were alike bound to take it. I have known soldiers of the Federal army, who followed the flag of the Union from the inception to the close of the war, take it. None can vote, or enter into business of any kind, without it. Swear, or be disfranchised—take the oath, or starve, and see our families starve. No other alternative was left us. But whether forcibly or voluntary, I have taken the oath, and I intend, in good faith, to keep it. My negroes, who remained with me, are treated as freemen. They are receiving wages for their labor. I have not a word to utter against any act of Congress, or proclamation of the President in regard to slavery. I have already voted for striking out every syllable in our Constitution on that subject. But the President has not demanded, nor does the oath we have taken reqnire of us, either in letter or spirit, to vote for any amendment of our Constitution, nor the passage of any law, on any subject. To support an existing law is what we have undertaken and sworn to do; not to pass another or similar one. We did not agree to do what may not have been legally done by others. Feeling, therefore, entirely free to act according to my own judgment, do the dignity and honor of Mississippi, and the best interests of her people, make this amendment necessary or proper, under existing circumstances? If there were no Federal pressure upon us, very few or none could be found in Mississippi to advocate such a measure as this. The only apology or excuse for it is, that our former relations to the United States cannot be restored, nor our members of Congress be admitted to their seats, nor civil law and order revived and permanently established among us, without it. If I could believe that, I might, and probably would, vote differently. But it is very clear to my mind that, the restoration of our former relations with the Federal Union cannot rightfully be made dependent, in any way, upon our action on this subject. According to the theory of the United States, Mississippi has never been out of the Union. Her act of secession was void, and her people never absolved from their allegiance to the Federal Government. Every act of Congress, proclamation of the President, and State paper, enacted or issued, from the beginning of the war to the appointment of Governor Sharkey, and providing for the election of delegates to this body, recognizes Mississippi as one of the States of the Union. It is only in that view the President could offer us amnesty, or prosecute any of our people for treason, or feel bound to guarantee a republican form of government to our State. Upon no other ground can the war against us be justified or excused. Without that it would have been wholly unprovoked, wicked, cruel and murderous. The United States cannot, will not, dare not now assert that Mississippi is not a State in the Union. To do so would be to affix the stamp of infamy upon themselves, in the judgment of the civilized world. I insist that we are now in the Union, and entitled to all the rights and privileges of any other State. Our people may have incurred penalties, and, if legally prosecuted and convicted, may have to suffer punishment; but they have forfeited none of their political rights as citizens. Mississippi is to-day, oppressed and overrun as she is by military power, the equal, under the Constitution, of any State in the Union.

No matter, then, whether we adopt this amendment or not, the representatives we may send to Congress cannot, without a palpable violation of the Constitution of the United States, be denied their seats. And this I understand to be the President's view. He advises the States in which he has appointed Provisional Governors to amend their Constitutions, by striking out the articles which recognize slavery, and thinks it would be better for them to do so. Not that they are bound to do so, or because he would, without that, oppose the admission of their representatives to seats in Congress. But he says he has no power over that subject, and Congress may not admit them. The inference is fair, if not entirely clear, that, if left to him, they would be admitted. "Each House," however, being "the judge of the elections, returns and qualifications of its own members," their admission or rejection is beyond his control, is all he says. No one, I suppose, would contend that either House of Congress has the right, under the Constitution, to reject a member duly elected and legally qualified, arbitrarily and without cause. They could uot refuse to admit him, because he was a Whig, Democrat or Republican, or because he came from a slave or free State. They have the right to enquire and determine whether he was elected at the time and place, in the manner prescribed by law, and whether those who voted for him were qualified electors, according to the law of the State in which he was elected, and whether he had been nine years a citizen of the United States, if a Senator, or seven years, if a member of the House of Representatives, and an inhabitant of the State in which he was chosen, at the time of his election. It is not at all probable that any objection can be justly made to any person sent by Mississippi to represent her in the next Congress. They will, no doubt, all be elected at the time, place, and in the manner prescribed by law, and by electors duly qualified, according to the law of this State prior to the 9th day of January, 1861, and who have taken the amnesty oath, under the proclamation of the President of the 29th day of May, 1865, and they will all, I take for granted, have the qualification of Senators and Representatives, respectively, required by the Constitution of the United States. Upon what ground, then, can they be refused admittance? Assuming Mississippi to be a State in the Union, the right of her delegation to Congress to all the privileges of members from any other State follows irresistably.

Suppose, however, they should be rejected, whether rightfully or not, what then would be our condition? All of our State, district and county offices will be filled, by officers duly elected, in strict accordance with the President's proclamation and the ordinance of this Convention, passed pursuant thereto, and their official character would unquestionably be fully recognized by the President. Our State Government, therefore, being regularly organized, according to his own views, there would be no good reason why the civil law should not be enforced here, in the same manner, and to the same extent, as in any other State. And I am not willing to believe the President would attempt, by mere despotic power or arbitrary act, to prevent or interrupt the administration of our State Government; and, without his sanction, certainly neither the military nor any other branch of the Federal Government could do it. Civil law would, consequently, be revived and enforced in the State, while we would be temporarily without representation in Congress.

It would then remain for the people of the Northern States to say whether they would sustain their representatives in a plain, palpable violation of the Constitution, and their solemn oath to support it. I know many believe, and I admit, not without very strong grounds for that opinion, that the Constitution has not been, for several years past, very sacredly regarded by the people of the North, and that public officials have almost ceased to consider it their guide or rule of action. It is certainly true that it has, in many instances, been very unceremoniously trampled upon. But that was during the existence of a gigantic war, that fearfully threatened the life of the nation; and it is probable the people thought it better to submit to even gross violations of the Constitution than, by forcible resistance, increase the danger of, and, may be, insure a permanent severance of the Union. With the return of peace, however, I trust different views will prevail. and I hope to see the people of the North, as well as the people of the South, once more return to their allegiance to the Constitution, and vigilantly and carefully guard and protect it against any and every assault or encroachment of Federal or any other power.

The people of the North have as much interest in upholding the Constitution as we have; and I am not prepared to believe they would sustain their representatives in so shameless a disregard of its plain provisions. Justice to us, their duty to the Constitution, and sound policy, would alike forbid it.

If we are not bound by the oath we have taken to vote for this amendment, and its adoption is not necessary to entitle our delegates to Congress to all the rights and privileges of members from other States, would it be likely to relieve us of military rule? Some gentlemen seem to believe that the suspension of the writ of *habeas corpus*, the denial of trial by jury, and the continuance of an army in the State, are all designed by the Federal Government to compel us to insert a free clause in our State Constitution. They surely forget that the proclamation of martial law and the suspension of the writ of *habeas corpus* were not limited to any State or section. They were not general in their operation, but embraced certain specified classes of persons, irrespective of their places of abode. We all know that hundreds of citizens of Northern States have been denied the privilege of the writ of *habeas corpus*, as well as the right of trial by jury. Leading prominent men, in no way connected with the army, have been tried there by Military Commissions, and convicted and punished. It is very manifest that these measures were not adopted, nor are they continued, with any reference whatever to any amendment of the Constitution of this or any other State.

Gentlemen also err, in my opinion, when they say the army is kept here to force us to abolish slavery. If that is the object of keeping troops here, as has been already worked by other States, why are they continued in Tennessee, when slavery was abolished by State action, a year ago ; or in Kentucky and Maryland, which were never considered insurrectionary States?

But why should the President, or Congress, want this, or any other State, to abolish slavery? That has already been done by a Presidential proclamation. If that act is legal, it is certainly unnecessary for us to do anything more than we have done. We have struck out every clause in our Constitution, in relation to slavery. Any further action on our part would be purely superrogatory. Whether slavery is legally abolished by the proclamation, or not, is not for us to determine. That is a question, as Mr. Lincoln told us, and our own distinguished Governor, in his proclamation, says, for the Courts. No one here, so far as I know, is disposed to raise that question. But if it ever should come up, it would be the duty of the Supreme Court, in the last resort, to determine it. And with that decision, whatever it may be, the whole country should be satisfied.

If any man believes his property in slaves has been taken away from him in relation of the Constitution ; or that he is legally entitled to compensation for them ; he is entitled in my opinion, to have the question tested in a legitimate way, before the proper tribunal, and by no vote of mine, shall that right be denied him.

The status of the negro, however, is a very insignificant matter, in my judgement, in comparison with the great principle of liberty involved here. It is not whether the negro shall be free—but whether we shall be slaves. Not whether the proclamation of the President is Constitutional; but whether we shall be permitted to live under whatever form of State Government, Republican in its character, and not inconsistent with the Constitution of the United States, and the laws passed pursuant thereto, we may think proper to adopt. The right of a State, to adopt such Constitution, as its citizens consider most advantageous to themselves, subject only to the limitation above stated, has never been questioned. And, I am not yet prepared, upon doubtful grounds of temporary expediency, to yield a principle of such vital importance. Believing the Federal Government has no right whatever to dictate to us, any amendment of our State Constitution; and that the States have exclusive jurisdiction of all questions like this; and not willing to yield a principle so essential to freedom, and the dignity and honor of the State, I feel compelled to vote against the amendment now proposed.

NINTH DAY.

WEDNESDAY, AUGUST 23, 1865.

The Convention met pursuant to adjournment.

Prayer by the Rev. Mr. Pressley, (member of the Convention.)

Journal of yesterday read and approved.

Mr. Simonton, from Committee on Enrolled Ordinances and constitutional amendments, submitted the following report:

MR. PRESIDENT:

The Committee on Enrolled Ordinances and constitutional amendments, respectfully report, that they have examined the following ordinances and constitutional amendments, and find the same correctly enrolled.

An Ordinance adopted by the Convention 21st day of August, 1865, in regard to Elections. Amendments to the Constitution of the State of Mississippi, adopted by the Convention on the 21st day of August, 1865, in regard to slaves, and conferring power on the Legislature in cases therein.

On motion of Mr. Simonton, the report of the committee was received and agreed to.

Mr. Sanders, of Attala, offered the following resolution, which was referred under the rule, to the Committee on State Constitution:

An Ordinance to amend the Constitution of the State of Mississippi, fixing the seat of government at the city of Jackson, in the county of Hinds:

Be it ordained by the people of the State of Mississippi, in Convention assembled, That the 3d article, 30th section of the Constitution of Mississippi, fixing the seat of government at the city of Jackson, in the county of Hinds, be and the same is hereby repealed.

Mr. Watson, of Marshall, offered the following resolution:

Resolved, That a Committee of three be appointed by the President, whose duty it shall be to prepare and report to the next Legislature, for its consideration and action, such laws and changes in existing laws of this State, as to said Committee may seem expedient, in view of the amendments to the Constitution made by this Convention.

On motion of Mr. Watson,

The resolution was adopted.

Mr. Yerger, of Hinds, offered the following resolution, which was adopted:

Resolved, That the Committee on Enrolled Ordinances and Amendments to the Constitution be instructed to have the Constitution of this State, as amended, correctly enrolled, which shall then be signed and attested by the President of the Convention, and be by him deposited in the office of the Secretary of State.

Mr. Hudson, of Yazoo, offered the following Ordinance:

Be it ordained, That the special Courts of Equity heretofore, and that may hereafter be established in this State by the Provisional Governor thereof, be and the same are hereby recognized to be in existence, but that in all cases, the right and benefit of exceptions, bills of exceptions, writs of error and appeals from said court or courts to the High Court of Errors and Appeals, for the revision and judgment of the latter court, shall be and are hereby secured to any party litigant in said court or courts, who may desire the same, as is now provided for and regulated by the laws of this State, in case of exceptions, writs of error, and appeals from the Circuit and Chancery Courts of this State, to the said Court of Errors and Appeals; and the said Court of Errors and Appeals shall take cognizance and jurisdiction of such cases, as in the case of Appeal and Writ of Error from the Circuit and Chancery Courts of this State: *Provided,* that such special courts, and the proceedings had therein, after the courts known to the Constitution and laws of this State are established, shall not be recognized beyond the then unfinished and instituted business of the same, and the records and papers of said special courts shall, upon their expiration, be deposited in the office of the several courts of this State, in whose counties the said special court or courts are or may be held, for the safe keeping thereof, and may be authenticated thereafter, as other records of said Circuit and Chancery Courts.

On motion of Mr. Hudson, the above ordinance was laid upon the table for the present.

Mr. Compton, from select committee, submitted the following report:

MR. PRESIDENT:

The Committee appointed to take into consideration the pay of the officers and members of this Convention, have had the same under consideration, and beg leave to report that in their opinion the compensation should be as follows, to-wit:

President	twelve	(12)	dollars	per diem.
Members (each)	eight	(8)	"	"
Secretary	fifty	(50)	"	"
Sergeant-at-arms	eight	(8)	"	"
Door-keeper	six	(6)	"	"
Pages (each)	two	(2)	"	"

The President and members to receive eight dollars for every twenty miles of travel in going to and returning from the Convention, on the most direct route.

All of which is respectfully submitted.

On motion of Mr. Compton, the report was received.

Mr. Hudson moved to lay the report upon the table,

Which motion was lost.

On motion of Mr. Compton, the report of the committee was adopted.

Mr. McBride, of Madison, submitted a Memorial from the members of the Board of Police of Madison county, relative to lawlessness and demoralization existing in said county.

The Memorial being read,

On motion of Mr. McBride, it was laid upon the table.

Mr. Malone, of DeSoto, offered the following resolution:

Resolved, That the thanks of the delegates of this Convention are due, and are hereby tendered to the Hon. J. S. Yerger, for the very able and impartial manner in which he has presided over its deliberations.

On motion of Mr. Matthews, of Panola,

The resolution was laid upon the table for the present.

On motion of Mr. Harrison, of Lowndes, the Convention resumed the consideration of the report of the Committee on State Constitution, relative to submitting certain amendments of the Constitution, together with the ordinances adopted by this Convention to the qualified electors of the State, for ratification or rejection.

On motion of Mr. Harrison,

The report of the Committee was agreed to.

On motion of Mr. Harrison, the Convention proceeded to the consideration of the ordinance to be entitled, "an ordinance to legalize and support the legislative enactments of Mississippi, passed since the 9th day of January, 1861, and for other purposes.

The ordinance being received,

Mr. Marshall, of Warren, offered the following as a substitute for the same:

The people of the State of Mississippi in Convention assembled, In order to quiet the public mind, and remove any doubt that may exist on the subject, do hereby ordain and declare that the official acts of all public officers, whether legislative, executive, judicial or ministerial, passed or performed since the 9th day of January, 1861; whether rightfully exercising the functions of their respective offices or not, be and the same are hereby legalized to the same extent, as if this State had never dissolved, or attempted to dissolve, its connection with the United States.

Mr. Marshall, of Warren—Mr. President:—According to the view I entertain, there is no action of this body necessary on that subject at all. We have a public statute that covers all the ground that was intended by the Committee, we could justly and legally cover. The statute as it now stands declares in substance, what is declared by my substitute. I think there can be little doubt, that the acts of all our officers, whether Mississippi be regarded one of the Confederate, or one of the United States, would be legal and binding, without any legislation on the subject by us. Such I hold to be the decision of all the Courts of Great Britain, on similar subjects; and such, I have no doubt, would be the decision of the courts of this country; but inasmuch as there may be some doubt on the subject, and inasmuch as some individuals may feel uneasy in regard to transactions that occured during the existence of the war; and to allay anixety that may arise on the subject, I have proposed this amendment. Some members have inquired, whether it would legalize legislative acts. I do not think there ought to be any doubt in the mind of any one on that subject. Members of the Legislature, as well as Judges, Justices of the Peace, and all other parties, acting by authority, would be regarded as public officers. This act embraces all public officers; no matter whether they be State, District or County; executive, legislative, judicial or ministerial. They are all embraced in the phraseology employed here, and it reaches, in a few words, the end intended to be accomplished by the whole bill, with the exception, that it does not legalize or validate contracts, that may have been entered into during the war; and that subject, I submit, the Convention has no power to control. If the contracts entered into by citizens of

Mississippi, are valid now, they cannot be invalidated; cannot be destroyed by any action of this Convention. If they are void now; no action of ours, can make them valid; and I do not think it necessary, to say anything by ordinance, on the subject.

Mr. Martin, of Adams—Mr. President:—I think it is far preferable to the report of the Committee, for some doubt would certainly arise, if the Convention undertook to make contracts valid; and more confusion would result from it, than by leaving the matter as it stands at present, without interfering with it at all. I think there ought to be an amendment to the substitute, so as to include legislative acts.

Mr. Marshall, of Warren.—It was designed to reach the end suggested by the amendment I offered. If a legislator is not a public officer, I would like to know in what light he should be viewed. If he be a public officer, then there can be no question, but that this covers all legislative acts.

Mr. Harrison, of Lowndes—Mr. President:—I am opposed to legalizing every act of the Legislature, and if that is the intention of the substitute, I shall be constrained to vote against it. I think in would be a very proper substitute for the second section of the bill. I have a substitute in my hand for the first section, and I think this would be proper for the second; but I shall vote against it as a substitute for the whole bill.

Mr. Marshall, of Warren: The object was to be brief, and use no more words than was necessary to convey the idea, but, if gentlemen prefer, the substitute may state all public officers,—legislative, executive, judicial, or ministerial, or use the words, "State, district, or county." The amendment is not intended, and does not purport to legalize any act that would not be legal, if the State had never dissolved its connection with the United States.

Mr. Barr, of Lafayette: For the purpose of taking the sense of the House on this subject, I move to lay the substitute on the table;

Which motion prevailed.

The first section of the Ordinance, as reported by the Committee, being under consideration,

Mr. Harrison, of Lowndes, offered the following as a substitute for the same:

Sec. 2. *Be it ordained by the people of the State of Mississippi, in Convention assembled*, That all laws and parts of laws enacted by the Legislature of the State of Mississippi, since the 9th day of January, A. D. 1861, so far as the same are not in conflict with, or repugnant to the Constitution of the United States, and the laws made in pursuance thereof, or of the Constitution of this State, as it existed on the 1st

16

day of January, 1861, or in aid of the late rebellion, except the laws in relation to crimes and misdemeanors, and except an act entitled an act to enable the railroad companies of this State, to pay the monies borrowed by them, "approved December 7th, 1863," be and the same are hereby ratified and confirmed, and declared to be valid and binding from their respective dates; and the same shall remain in full force and effect, until altered or repealed according to law.

MR. HARRISON, of Lowndes—Mr. President: This substitute proposes not to ratify the criminal laws of the land, at least those adopted since the first of January, 1861, for the reason that it would be an *ex post facto* law, in my opinion, and unconstitutional. If the law is valid, there is no use in ratifying it, and I do not wish to commit myself, or the Convention, by doing what I consider purely unconstitutional. I therefore insert, "except the law in relation to crimes and misdemeanors."

Mr. Jarnagin, of Noxubee, offered the following amendment:

Strike out the words, "in aid of the late rebellion."

MR. JARNAGIN, of Noxubee: In offering this amendment I would simply remark, that the substitute leaves to the decision of every individual the question, whether these particular laws were in aid of the rebellion, or not. Now I think there are a great many laws passed by the Legislature since the 9th January, 1861, in regard to which it would be very difficult to discriminate whether they were in aid of the rebellion, or not. For instance, in regard to the issuance of the cotton money, it might be difficult to determine whether it was in aid of the rebellion, or not. The necessity certainly arose from the rebellion. A large amount of money was issued, to be expended for the benefit of the indigent of the State of Mississippi. The question would arise whether the act was passed in aid of the rebellion. It clearly grew out of the rebellion, and there would have been no necessity of legislating upon that subject, and divers other subjects, if we had not been in a state of rebellion. If we can possibly make it more plain, and designate in a general way what statutes are intended to be valid, or what not, it will be much better. It leaves the whole question open for the courts to decide, and for every individual to form his own judgment whether any particular law was in aid of the late rebellion, or not. I wish to make it as definite as possible, and move to strike out the words, "in aid of the late rebellion."

MR. HOUSTON, of Monroe—Mr. President: I shall vote against the amendment offered, for it seems to me that these, like all other laws, will be for the consideration of the courts of the country. There is nothing more indefinite in that part of the ordinance, than there is in the portion of it which speaks of the validity of the laws which are not unconstitutional with the Court of the United States, or the State of Mississippi. Who is to decide what laws are in contravention of the Court of the United States, and the State of Mississippi? It is as much a question for the Conrts to decide what was.

On motion of Mr. Cooper, of Rankin,

The amendment was laid on the table.

The question recurring on the substitute offered by Mr Harrison,

Mr. Potter, of Hinds, offered the following amendment:

Strike out the words, "so far as the same are not in conflict, &c., to the words, "late rebellion," inclusive, and insert in lieu thereof, the words, "which would have been valid if enacted in time of peace."

Mr. Yerger: For the purpose of testing the sense of the Convention, I move to lay the amendment on the table. Carried.

Mr. Hudson, of Yazoo, offered the following amendment to the first section, which was adopted:

Provided, That the acts of the Legislature of this State, passed in April, 1864, for the suppression of distilleries, and the sale of spirituous liquors, and declaring the same to be a public and common nuisance, and all acts and laws authorizing the payment of dues to the State in Confederate money, or notes, shall no longer be in force, but are hereby declared henceforth inoperative.

MR. WATSON, of Marshall: I cannot vote for the substitute in the form which it now stands. I regard every distillery that has been established in the State, as an unmitigated evil and nuisance. I cannot, by my vote, even under the circumstances in which we are now placed, legalize the distilleries that have been erected, and have been pouring forth their poisonous streams upon our population.

MR. BARR, of Lafayette: I move to reconsider the vote adopting the proviso.

On motion of Mr. Morphis, of Pontotoc, the proviso was laid on the table.

Mr. Yerger offered the following amendment to the substitute offered by Mr. Harrison.

Provided, That all acts and laws authorizing the payment of dues to the State in Confederate money, or notes, shall no longer be in force, but are hereby declared henceforth inoperative.

MR. HUDSON, of Yazoo: The object of the Proviso was to accomplish that which the gentleman from Marshall, [Mr. Watson] upholds. It was to suppress the distilleries of the

State—the monopolists on that subject—and I propose to silence them at once. At this time, especially, I think they are an element of the greatest danger in our country. As to my amendment to suppress these things, I agree to go so far as any one else on that subject, and it was with a view to that end—not only of suppressing other distilleries, but those authorized to distil, that I offered the proviso.

Mr. Watson, of Marshall—Mr. President:—The gentleman from Yazoo, I dare say, is correct in his understanding of this whole subject. I was in error to some extent. Now, sir, I do desire to suppress the two State distilleries, and I do not wish to abrogate the law passed for suppressing the many distilleries which had been established in the State. If the proviso offered by the gentlemen from Yazoo, (Mr. Hudson,) had been adopted, all the laws prohibiting distilleries would have been repealed; and any one would have been at liberty to have established a distillery. That would have opened the very flood-gates of evil. It is true, that was done, without perceiving what the proviso of the gentleman from Yazoo intended to do, under these circumstances, I shall move to amend the substitute before the house.

Mr. Watson, then offered the following as an amendment to the amendment offered by Mr. Yerger, which was accepted by the latter:

And provided, That all laws authorizing the distillation of spirits, on State account, etc.

Mr, Jarnagin offered the following amendment, which was also accepted by Mr. Yerger,

Provided further, That this ordinance shall not make valid any act passed by said Legislature, which may conflict with any ordinance passed by the Convention.

Mr. Watson offered the following additional proviso:

Provided further, That all laws for the suppression of distilleries and intemperance, passed in the year 1863 and 1864, are hereby revived as valid acts of the Legislature.

Mr. Harrison, of Lowndes—Mr. President:—I have read the laws myself, and can state that they were intended as war measures, and did not profess to be for the suppression of intemperance; but were passed to prevent the distillation of spirits, from peaches, apples, and any kind of fruit or vegetables. They were war measures to prevent our soldiers from being demoralized. There are a great many provisions in the laws, it would be competent for the Legislature to repass. I profess to be a friend of temperance myself; at the same time, I do not see any reason why a man may not be allowed to distil a few peaches or apples, when the State has been thrown open for the introduction of foreign spirits. The laws are of no practical effect, and the Legislature meets in time to pass proper laws on that subject. The only effect of the law is to run from this time to the meeting of the Legislature, and I see no reason why we should press the question on this Convention, at this time.

Mr. Watson, of Marshall—Mr. President:—I am aware that unless these laws are of such a character as to be valid, and operate under the circumstances in which they have heretofore existed: in other words, if in violation of the Constitution of the United States, or the State of Mississippi, or if intended to aid the rebellion, then they would be held void; but, in my judgment we shall accomplish much, if we put them in force from this time, until the Legislature meets. In the town of Holly Springs, we have some half dozen retail establishments, for the sale of liquor, and several of them are kept by negroes. Intemperance there, has became a very great evil. Now, I desire to suppress this intemperance. We have a distillery or two, in the county there, doing much mischief. I desire these evils to be suppressed, and I never knew a law that was intended to suppress intemperance, that did not advance the public good. On the day of our election, by an order from the military authorities, the groceries and drinking establishments were closed; and, sir, the order, propriety and sobriety that characterized every man in town, on that day, was most remarkable; and I asked myself how it was possible, when that good effect resulted from the suppression of intemperance, was so manifest and incalculable, that the people having the subject under their own control, would suffer themselves to be inflicted by this great evil. I want something done to-day, to arrest it for the present, until proper legislation can be had.

Mr. Morphis, of Pontotoc, moved to lay the amendment upon the table,

Which motion was lost.

The question recuring on the adoption of the amendment, it was decided in the negative.

The question was then taken on the amendment offered by Mr. Yerger, and decided in the affirmative.

On motion of Mr. Harrison, the first section, as amended, was then adopted, and is as follows, to-wit:

Sec. 1. *Be it ordained by the people of the State of Mississippi in Convention assembled,* That all laws and parts of laws, enacted by the Legislature of the State of Mississippi, since the 9th day of January, 1861, so far as the same are not in conflict with, or repugnant to, the Constitution of the United States, and the laws made in pursuance thereof, or of the Constitution of this State as it existed on the 1st day of January, 1861, or in aid of the late rebellion, except the laws in relation to crimes and misdemeanors, and except an act entitled "An act to enable the railroad companies of this State to pay the monies borrowed by them," approved December 7th, 1863, be and the same are hereby ratified and confirmed, and declared to be valid and binding from their respective dates; and the same shall remain in full force and effect until altered or repealed according to law: *Provided*, That all acts and laws authorizing the payment of dues to the State in Confederate money or notes; and all laws authorizing the distillation of spirits on State account, shall no longer be in force, but are declared henceforth inoperative: Provided further, That this ordinance shall not make valid any act passed by said Legislature, which may conflict with any ordinance passed by this Convention.

The second section being taken up,

Mr. Harrison, of Lowndes, offered the following as a substitue for the same:

SEC. 2. *Be it further ordained*, That the official acts of all acting public officers of the State of Mississippi, in possession of any office, and exercising the functions thereof, since the 9th day of January, A. D. 1861, and done and performed under color of the laws of said State, and in pursuance thereof, and not inconsistent with the Constitution of the United States, and the laws made in pursuance thereof, or in aid of the late rebellion, be hereby legalized, ratified and confirmed, and declared to be lawful acts in regard to the persons interested therein, or affected thereby, whether such person be lawfully entitled to hold such office or not, and whether such persons be lawfully qualified or not.

Mr. Houston, of Monroe, moved to amend the substitute by inserting after the words, "the Constitution of the United States," the words: "or the Constitution of the State of Mississippi."

The amendment being accepted by Mr. Harrison,

Mr. Cooper, of Rankin, moved to lay the substitute on the table,

Which motion was lost.

The third section was then taken up, when—

Mr. Harrison, of Lowndes, offered the following substitute for the same:

SEC. 3. *Be it further ordained*, That all official acts, proceedings, judgments, decrees and orders of the several courts of the State, including the boards of county police, regular upon their face, and rendered under color, and in the ordinary course of law, together with all sales made by judicial officers, executors, administrators, guardians, and all other persons acting in a fidicuary or ministerial capacity, in regular and due form, and where the same have been executed by the payment of the purchase money, are hereby legalized, ratified, and confirmed: subject, nevertheless, to the right of appeal, writs of error and supersedeas, according to the ordinary rules and forms of law.

Mr. Barr, of Lafayette, offered the following amendment, which was accepted by Mr. Harrison;

Provided, That in all cases in which judgments have been rendered in the Circuit Courts in this State since the 9th day of January, 1861, and prior to this date, the party against whom such judgment has been rendered shall be entitled to a new trial, upon his filing an affidavit that he was unavoidably absent from the court where the judgment was rendered, at the time of its rendition, and that he had no attorney present in the court, and that he believes that the judgment is unjust.

Mr. Barr, of Lafayette—Mr. President:—I desire simply to state, that this is intended to cover cases where judgements were rendered by the Circuit Courts, and the parties were absent at the time. It has come to my knowledge, that in two instances, judgments have been rendered in the Circuit Courts, in which great injury has been done to the parties, who were not there. It is but just, that these parties, who were necessarily absent, when the judgemnts were rendered; who were not represented, and had no hearing, personally or by attorney, shall, upon making the affidavit, have a new trial.

Mr. Harrison, of Lowndes—I accept the amendment. I think the word is broad enough to cover all official acts of every description.

Mr. Houston, of Monroe—For that very reason, I shall feel myself constrained to vote against the substitutes. It leaves the question open for litigation, and great hardship might be done to parties, who had made purchases. It may be determined by the Courts, that the sales are legal; and in many cases, property was sold for ten times its real value, in coin. Payment was made in Confederate notes, while the only money known to the Constitution is gold and silver. It would be a very great hardship, to leave that an open question; perhaps to be decided by the Courts, that the parties were paid for the property purchased in good money, at Confederate prices. For that reason, I desire something should be said in reference to that, and that it shall not be left an open question, so that the value of the property, at the time of the sale, may be investigated by the Courts of the country; and the party may not be compelled to pay more than what was the real value in Constitutional money. "Dollars" in notes, means dollars in gold and silver. I shall have to vote against this proposition, unless there can be some amendment inserted to allow these questions to be investigated, and inquiry made as to the real value of the property.

Mr. Harrison, of Lowndes.—I would suggest to the delegate, that in my judgment, he is doing what he does not intend—running on the evil he desires to avoid. We leave the question where the party has purchased with Confederate money, to be litigated. If the gentleman can devise any proviso, by which the desired end can be reached, I have no objection, and should be glad to have it done; but I have not been able to frame one. My idea is to leave it to stand where the law places it. If the sale was made by an officer who was not authorized to do it, let the party plead that fact. If he agreed to pay five times the value, in Confederate money, he must plead that; but I know of no amendment by which that can be reached. I do not think the gentleman ought to vote against the whole proposition for this reason.

Mr. Houston, of Monroe.—I understand the substitute to be this: That all the action, not only of the Courts, but of administrators, executors, and all persons acting in a fidiciary capacity, shall be ratified by this ordinance. If you ratify these acts; if the administrator or executor has gone on under the order of the Court, and sold the property; we ratify his act in the sale, as well as the act of the Court, in making the order. We have ratified the whole transaction, and thereby made the parties purchasing the property, liable to pay for the property, under that purchase. The difficulty which I have, is where the party has given his note for so many dollars. How can the party get testimony before a Court, to say it did not mean gold and silver? For the purpose of avoiding this difficulty, I propose this amendment:

Provided, That in cases of sales made as aforesaid, and in all other cases in which parties have executed notes or obligations for the payment of money, parol testimony shall be admitted to show the real value of the property at the time of sale, and that shall be the measure of indebtedness of the parties.

Mr. Yergee, of Hinds.—I shall not support the proviso offered by the gentleman from Monroe, (Mr. Houston.) In the first place, I do not think we ought to legislate at all, in reference to private sales; but leave them to stand where they stood, under the laws, at the time. In regard to judicial sales, I think it is right and proper, where the contracts have not been executed, that the parties should be relieved, unless they agree to a fair value of the property, at the time of the sale. If the proviso is not adopted, I shall offer one that will probably cover the ground.

Mr. Simonton, of Itawamba, offered the following amendment, which was accepted by Mr. Houston:

Provided further, That executors, administrators and other officers acting in a fiduciary capacity, shall have power to compromise and agree with persons against whom they hold notes, bonds, judgments, or other evidences of debt, as to the real value of the property for which such evidences of debt were given, subject to the approval of the judge of probate of their respective counties.

Mr. Hudson, of Yazoo.—The substitute does not give any reason for the absence of the party. I think he ought to be required to state that he was unavoidably absent; or not able to be present, in consequence of which injustice was done. As it now stands, he may have been able to be present, and was unintentionally absent. I insist that he should be required to say that he was unavoidably absent.

Mr. Jarnagin, of Noxubee.—If I understand it from the reading, it is to ratify the acts of the executors and administrators, in a sale where the money has been paid, so far as the administrator or executor is concerned. Almost all the sales which took place after January 9th, 1861, were sold, not on time, but for cash. If the order of the Probate Court is ratified making the acts valid, it will do great injustice to the minor children. For instance, an administrator sells to the amount of $30,000 or $40,000, which was received in Confederate money, which is now in the hands of the administrators.—Shall we look alone to the relief of the administrator? In other words, does this go so far as to legalize the acts of the administrator, and authorize his setttlement with the Probate Court, by bringing in this Confederate money? If you do this, you bankrupt all these estates. If he has acted in good faith, and kept the money in hand, of course the children will not get a dollar. I wish to leave the administrator or executor without any ratifications whatever of his acts by us.

The amendment was then adopted.

Mr. Watson, of Marshall—Mr. President:—I beg to submit a proposition in lieu of the amendment of the delegate from Monroe, (Mr. Houston.) I think that gentleman goes a little too far. If a party sees fit to pay a thousand dollars in specie, for property worth five hundred, we cannot help it, or interfere with such a contract, or impair its force or obligation. But we can do this: The parties generally contemplated nothing but Confederate money. I know instances in which a party agreed to give two thousand dollars for a house, which both parties understood was worth $150 or $200, in specie, and they contemplated payment in paper money; yet the note was written for two thousand dollars, without specifying Confederate money; and by the laws there is no relief; it is a writing, and there is no fraud, surprise or mistake. The parties wrote down one thing and meant another. It is admissable by law, to say parol testimony shall be heard to establish the true intent and meaning, and say what in specie is the proper amount to be recovered to do justice, and to meet that case, I propose this amendment as a substitute for the original proviso, which I hope the gentleman will accept:

Provided, That in cases of sales made as aforesaid, and in all other cases in which a party has executed a note or agreement in wrting for the payment of money, parol testimony shall be admissable to prove whether or not such contract contemplated specie or currency, and to show what amount in specie the payee or obligee has a right equitably and justly to demand or recover.

Mr. Houston, of Monroe—I cannot accept the substitute for this reason : It can conceive of no mode by which we can get at the true intent and meaning ot parties in all casses. Very often, Probate Courts have made orders for the sale of property, for Confederate money, Again, they have made orders for the sale of property, for gold and silver; and again, on credit, without specifying in what it should be paid. Suppose in a case of that character, parties go and make a purchase at that sale; how are we, by parol testimony, to ascertain what was the true intent and meaning of the parties. There was no agreement between them. The property was offered for sale, by order of the Court. which we render valid, by our action, and the other party goes up, and purchases it at a price, greatly beyond its real value, in the legal currency of the country, and we have no means of arriving at the fact of what was the agreement between them. One party may have intended to pay in Confederate money, and there was no agreement between them. But, in the proviso I have proposed, amending it, we can arrive at substantial justice to all parties.

Mr. Jonhson, of Smith.—There have been so many amendments and provisos offered, that is a difficult matter for me to tell what is before the Convention. There are still other amendments proposed, and I move that this section and amendment be re-committed to the Committee, with instructions to report as soon as possible.

The motion to refer was lost.

Mr. Watson, of Marshall—Mr. President:—I think it ought

to be competent to prove what was the intention and meaning of the parties. A sale is advertised; parties assemble, and a horse is brought out, and they begin to bid, $500, $1000, $1,500 or $2000; when every one knows, if specie was in contemplation with the parties, they would bid, $50, $60, $70 or $80. Persons present could determine, whether or not, the sale contemplated specie or currency; and so in transactions between other parties. The time at which the transaction was made; the circumstances concerning it; the fact, that everything was contracted with reference to Confederate money; are facts, which would abundantly satisfy any jury, as to whether the contract contemplated specie or currency; and while we have a right to reduce the recovery to what is justice and equity, we have not a right to go back and determine what the purchaser agreed to give more than the object was worth. It is impairing the obligation of contract. The note has been given for $2000; and it obviously contemplated Confederate money. The true plan is: what was the $2000, worth in specie; and not what the horse was worth; which would be attempting at once to impair the obligations of a contract.

Take the other view, and ascertain what the parties really intended to get on the one hand, and to receive on the other, and reduce that to the specie standard, and we are just enforcing contracts which we have a right to do.

Mr. Jarnagin, of Noxubee.—There are a great many contracts, where the debt is not due, in which Confederate money was specified. I seems to me, the amendment does not go far enough; and I shall be compelled to vote against it, unless it goes farther than is contemplated.

The amendment was adopted.

Mr. Jarnagin, of Noxubee, offered the following amendment:

And provided further, That any executor, administrator, guardian or other fiduciary agent, who shall have been guilty of any neglect of legal duty, in his or her fiduciary capacity, shall not be legally hereby protected against the legal consequences of such neglect or failure in his or her legal duty.

Mr. Harrison, of Lowndes, moved to lay it on the table, which was carried.

The third section, as amended, was then adopted, and is as follows:

Sec. 3. *Be it further ordained,* That all official acts, proceedings, judgments, decrees and orders of the several Courts of this State, including the Boards of County Police, regular upon their face, and rendered under color, and in the ordinary course of law, together with all sales made by judicial officers, executors, administrators, guardians, and all other persons acting in a fiduciary or ministerial capacity, in regular and due form, and where the same have been executed, by payment of the purchase money, are hereby legalized, ratified and confirmed; subject, nevertheless, to the right of appeal, writs of error and supercedeas, according to the ordinary rules and forms of law: *Provided*, That in all cases, in which judgments have been rendered in the Circuit Courts, in this State, since the 9th January 1861, and prior to this date, the party against whom such judgement has been rendered shall be entitled to a new trial, upon his filing an affidavit that he was unavoidably absent from the Court when the judgement was rendered, at the time of its rendition, and that he had no attorney present in the Court, and that he believes that the judgment is unjust: *Provided, further*, That in cases of sales made as aforesaid, and in all other cases in which a party has executed a note or agreement in writing, for the payment of the money, parol testimony shall be admissable to prove whether or not, such contract contemplated specie or currency, and to show what amount in specie the payee or obligee has a right equitably and justly to demand or recover: *And provided further*, That executors, administrators and other officers acting in a fiduciary capacity, shall have power to compromise and agree with persons, against whom they hold notes, bonds, judgments or other evidences of debt, as to the real value of the property, for which such evidences of debt were given; subject to the approval of the Judge of Probate of their respective counties.

On motion of Mr. Harrison,

The 4th, 5th, 6th, 7th, and 8th sections of the ordinance as reported by the Committee, were stricken out.

Mr. Harrison, offered the following as a substitute for the 9th section:

SEC. 9. *Be it further ordained*, That all marriages entered into in this State since the 9th day of January, 1861, by persons capable of contracting, are valid and binding, and are hereby ratified and confirmed, and declared to be legal and valid from their respective dates, whether celebrated with the usual forms and ceremonies or not.

Mr. Simonton, of Itawamba, offered the following amendment, which was adopted:

SEC. 5. *Provided*, That it is not intended by this ordinance to validate or invalidate the act of any officer or person acting as an officer, in receiving any monies payable to the State from the railroad companies, but to leave the same subject to adjudication by the courts in the future.

The question was then taken on the adoption of the ordinance as amended, and decided in the affirmative.

Mr. Simonton, of Itawamba, offered the following resolution,

Which was adopted:

Resolved, That the President be authorized and directed to order the printing of a sufficient number of blank writs of election, with the ordinance in regard to elections, passed by this Convention attached, to be filled up by him, and directed to the Sheriffs of the several counties in the State.

On motion of Mr. Peyton, of Copiah.

The Convention adjourned until 4 o'clock, P. M.

FOUR O'CLOCK, P. M.

The Convention met pursuant to adjournment,

The President appointed as the Committee to prepare and report to the next Legislatue, for its consideration and action, such laws and changes in existing laws of this State, as to said Committee may seem expedient, in view of the amendments to the Constitution, made by this Convention: Messrs. A. H, Handy, of Madison; E. J. Goode, of Lawrence; and W. Hemingway, of Carroll.

Mr. Simonton, from the Committee on Enrolled Ordinances and Constitutional Amendments, submitted the following report:

MR. PRESIDENT:—

The Committee on Enrolled Ordinances and Constitutional Amendments respectfully report: That they have examined an ordinance adopted by the Convention, on the 22d day of August, 1865, entitled an ordinance in relation to the Ordinance of Secession, and the other ordinances and resolutions, adopted by a former Convention, held in the City of Jackson, on the 7th day of January 1861, and on the 25th day of March, 1861, and find the same correctly enrolled.

On motion of Mr. Simonton,

The report was received and agreed to.

Mr. Johnson, of Marshall, offered the following resolution:

Resolved, That in the opinion of this Convention, the accumulation of a redundant population of Freedmen, in particular localities; and thereby the fearful prevalence of pauperism, should be guarded against if possible; and this end, that a judicious system of *colonization* should be adopted; and the Senators and Representatives, who shall be elected from this State, be requested to promote the same.

On motion of Mr. Barr, ot Lafayette,

The resolution was indefinitely postponed.

Mr. Harrison, from the Committee on State Constitution, submitted the following report:

MR. PRESIDENT:

The Committee on the Constitution, to whom was referred "an ordinance to amend the Constitution of the State, fixing the seat of Government, at the City of Jackson, in the County of Hinds," beg leave to report: That they adhere to the opinion expressed in their first report, submitted on a former day, "that it is not necessary or proper, at the present time to enter into other or further alterations or amendments of the Constitution upon its general provisions," and accordingly they recommend that the proposed ordinance do not pass.

On motion of Mr. Harrison,

The report was received and agreed to.

Mr. Peyton, of Copiah, offered the following ordinance:

SECTION 1. *Be it ordained and declared, and it is hereby ordained and declared,* That the 18th section of the 4th article of the Constitution of the State of Mississippi, be so amended as to read as follows, to-wit: A Court of Probates shall be established in each county in this State, with jurisdiction in all matters testamentary, and of administration in minors' business, and allotment of dower, in cases of idiocy and lunacy, and of persons *non compos mentis*. The Judge of said Court shall be elected by the qualified electors of the respective counties for the term of two years.

On motion of Mr. Watson, of Marshall, the above ordinance was refered to the Committee on State Constitution, with instructions to report favorably thereupon.

Mr. Cooper, of Rankin, offered the following ordinance:

An Ordinance to be entitled an ordinance, to enable the Sheriff and Clerk of Hancock county, to execute official bonds.

Be it ordained, That the penalty of the official bond of the Sheriff of Hancock county be reduced to five thousand dollars; and the penalty of the official bond of the Circuit and Probate Clerks of said county be reduced to twenty-five hundred dollars, each, until the Legislature of the State of Mississippi, shall by law, increase or otherwise change them or either of them.

Mr. Watson, of Marshall, presented a communication from Gen. A. M. West, which was read for information.

Mr. Johnson, of Smith, called up the following ordinance, submitted by him this morning:

An ordinance to submit Article eight, of the Constitution, proposed and adopted by this Convention, to the qualified voters of the State, for their adoption or rejection.

SECTION 1. *Be it ordained by the Convention*, That article eight of the Constitution, adopted by this Convention, the 21st day of August, A. D. 1865, be submitted to the qualified voters of the State, at the general election, to be held the first Monday of October next, for their adoption or rejection.

SEC. 2. The returning officers of the several election precincts of each county shall propound to each voter, as he presents his ballot: "AMENDMENT, OR NO AMENDMENT;" and the voters who may be in favor of adopting said Article eight, as a part of the Constitution of the State, shall answer: "Amendment;" and those who may be opposed to it, shall answer: "no Amendment."

SEC. 3. The Clerks of election of each county shall keep a correct account of the number of votes cast, for and against said Article eight, and the returning officer of each county shall make due return thereof to the Secretary of State; and if it appears from the full returns that of those who voted on said proposition, a majority voted in favor of said Article eight; then the Governor of the State, shall issue his proclamation, declaring that fact, and that said article is a part of the Constitution of the State; but if it appears that a majority voted against said article, then the Secretary of State shall make report thereof to the next Legislature, and it shall be the duty of the Legislature to strike out said article from the Constitution.

SEC. 4. It shall be the duty of the President of this Convention, to call the attention of the Sheriffs to this Ordinance, in the writs of election, which this Convention has directed him to issue.

Mr. Yerger, of Hinds, moved to lay the ordinance upon the table,

Which was decided in the affirmative, by yeas and nays, called for by Messrs, Johnson, of Smith; Johnson, of Marshall; and Brown, as follows, to-wit:

YEAS—Mr. President, Messrs. Billups, Binford, Brandon, Byars, Cason, Cooper, of Rankin, Cooper, of Panola, Crum, Goode, Gully, Hall, Hamm, Harrison, Hemingway, Horne, Houston, Hurst, Hudson, Jarnagin, Johnston, of Hinds, Johnson, of Choctaw, Jones, King, Lewis, Loper, Marshall, Martin, of Adams, Martin, of Sunflower, Matthews, Montgomery, McBride, Niles, Owen, of Tunica, Peyton, Pressley, Quin, Rushing, Sanders, of Attala, Sessions, Simonton, Slover, Maury, Stricklin, Tate, Webb, Wilson, Wooley, Wylie, Yerger. —50.

NAYS.—Messrs. Barr, Bailey, Blackwell, Bond, Brown, Carter, Compton, Crawford, Cummings, Dorris, Dowd, Duncan, Franklin, Gaither, Gowan, Griffin, Heard, Hill, Johnson, of of Marshall, Kennedy, Lambdin, Lewers, Lindsey, Malone, Morphis, Owens, of Scott, Phipps, Potter, Reid, Reynolds, Rives, Sanders, of DeSoto, Sparkman, Stanley, Stone, Swett, Trotter, Wallace, Wall, Watson, White, Wier, Woodward.—44.

Mr. Harrison, of Lowndes, from the Committee on State Constitution, submitted the following report:

Mr. President:—

The Committee to whom was referred an ordinance, in relation to changing the 18th section of the 4th article of the Constitution, report: That they recommend that the same do pass.

On motion of Mr. Yerger, of Hinds,

The report was received and agreed to.

On his further motion, the ordinance was adopted.

The ordinance offered by Mr. Hudson, in relation to Special Courts of Equity, was then taken up.

On motion of Mr Hudson,

The ordinance was adopted,

Mr. Reynolds, of Tishomingo, called up the resolution instructing the Committee on State Constitution, to report an ordinance, extending the jurisdiction of Justices of Peace.

Mr. Johnson, of Smith, moved to reconsider the vote, by which the report of said Committee on this subject was agreed to on a former day.

Mr. Harrison, of Lowndes.—I am utterly opposed to taking away the right of trial by jury, where it is conferred by the Constitution of the United States, and the State of Mississippi, and giving it to the Justices of the Peace. So far as I am individually concerned, I have never had any great admiration for these judicial tribunals; though they are very necessary and proper, and very respectable. It is proposed to change the jurisdiction of Justices of the Peace, in cases of promissory notes and obligations, from $50 to $150. It will be a peculiar hardship on the poor man. They serve their process, in from five to ten days, and can give judgment in ten or fifteen days.

Mr. Duncan, of Tishomingo.—A man goes into the Courts of the country, on a note of $50, and will have to pay an Attorney from $5 to $10; so that it would cost from $15 to $20, in the Court. It is to save cost that the amendment is proposed. A little money goes a long ways now, with a large majority of the citizens of the State. A Convention may not be assembled again for twenty years; and I hope this act of justice to the people will be extended to them by this body.

Mr. Harrion, of Lowndes.—The idea that because a man has a note, there is no litigation, I do not think at all conclusive. It is merely evidence of indebtedness, and that is all, and if the object is to decrease the cost, the Legislature can make the cost less in the Circuit Court; but the mere idea that if it is brought into the Circuit Court, it will save cost, would not be sufficient, I think to justify us in taking this step.

Before a Justice of the Peace, these things will be expedited in favor of the creditor.

Mr. Brown, of Yallobusha.—I think the jurisdiction of a Justice of the Peace should be extended. If an officer is capable of giving a correct decision upon an account of $50, he can do it where $500 is involved; but limiting it to $50, the remuneration is so small, that it is impossible to get a man who is qualified, to discharge the duties of the office, and to accept it. It is a farce as it stands, and yet, we cannot well dispense with it. If the right of appeal is allowed, the party can take it to another Court, and employ counsel, and I think it is right the jurisdiction should be extended.

Mr. Johnston, of Hinds.—The right of appeal exists from the Magistrate's Court very properly, and it seems to me that this would be unjust to the debtor, in this: that it would increase the cost. If a man was sued for a debt of one or two hundred dollars, and judgment rendered, an appeal would be taken to the Circuit Court, and there is a double bill of costs. If an Attorney could be dispensed with at the Magistrates, it certainly could not be dispensed with at the other Court.

Mr. Reynolds, of Tishomingo.—I think we had better extend the jurisdiction of Magistrates. I was ten years in the Legislature, and I do not think that there was a year in which there was not a bill introduced to extend this jurisdiction. If the people desire it, let them have it. I do not think the Convention should refuse to comply with the demand; for if the Magistrate has the right to try cases without the interposition of a jury, the right of appeal exists. I am satisfied whether it will diminish cost or not; whether it will be in favor of the debtor or creditor, the people all demand and want it. It will require but little trouble for it to be done by this Convention, and I think it should be done. No harm can result, and protection to the debtor and creditor, plaintiff and defendant, would be given by securing the right of appeal.

Mr. Johnson, of Smith—Mr. President: There are two strong objections to this amendment at this time—admitting that it would be proper at ordinary times.

In the first place, it opens the question of general amendments to the Constitution—for I suppose there are very few members here, but what might wish to introduce an ordinance proposing some change therein.

Another objection is this: Some persons apprehend that suits will be prosecuted as soon as the courts are restored, on account of notes held, and that there is, consequently, great danger of a sacrifice of property. I think this very probable, for persons can prosecute suit to judgment in the course of eight or nine days, and have execution issued in ten or fifteen. I was informed by a member of this Convention, that he had placed in his hands, a short time ago, one hundred and twenty-five thousand dollars, in notes, &c., for collection. Now, if people holding these large claims, proceed, forthwith, to sue upon them before Justices of the Peace, they get judgment and execution in so short a time that there is unquestionably danger of a great sacrifice of property.

MR. MARTIN, of Adams: From my experience at the bar, my business and that of other members of the legal profession, would be increased by sustaining the proposition; but, as a member of the Committee, I have committed myself on the subject. I shall vote against it, so that we cannot be accused of voting otherwise than disinterestedly in regard to this matter. I think the jurisdiction now given to magistrates is about as extended as it ought to be, and if we open these subjects for legislation, there is no telling when we can get through. I am opposed to going into general amendments to the Constitution.

MR. MORPHIS, of Pontotoc—Mr. President: Not being a lawyer, I do not look upon this subject from the same stand point as the last gentleman. My experience has been, that men are apt to act from a little selfish interest; and lawyers being interested in litigation, it is my opinion, that it would bring about more litigation,—these gentlemen would be likely to favor it,—from which reason I believe that this project does not commend itself to them in a pecuniary point of view. I know that my constituents would be much pleased to have the proposed step taken, and therefore I shall vote for a reconsideration.

MR. JOHNSTON, of Hinds—Mr. President: The remarks of the gentleman impugning the motives of those who take a different view of the question from himself, are entirely uncalled for. Certainly we should all be actuated by a desire of doing that which is for the good of the people, but the gentleman seems to assume that the legal profession seeks only its own aggrandizement, and that he is the peculiar guardian of the rights of the people—which I deny — considering myself as much the friend of the people as he possibly can be.

So far as I am concerned, the practice in the magistrates' courts is of no immediate importance; but I believe, with the gentleman from Adams, [Mr. Martin] that an extension of their jurisdiction would increase our practice. Where magistrates are invested with extraordinary power, the parties may undertake to manage their own cases, and so certainly as they do, they must employ an attorney, and pay him a large fee to unravel the case, when it is appealed to the Circuit Court. I am not in favor of an extension of this jurisdiction, for this simple reason—that I think it would be a great injury to the people, if done. If they have been trying to do so, for the last fifteen or twenty years, the legislation taken thereon, goes to show that the *people* have opposed it.

In conclusion, I would suggest to the gentleman from Pontotoc, [Mr. Morphis] that some thirty-six members of this Convention are lawyers, who have been *trusted by the people of the State*, and that in face of that fact, the gentleman should not attribute to us such narrow and selfish views.

Mr. Cooper, of Rankin—Mr. President: I am opposed to the reconsideration of this matter, because I think that if there ever was a time when the people of the country should receive indulgence from creditors, now is the time. If the legislature should give the extended jurisdiction proposed, to these magistrates, it would enable those persons holding large amounts of notes to force collection from the people.—For that reason, if for no other, I am opposed to meddling with the law as it now stands.

The question was then taken on the motion to reconsider, and decided in the negative, by the following vote—the yeas and nays being called for by Messrs. Duncan, Slover, and Morphis:

Yeas.—Messrs. Blackwood, Bond, Brown, Byars, Cason, Cooper, of Panola, Crawford, Crum, Cummings, Duncan, Hill, Johnson, of Marshall, Kennedy, Lewers, Lindsey, Malone, Matthews, Morphis, Pressley, Reynolds, Sanders, of DeSoto, Simonton, Slover, Sparkman, Stanley, Tate, Wallace, White, Wier, and Wylie—31.

Nays.—Mr. President, Messrs. Barr, Bailey, Billups, Binford, Brandon, Carter, Compton, Cooper, of Rankin, Davis, Dorris, Dowd, Franklin, Gaither, Gowan, Goode, Griffin, Gulley, Hall, Hamm, Harrison, Heard, Hemingway, Horne, Houston, Hudson, Hurst, Jarnagin, Johnston, of Hinds, Johnson, of Choctaw, Johnson, of Smith, Jones, King, Lambdin, Lewis, Loper, Marshall, Martin, of Adams, Martin, of Sunflower, Maury, Montgomery, Mayson, McBride, Niles, Owen, of Tunica, Owens, of Scott, Peyton, Phipps, Potter, Quin, Reid, Sanders of Attala, Sessions, Stone, Stricklin, Swett, Trotter, Wall, Webb, Wilson, Woodward, Wooley, and Yerger.—64.

Mr. Watson, of Marshall, offered the following ordinance:

Be it ordained by the people of the State of Mississippi in Convention assembled, That the 25th section of article 3, of the State Constitution, so far as it prohibits an increase of the compensation of members of the Legislature from taking effect during the session at which it is made, be and the same is hereby suspended, until after the close of the next session of that body.

On motion of Mr. Watson, the rule requiring constitutional amendments to be referred to the select committee on that subject, was suspended.

Mr. Hudson moved to refer the Ordinance to said Committee,

Which motion was lost.

The question was then taken on the adoption of the Ordinance offered by Mr. Watson,

And decided in the affirmative.

Mr. Barr, of Lafayette, offered the following:

"Amend the 7th section of the 4th article of the Constitution of the State, so as to read thus:

"The High Court of Errors and Appeals will be held at least once in each year, at the seat of government; and at such other place or places in the State, as the Legislature may direct.

MR. WATSON, of Marshall—Mr. President: As the Constitution now stands, it is not competent for the Legislature to order a session of the High Court of Errors and Appeals to be held at any place but at the seat of government. This inconvenience was felt to be so great, that some years ago, the legislature passed a law requiring that Court to meet at Oxford, to hear arguments, &c., but they could render no decision there, under the Constitution, and therefore had to return here in order to do so. It worked so badly that the law was repealed.

I believe that Mississippi is now the only State in the Union whose High Court of Errors is held at but one point.

One great objection against holding the Court at more than one place, is the usual want of a library. At Oxford, the University has a very good library, and that was constantly on the increase before the war. There are also two very good buildings which the trustees could convert into a court room, and accommodations for the members of the bar and bench. The High Court would be a matter of interest in connection with the law class of the University, and the arrangement would, besides all this, accommodate a large number of the citizens of the State.

I therefore wish to have the prohibition removed, so that the Legislature can at least exercise its discretion on that subject.

On motion of Mr. Barr, the rule requiring amendments to the Constitution to be referred to the select committee on that subject, was suspended.

On his further motion, the Ordinance was adopted.

Mr. Hudson offered the following resolution,

Which was referred, under the rule, to the Committee on State Constitution:

Resolved, That the Committee on Constitution be instructed to inquire into and report to this Convention, whether it is expedient or necessary to increase the salary of any or all officers in this State, and if it is deemed expedient or necessary, to report such increase as they may deem proper.

On motion of Mr. Compton, the Convention adjourned until 9 o'clock to-morrow morning.

TENTH DAY.

THURSDAY, AUGUST, 24TH., 1865.

The Convention met pursuant to adjournment.

Prayer by the Rev. John Hunter.

Journal of yesterday read and approved.

Mr. Simonton, from the Committee on Enrolled Ordinances and Constitutional Amendments, submitted the following report:

MR. PRESIDENT :—

The Committee on Enrolled Ordinances and Constitutional Amendments respectfully report: That they have examined the following Ordinances, Constitutional Amendments and Resolutions, and find the same correctly enrolled:

Report of Committee in regard to the pay of officers and members of this Convention, adopted August 23d, 1865.

Resolution appointing a Committee of three, to recommend changes in the laws of this State, to the next Legislature, adopted 23d August, 1865.

An Ordinance in regard to the Special Courts of Equity, adopted 23d August, 1865.

An Ordinance to legalize and support the legislative enactments of the State of Mississippi, passed since the 9th day of January, 1861, and for other purposes, adopted 23d August, 1865.

An Ordinance to enable the Sheriff and Clerks of Hancock county to execute official bonds, adopted 23d August 1865.

An Ordinance to amend the seventh section of the fourth article of the Constitution, adopted 23d August, 1865.

An Ordinance to amend the eighteenth section of the fourth article of the Constitntion, adopted 23d August, 1865.

Report concerning Short-Hand Reporters, adopted August 17th, 1865.

An Ordinance suspending the twenty-fifth section of article three of the Constitution, in regard to the compensation of members of the Legislature, adopted 23d August, 1865.

On motion of Mr. Simonton,

The report of the Committee was received and agreed to.

Mr. Potter, of Hinds, presented a memorial, signed by four thousand six hundred and thirty-three ladies of the State of

Mississippi, in behalf of Jefferson Davis and Charles Clark, of this State.

The memorial having been read,

Mr. Wilson, of Yazoo, offered the following resolution:

Resolved, That the memorial just read, be respectfully referred to the President of the United States, to be considered of by him; and to that end, that the President of this Convention do transmit the same.

MR. POTTER, of Hinds.—Mr. President:—I desire to say a word in relation to this matter. The business of the preparation of this memorial was begun on Friday last, and it now contains more than forty-six hundred signatures of the mothers and daughters of this State. It comes commended to a most respectful consideration on our part, by the great worth of these memorialists. I have do doubt, but that if more time had been allowed, these signatures might have been multiplied, by thousands and tens of thousands. Aye, sir, I may say, that no lady would have refused to append her name to that petition, for mercy to those of its citizens, in their now silent and desolate condition. The memorialists are not unaware of the position assumed by members of this Convention, in regard to that matter. They know that on consultation, previously, among ourselves, it has been deemed appropriate that a private memorial, containing this same prayer, should be signed by the several members of this body. I am proud to say, sir, that the memorial thus prepared for our signatures, contains the name of every member of this Convention, with the exception of perhaps some ten, and of those a portion were absent before the memorial was prepared. So far as regards the expression of our views—so far as the present President can gather any idea of our sympathy with this movement, it is contained in the memorial which most of us have signed. I, Mr. President, have not been able to bring my mind to see the distinction which some suggest to exist between official action on a memorial prepared for our signatures, and private action as individuals. If we had adopted that as a memorial of this Convention, it would have expressed our feelings, our wishes, our sympathies, to the same extent —in precisely the same degree. I would state that this memorial had been prepared before the views of the Convention had been known upon the matter—before this course of policy, which I have mentioned, was adopted by us as individuals, and comes here addressed to the Convention, as the official body of the State; and the question now is—what is the most appropriate disposition that can be made of it? The ladies do not ask that this Convention should act upon it, under the circumstances. It is necessary, however, that some proper and respectful disposition should be made of it, and it seems to me, sir, that the course suggested by the delegate from Yazoo, (Mr. Wilson,) is the exact course to be taken in reference to it, in view of all existing circumstances. I could have wished to have gone a step further, and to have inserted in that resolution, an expression of the hearty wish of the individual members of this Convention, that the prayer of the memorial be granted.

I hope, sir, without discussion, without opposition, with this brief explanation of the condition of things, members will agree to sustain the motion, made by the gentleman from Yazoo.

Mr. Crawford, of Jones.—Mr. President:—This matter was brought up a few days ago, and I thought the action of this Convention then had settled the question forever, so far as the Convention, as a body, was concerned; but, under other circumstances, it is introduced again, to-day, as a memorial of the ladies of Mississippi. With all due regard to the source from which it comes, I beg leave to express my opinion, as to the propriety of any action being taken upon this matter by us, as a Convention of the State of Mississippi—and that is, with the highest feeling of respect for those who have presented it here, and my heartfelt sympathy for the cause—that we should take no official action in regard to it, for the reason, that I do not believe that such action would be in furtherance of the object. I shall therefore, as a member of this Convention, oppose the motion of the gentleman from Yazoo, while I am willing, as an individual, and in any private capacity, to do all things in furtherance of the release of these gentlemen, who stand high in the opinion of the people of Mississippi.

Mr. Simonton, of Itawamba.—Mr. President:—I desire to offer a resolution as a substitute for that offered by the gentleman from Yazoo, (Mr. Hudson.) It reads as follows:

Resolved, That the memorial ot the ladies of Mississippi to this Convention, in regard to Mr. Davis and Mr. Clark, be respectfully referred to his Excellency, Andrew Johnston, President of the United States, with a request that a copy may be transmitted to each of the gentlemen mentioned therein.

I know something of the feelings that these gentlemen must have. I know something of the feeling that will be awakened in their breasts, by knowing that the people of the State of Mississippi—although they did not affiliate, or perhaps sympathise with the movement of which President Davis and Clark were the leaders—yet, as citizens of Mississippi, and what was once a rebel State—that they do sympathise with them; and I desire, that not only may this memorial go before his Excellency, the President of the United States, but that those worthy gentlemen may know that we all sympathise with them in their present position.

MR. WATSON, of Marshall—Mr. President:—I prefer the original resolution to the substitute, presented by the gentleman from Itawamba, (Mr. Simonton,) and for this reason. The substitute imposes upon the President of the United States, a duty which might not be acceptable to him. We can ourselves, in some other way, have a copy of this memorial sent to these gentlemen. The request, as presented by the substitute, is rather an extraordinary one, under the circumstance. And for that reason, we should not prefer it, if for no other.

MR. SIMONTON, of Itawamba.—Mr. President:—I meant to simply suggest, that we might be permitted to forward a copy. I will therefore, change the phraseology, to make the resolution conform to my intentions.

The proposed change being made the resolution was adopted.

Mr. Johnston, of Hinds, from the Committee on ordinances and laws, submitted the following report:

Mr. PRESIDENT:—

The Committee of fifteen, appointed to consider what action should be had in reference to the Ordinance of Secession, and the legislative and judicial action of the State, since the 9th day of January, 1861, and to whom was referred a resolution, proposing to punish the crimes of grand larceny, robery, rape, arson and burglary, with the penalty of death, by hanging, beg leave, respectfully to report: That they have considered theaforesaid resolution, and are of the opinion, that it would be improper to extend the death penalty to those offences The Legislature of the State, has full power to prescribe the punishment for crimes, and the Committee consider that the subject matter of the resolution referred to them should be left to the action of the Legislature. The Committee therefore reccommend that the said resolution do not pass.

Your Committee have disposed of all the business before them; and they pray that this report be received and agreed to, and that they be discharged from further service.

MR. HOUSTON, of Monroe—Mr. President:—I am satisfied that the report is not in accordance with the best interests of the country, as it is at present situated. I do believe that there are some of those crimes, at least, which should be punished with the death penalty. I thought, on yesterday, that this Convention would take no action on this subject. I believe it more properly comes before the Legislature, and I am unwilling, by any action of this body—by receiving and agreeing to this report—to indicate to the Legislature that may hereafter convene—that the views of this Convention, were adverse to the application of the death penalty to certain of these crimes. Under the Constitution of the conutry, as it was before the war, this would be regarded as bloody legislation—to attach the death penalty to any of these offences; but we must look to what would be for the greatest good and protection to the country—leaving the Legislature to act without any seeming dictation from us, or even suggestion.

Taking this view of the matter, I beg leave to submit the following resolution :

Resolved, That the subject matter of the report of the Committee of fifteen, on the subject of the punishment of crime, be re-submitted to that Committee, with instructions to take no action in the premises, but leave the matter for the action of the Legislature when convened.

Mr. Hudson, of Yazoo—Mr. President:—I must confess that I am opposed to this report. As the law now exists, we may be plundered by thieves—our houses may be burned down at mid-night, over the heads of ourselves and our slumbering families—and what is the penalty attached by law, to the commision of such offences? Our wives, our sisters and daughters may be subjected to violence; and what is the penalty? Simply, in either of these cases—imprisonment in the State Penitentiary! But no such institution now exists, and how then, if the Courts convict these wretches now roaming over the country, are they to be punished? They must be committed to the county jails, which are wholly insufficient, and too insecure to present any barrier to the escape of these villains. Is then the punishment which must now be inflicted commensurate with that deserved? No! No!

I do not believe that at any time, has the punishment been what it, as prescribed by law, should be. What reformations have ever occured in the State Penitentiary? None—but those incarcerated come forth as monuments of their own infamy—again, to carry on their depredations, and repeat their previous offences. They are simply held in such condition, that they cannot for the time being commit crime.

The Proclamation of Gov. Sharkey,. shows that there are bands of desperadoes, thronging the community, and the object of the ordinance proposed—and it may be repealed by the Legislature, as soon as that body meets—is that this penalty may operate *now*, upon offences committed *now ;* and from this time until the law is repealed. Our wives and daughters dare not go from home, without an escort to protect them from being deprived of all that is precious to women. Our citizens cannot go to market with one or two bales of cotton, without being deprived of it—their own teams being used to carry away the staple, which is the only support of their needy families. But there is no punishment affixed to the commission of these deeds, that can have the slightest possible effect in preventing them, or diminishing their frequency!

MR. JOHNSTON, of Hinds—Mr. President:—I know the desire of this Convention to adjourn, and shall consume, but a very few moments, in presenting some views which governed the Committee in submitting the report under consideration.

The picture of depredation and crime prevailing in the State, alluded to by the gentleman from Yazoo, (Mr. Hudson,) has not been over-wrought. I am painfully aware of the fact that the extraordinary times through which we have passed, have resulted in the prevalence of crime throughout the country, and that the laws are, have been, and will be, for some time, violated with impunity. But, Mr. President, how can the resolution offered by the honorable gentleman from Yazoo, affect this matter? What good or beneficial effect could its adoption have at the present time? It is not the degree of punishment, but its certainty, which tends to diminish the crime of the country; and when you affix the death penalty to the commission of small offences, the juries of the country will not convict the offenders at all, when put on trial, if they know the death penalty is to follow. For example—that resolution reported against by the Committee, makes grand larceny punishable by death. If a citizen, therefore, should steal goods of the value of twenty dollars and upwards, it is made grand larceny, and he is convicted of the theft by that jury—he is executed for that offence. This is too bloody an act for me to sanction at any time; and the juries of the country will say: "although our minds are well nigh satisfied of the guilt of this individual, we will not bring in a verdict of guilty; because by that, he must suffer death; and we cannot consent that a human being should be executed, simply for that." The history of criminal jurisprudence will show that those who are constituted by nature and habit, to be great public offenders, are not to be deterred from the commission of crime, by any punishment that can be named. Even the faggot would not deter them from the committal of the deeds to which they are impelled by their constitution and nature.

A great number of offences were, in former days, visited with the death penalty, in England,—such as counterfeiting the coin of the realm, theft, larceny, &c.,—all of which were punished in this manner. Yet, in this enlightened age of the world, there has been, and still is, a constant tendency to diminish the offences upon which the extreme penalty of the law is visited. Besides, there are a great many of the most enlightened and philanthropicl men of the age, who believe that it is not in the justly exercised power of man to take the life which the Great Creator has vested in a fellow man; and, in short, it is a growing sentiment—that the death penalty ought not to be executed in any case. However that may be—whatever may be the opinions of men in regard to that proposition—it is certainly true that the course proposed by the gentleman from Yazoo, will not remedy the evil of which he justly complains.

Suppose this Convention, to-day, was to adopt this resolution, and affix the death penalty to all these specified offences. Would that stop the robbery going on through the country, or the arson or would it tend to disperse the organized bands of thieves and murderers who are traversing the State, brought into existence by the civil war raging in our midst? Such demonstrations are the result of great civil commotions, and it is not to be supposed that it would be otherwise. It would have *no* effect upon those organizations, or tend to diminish crime at all. The mere affixing of the death penalty would have no influence upon those bad men who are banded together in committing deeds of lawlessness, and nothing would therefore be gained by the adoption of the resolution under consideration.

The committee took this view—that it is in the power of the Legislature of the State of Mississippi, to affix the punishments due to the different grades of crime. That Legislature is soon to assemble, and this matter ought to be entrusted to them, because it comes peculiarly within the powers conferred upon them, and the duties which devolve upon them. We therefore thought that this Convention ought not to legislate in regard to the matter at all, but leave it to that body, which has no constitutional restrictions as to the manner in which they shall dispose of this question.

The gentleman has said that the offences enumerated in his resolution, are penitentiary offences now, but that there being no penitentiary, there is no mode of punishing these crimes; but when a man is convicted according to the present criminal code, although the penitentiary is not, at this moment, in a condition to receive them, they are notwithstanding, held in custody and confinement until such time as that place can be prepared for their reception—until the penitentiary is rebuilt and placed in condition for labor to be resumed there. We took it for granted, that one of the first acts of the Legislature, which is soon to assemble, would be to repair the penitentiary, rebuild the ruined walls, replace the machinery of industry there; so that individuals violating the laws might be speedily taken from the county dungeons and placed in quarters suitable to their conditions. Doubtless, it will be but a very few months before the penitentiary will again be in operation.

These were the views that actuated the committee to report adversely to this petition, and I am free to say that, if by voting for the adoption of the resolution, I could remedy the great evils of which the gentleman complains, I would support it; but, I feel certain, in my own mind, that the adoption of the resolution could have no such effect.

I know that the intentions of the gentleman are good—that he offered this in a proper spirit—but still I think he is very much mistaken in the effect which would result from his doctrine. I therefore hope that the Convention will sustain the report of the Committee, which I had the honor to submit this morning.

MR. MARTIN, of Adams—Mr. President: I shall feel myself obliged to vote against the adoption of the report of the Committee.

All of us know that the sensibilities of our people have led us to let loose upon society, criminals, who ought to have suffered the death penalty. We know there is a spirit of repugnance on the part of the people, to the infliction of the extreme penalty—at least there was before the war—but now that we have come out of that, we find that it has changed the opinions of our citizens, in many respects.

I, for one, think that this Convention should act upon this question—to give to the people of this State who are disposed to be orderly, and return to their peaceable occupations, an assurance that we intend that peace, and law and order, shall prevail. This is the first opportunity that has been presented for the people of this State to say what they mean to do on this subject of lawlessness within our borders; and let the gentlemen who are stealing and robbing throughout the country, understand that it is our intention to inflict upon them the certain extreme penalty, and that speedily. It has become more necessary that we should do this now, because of the effects of this struggle through which we have passed; for any man who has been in the army, has seen how the moral restraints that usually control are thrown off,—how men have forgotten the lessons learned when they were pursuing their peaceable occupations, and have been guilty of crimes that, in ordinary times, would have consigned them to the penitentiary. I think that if ever the time did exist, for inflicting severe punishment, it does now, and I believe that our jurors will act up to their duty, and the necessity of the times. I trust that the best men will be selected to fill the public offices of the State, who will understand that their duty requires that they should punish—and that, severely.

As has been remarked, it is perfectly useless to attempt to confine these desperadoes in the county jails of the State—for they present no difficulty to these men enlarging themselves. In nine out of ten counties in this State, the jails are not of sufficient strength to keep any one of ordinary ingenuity in them for twenty-four hours. If, then, we wait until the penitentiary is completed, they will inevitably escape their just deserts.

I think, therefore, that we shall be compelled for the present, and until we find that we are extirpating these gentry, to resort to extreme measures, and I shall therefore vote against adopting the report of the committee.

Mr. Yerger, of Hinds—Mr. President: I should feel myself obliged to vote against the adoption of the resolution offered by the gentleman from Monroe, [Mr. Houston] if I entertained views of policy different from those expressed by the committee—which I do not.

I think a mistake, and, to some extent, a mischievous and dangerous idea prevails, with regard to the power and jurisdiction of this Convention. It is not, as it is sometimes styled, a Convention of the State of Mississippi, but it is a Convention of the delegates of the people of Mississippi. It is not a Convention of the delegates of the people of Mississippi, for purposes of general alteration or change in the organic law of the State; but it is a Convention for a specified and definite purpose, and for that purpose alone have we been sent here. That purpose is indicated in the Proclamation of the President of the United States, authorizing the calling of this Convention, which is, that the Convention shall be held for the purpose of altering or amending the Constitution of the State, and with authority to exercise, within the limits of the State, all necessary and proper power to enable the loyal people of the State of Mississippi, to restore the State to her constitutional relations with the Federal Government, and to present such a republican form of government as will entitle the State to the guarantee of the United States therefor, and its people to the protection of the United States against invasion and domestic violence. This is the power of attorney, which the people of the State of Mississippi have granted to us, under the Proclamation of the President. We are sent here by them to do a specified act, and that part of their sovereign power, and no more, has been delegated to this Convention.

I therefore protest against an attempt on the part of this Convention, to undertake an alteration generally, which was not a power entrusted to it by the people, or to change and alter the organic law generally, which was not a part of the purpose for which it was assembled, or of the power delegated to it, by the people—because, in my opinion, all acts going beyond the legitimate purpose and scope specified in the President's Proclamation, would be mere acts of usurpation, and not obligatory upon the people, unless ratified by them—for they have sent us here for no such purpose. We are not a Legislature, or sent here to legislate with regard to the general laws and policy of the State.

MR. HUDSON, of Yazoo—Mr. President: I am much opposed to leaving this subject to the Legislature, and will remark, in addition to what I have already stated—that until the Legislature meets, the penalty remains the same as ever; and although the Courts will not be revived until after the general election, still, the parties committing the offences enumerated, will incur the penalty of this proposed Ordinance, and the Courts will be enabled to disperse these organized bands of desperadoes.

I do not believe that honest and intelligent jurors will hesitate to pronounce a just verdict, without regard to the penalty which will follow the announcement of it, for they will see that the salvation of the country depends upon a manly discharge of their duties.

But it is said that this is a Convention with special and limited powers—that the grant comes from the President of the United States—that this is not a Convention of the State, and therefore we should not meddle with these matters. The very last words of the Proclamation are—"to protect this State against domestic violence." One of the special grants conferred upon us, and one of the grand objects for which we are assembled, is to protect the State from domestic violence; and in adopting this resolution, and destroying these bands of robbers, we are carrying out that very object. I insist that we should take this view of the subject, and not refer this matter to the uncertainty of the future. This will be done by voting down this proposition of the gentleman from Monroe, when I shall recall this ordinance for further action.

MR. STONE, of Copiah—Mr. President: It has occurred to me, that gentlemen have not taken the right view of this matter. The argument is, there is no jail, and no opportunity of confining or punishing these individuals—but we should first get them. I ask why—while these crimes are so prevalent—the people of Mississippi do not now rise in the majesty of their strength, and attempt to arrest these desperadoes? Does the proposition of the honorable gentleman affect that matter? Why is it necessary to pass this law while the country is sitting down so quietly under these robberies and larcenies? If the people will take this in hand, they can confine these men, the same as if this law was passed, until the courts are organized, and they are brought before the tribunals of the country.

If the gentlemen will introduce an ordinance forming an

armed force for the purpose of arresting these desperadoes, I will join it, but, until then—until the people are aroused and take this matter in hand—there is no necessity to pass this Ordinance, for it would sleep until the country is aroused, and proper steps taken.

On motion of Mr. Johnson, of Smith,

The report of the Committee was laid upon the table.

The following communications from his Excellency, Wm. L. Sharkey, Provisional Governor, were read, and ordered to be spread upon the Journals:

EXECUTIVE OFFICE,
Jackson, Miss., Aug. 24, 1865.

Hon. J. S. Yerger, President of the Convention:

SIR: I most respectfully request of the Convention, that I may be furnished with a perfect copy of the Constitution, as amended, together with a copy of the Ordinances, to be forwarded under the Seal of the State to the Department of State, at Washington.

I have the honor to be,
Your obedient Servant,
W. L. SHARKEY,
Provisional Governor of Miss.

EXECUTIVE OFFICE,
Jackson, Miss., Aug. 24, 1865.

Hon. J. S. Yerger, President of the Convention:

SIR: I enclose a dispatch just received from the President, which you can have read to the Convention, if you think proper. There is, however, a deficiency in the dispatch, forty words being missing.

Your obedient Servant,
W. L. SHARKEY,
Provisional Governor of Miss.

Mr. Hudson, of Yazoo, offered the following Ordinance:

Be it Ordained, That the Legislature of this State shall have full and complete, ample and plenary power and right to ascertain, adjust, and settle any and all pecuniary liabilities and indebtedness of this State, or the citizens thereof, to the Government of the United States of America, under and by reason of the revenue laws of the latter, either past, present or future; and to provide by law, or otherwise, in such way and manner, and on such terms as the Legislature may, in its opinion, deem, or declare to be most wise, judicious and expedient for the ascertainment, adjustment, and present or ultimate settlement and payment of the same: hereby intending to confer, and actually conferring upon the Legislature of this State, full and absolute power and right, to pledge and use the faith and credit of the State, and to do and perform whatever is or may be necessary or expedient in the premises aforesaid.

Mr. Yerger, of Hinds, moved to lay the Ordinance on the table,

Which was lost.

On motion of Mr. Hudson,

The Ordinance was adopted.

The following communication from Hon. A. H. Handy was read:

JACKSON, Miss., August 24, 1865.

Hon. J. S. Yerger, President State Convention:

SIR: I deem it proper, without delay, to inform you, that my private engagements are such that I will be unable to perform the trust contemplated by the resolution of your honorable body, for the appointment of a Committee of three, "to prepare and report to the next Legislature for its consideration and action, such laws and changes in existing laws of this State, as to said committee shall seem expedient in view of the amendments to the Constitution made by said Convention."

I must, therefore, most respectfully decline the appointment tendered to me as a member of that committee by you.

With my acknowledgments for the honor done me in the tender of the appointment, and with the expression of my regret at my inability to accept it,—

I have the honor to be, with high respect,

Your obedient Servant,

A. H. HANDY.

The President appointed the Hon. Robert S. Hudson, of Yazoo county, to fill the vacancy occasioned by the non-acceptance of Mr. Handy.

Mr. Simonton, of Itawamba, moved to reconsider the vote on yesterday, by which the Committee on Enrolled Ordinances and Constitutional Amendments were instructed to have the Constitution of the State and Amendments thereto, enrolled, and filed in the office of Secretary of State.

The motion being agreed to,

Mr. Cooper, of Rankin, offered the following resolution, which was adopted:

Resolved, That the Hon. William Yerger, Hon. Amos R. Johnston, and Hon. George L. Potter, be appointed a special Committee, who shall, as soon after the adjournment of this Convention as practicable, see that the Constitution of the State of Mississippi, as amended and adopted by this Convention, is properly enrolled in duplicate, and signed and attested by the President of the Convention, to present one copy thereof, to the Provisional Governor, and request him to forward the same to the President of the United States, and file the other copy thereof, in the office of the Secretary of State; and said Committee shall also see that all the Ordinances adopted by this Convention are properly enrolled and attested in duplicate—one copy thereof, to be presented to the Provisional Governor, and the other to be deposited in the office of Secretary of State.

Mr. Sanders, of Attala, offered the following resolution:

Resolved, That this Convention adjourn to-day, at two o'clock, P. M., to be called together by the President of the Convention, if the exigencies of the country require it; and if no such necessity arise within six months from this date, then this Convention shall stand adjourned, *sine die*.

Mr. Hudson moved to amend the above resolution, by striking out two o'clock, and insert three o'clock,

Which was lost.

Mr. Johnson, of Smith, moved to amend by striking out "two o'clock," and insert "one o'clock,"

Which was lost.

On motion of Mr. Hudson, the resolution was adopted.

Mr. Malone, of DeSoto, called up a resolution of thanks to the President of the Convention, offered by him on a former day.

On motion of Mr. Malone, the resolution was unanimously adopted.

Mr. Yerger, of Hinds, offered the following resolution:

Resolved, That the President of this Convention appoint four Commissioners, to confer with the authorities of the United States at Washington, relative to the utility and necessity of rebuilding the levees on the Mississippi river, and that they endeavor to obtain, by loan, or otherwise, such funds as may be necessary for that purpose, and also make an arrangement, if possible, to procure a competent force of laborers to finish the work during the present year. But, in the event of any loan or debt being created for the purposes aforesaid, the taxes necessary to reimburse, or pay the same, shall only be levied, by the Legislature, upon such counties or districts as may be protected by the levees from inundation.

Mr. Yerger, of Hinds—Mr. President: I presume, there will be no objection on the part of any member of this Convention, to the resolution, as it contemplates a matter affecting so importantly the welfare of the whole State.

The counties on the Mississippi river, have had their levees entirely destroyed by the action of the authorities of the United States Government, for military purposes, or by the receding of the banks by the action of the river during the last five years, during which time there has been no repairs. It is certainly impossible that that section of the State can be cultivated, unless the levees are repaired, and it is equally impossible, at the present time, that citizens residing and owning property there, can repair them, unless they can obtain means from the General Government. The whole State cannot be taxed for this loan, and if there has been any idea of that kind entertained by any member of this Convention, I will simply state that, if the loan is paid, the tax to be paid at any time shall be laid alone on the levee district, which was heretofore taxed by this State for the building of the levee on the Mississippi river.

MR. MARTIN, of Adams—Mr. President: I have lately been in the levee country, referred to, and have found that the state of affairs is as has been first described. I find that the negroes on the plantations in that section of the country will not undertake to work places next year, or make any contracts to do so, unless those levees are repaired, because they are not willing to run the risk of receiving pay from planters who probably own nothing, or to work on shares, when the crop is subject to so many contingencies. Unless some action is taken, and aid furnished from some quarter, these plantations must be abandoned.

MR. POTTER, of Hinds—Mr. President: I confirm heartily the objects of this resolution. I am not, personally, interested in a single foot of land whose value will be affected by the action proposed; but I conceive that I have the slightest possible interest in the object sought to be accomplished. I think that every citizen of the State is interested, in like manner. It certainly, Sir, is for the interest of all portions that this once rich and productive territory, known as the swamp district, should be restored, in some degree, at least, to its former prosperity. Now we are all interested in seeking that result; because, if we restore these lands to their former value and productive condition, we create an immense fund for the purposes of State revenue. Therefore, we are all interested, in this view, in the progress of improvement.

Delegates should bear in mind that we have not only State taxation to regard hereafter, but taxation on the part of the Federal Government. It is our policy, and should be the earnest desire of every delegate to create, in any part of the State where it has been created, the largest possible taxable capital, and I know of no measure that will benefit the people more in regard to State taxation and Federal taxation—no measure that will so greatly relieve us from the burdens of heavy taxation, as the one proposed by the delegate from Hinds, [Mr. Yerger.]

Again, it is but a measure of justice to the parties more directly interested in those lands. That country has been desolated, not only by deluges of water, but by deluges of war. It is the purpose to do, by this measure, something for its relief, and to do it in such a way, that the balance of people of the State shall not be taxed one dollar, and yet, so that our fellow citizens in that district shall be greatly benefitted.

For other reasons which I might give, I hope the members of this Convention will adopt this resolution.

Mr. Maury, of Claiborne—Mr. President: It cannot be doubted, that the region of country contemplated by the resolution, will be vastly benefitted by its adoption, but neither can it be doubted that every other portion of the State would be equally benefitted by the expenditure of money thereon. This is not the first time that I have listened to arguments such as have been delivered here to-day, for I heard them many years ago, and that too, in Mississippi, and money has been borrowed for the purpose of furthering the prosperity of the State, increasing the facilities of the people, and the fertility of the land.

This is not the time to enter upon measures of this description. What is now the indebtedness of the State of Mississippi? Who can conjecture? Can any one mention it? Has the debt of the Planters' Bank been paid—that was borrowed by virtue of a provision passed by a Convention of the State? Has the debt incurred by the people of Mississippi, for the purpose of establishing the Union Bank, been paid? This money was to be used to develop the hidden resources of the country. What has become of it? Where has it gone? Since the passage of those laws, the prosperity of the country has suffered much more than it would if the people had been left to their individual resources, industry, and enterprise!

I object to any such measure, until we redeem our credit, and I hope the proposition will find no favor in the Convention, for we have not been sent here to borrow money.

Every portion of this State has been desolated. You, and you, sirs, and every member of this Convention, would like to have our former prosperity re-established. But, that re-establishment should not be attempted by borrowing money—at any rate, at the present time—for the people can send their representatives here to do that, if they wish really to have it done; but it is not proper for this Convention to saddle upon them this debt, without their concurrence, either express or implied.

Mr. Brown, of Yalobusha—Mr. President: I wish to give my reasons for voting against this proposition. I would like to see the levee repaired, and that fertile region of country adjacent to it, guarded against destruction. But, I do think that, in our exhausted condition—not knowing at the same time what control we can exercise over labor, with a heavy debt already upon our shoulders, and the certainty of being required to assume and liquidate another, I think it would be unwise—and for this reason, too: It is known that Government plantations are located upon the river, and perhaps the Government will repair that levee, rather than abandon them, as it otherwise must do. Now is a very appropriate occasion for the United States Government to re-establish the policy of internal improvements, on the part of the Federal Government. This is the only occasion that may arise during years, which will induce the Federal Government to take that step, and I believe that it will take that step now; but, at any rate, I would have any legislation upon this matter deferred for the present.

Mr. Weir, of Yalobusha—Mr. President: I offer the following proviso to the resolution of the gentleman from Hinds:

Provided, That the aforesaid Commissioners shall not be authorized to pledge the faith of the State for the payment of any money by them borrowed, or aid procured for the purposes expressed in this Ordinance.

The proviso being accepted by Mr. Yerger, the resolution was adopted.

Mr. Watson, of Marshall, offered the following resolution:

Resolved, That it shall be the duty of the next Legislature to appropriate, for the purpose, whatever sum may be necessary to pay to the Committee appointed by this Convention, on the subject of the revision of the statutes of the State, a compensation of ten dollars per day each, for the time during which they may be employed in their said duties.

On motion of Mr. Watson,

The resolution was adopted.

Mr. Cooper, of Rankin, offered an ordinance proposing to re-instate Mr. Thos. Palmer, to citizenship in this State.

Mr. Cooper, of Rankin—Mr. President:—The object of this ordinance is apparent. Mr. Palmer was an old citizen of this State; but in 1858 removed from the State. He has returned; designs establishing his home amongst us again, and merely desires to have his civil disabilities removed.

Mr. Yerger, of Hinds.—Mr. President:—Mr. Palmer was, for many years, a resident of this place, and sustained the highest moral character—being a man of the strictest integrity. Some six or eight years ago, he removed to Missouri—where the wai, of the last four or five years has been of such a character—the country being overrun by both parties—that he now desires to again come among us. He is an old man, between 68 and 70 years of age; and wishes, during the remainder of his years, to be a citizen of the State.

Mr. Barr, of Lafayette—I have no doubt, Mr. President, that the object of the resolution is a worthy one; but I am opposed to special legislation. I move to lay it on the table.

The motion was carried.

Mr. Johnston, of Hinds, offered the following resolution:

Resolved, That Leo. Phillips, Louis Fite, George Donnell and Charles E. Tolbert, the pages of this Convention, be each allowed the sum of two dollars per day, as extra compensation, in consideration of their faithful services.

Mr. Crawford, of Jones, moved to lay the resolution on the table,

Which motion was lost.

On motion of Mr. Johnston,

The resolution was adopted.

Mr. Compton, of Marshall, offered an ordinance, which was adopted, making certain appropriations, in the aggregate, as follows:

E. M. Yerger, publisher Daily News	$1,119 00
A. N. Kimball, " Mississippian	200 00
J. J. Shannon & Co " Clarion	200 00
T, C. McMakin, for sundries	175 00
J. K. Yerger, postmaster	24 82
A. Reed, (freedman)	50 00
A. Moore, "	50 00
	$1.818 82

Mr. Watson, of Marshall, offered the following resolution:

Resolved, That the official Reporters of the debates of this Convention, be allowed five days after to-day, for the purpose of extending, and revising their notes; and that they also be allowed a compensation each of ten dollars per day, in addition to the allowance heretofore made them, and that the time of their services be computed from the organization of the Convention.

Mr. Watson, of Marshall—Mr. President:—The Reporters of this body, were employed on the fourth day of its sessions; but were present from nearly the first day of the session, and ready to perform any duty that might be assigned to them. They have on hand, an amount of notes, the volume of which is such, that a number of days must necessarily be consumed in transcribing them properly.

I also think, sir, that in view of the character of their labors, and the per diem of others connected with this body, that too little was allowed them originally; and as a member of the Committee, I shall now vote for an additional allowance to be granted them.

Mr. Yerger, of Hinds,—I second that resolution, Mr. President, and move its adoption.

I will state to the Convention, what I suppose, however, almost every member has observed for himself, that a more laborious, dilligent and faithful work, was never performed in the same time, and in the same efficient manner, than that accomplished by our Reporters, Messrs. Burnham & Bartlett.

I will state in addition, that I do not think I ever have been connected with a legislative body in which half the amount of business was required to be reported in the same length oi time, that this Convention has thrown upon the Reporters here. Our sittings have been continuous during almost the entire long summer days, and in consequence of it, they have done a great deal more work, and double what is usually done before legislative bodies. I therefore hope that the Convention will pass the resolution.

Mr. Martin, of Adams—Mr. President:—I feel in some degree responsible, as a member of the Committee, for having secured the appointment of our Reporters, and I am glad to say that our course has been vindicated, by the promptness with which they have fulfilled their duties, and by the excellent reports they have furnished us, so far as we have gone. I had no idea at the outset, that their labor would be so arduous as it has been; but have been convinced that their compensation, as fixed by the original contract, has been wholly inadequate.

Believing that the skill they have displayed merits a reward in proportion to their labor, I heartily concur in the propriety of adopting the resolution.

The question was then taken on the adoption of the resolution, and decided in the affirmative.

Mr. Hudson, of Yazoo, offered the following as a proviso to resolution, relative to the adjournment of the Convention.

Provided, That in case of the death of the President, the Convention may be called by the Governor of the State.

On motion of Mr. Hudson, the proviso was adopted.

Mr. Simonton, of Itawamba, offered the following resolution, which, on his motion, was adopted:

Resolved, That a Special Committee of three be appointed to take into consideration, the printing of the journals and debates of this Convention, with directions to report an ordinance or resolution at an early moment.

Mr. Brown, of Yalobusha, offered the following resolution, which, on his motion was adopted:

Resolved, That J. L. Power, Secretary of the Convention, be allowed five extra days, after adjournment, to complete the duties assigned him, and that he be allowed for such services, the same rate of compensation agreed to by the Convention yesterday.

Mr. Compton, of Marshall, offered the following resolution:

Resolved, That the thanks of this Convention be tendered to Mr. J. L. Power, Secretary, and Mr. R. C. Miller, his Assistant, for the prompt, efficient and courteous manner in which they have discharged their duties.

On motion of Mr. Hudson,

The resolution was unanimously adopted.

The President announced as the Committee on printing the journal, ordinances and debates of the Convention, Messrs. Simonton, Cooper of Rankin, and Hudson.

Mr. Matthews, of Panola, offered the following resolution:

Resolved, That the thanks of this Convention are due, and are hereby extended to Gen. T. C. McMakin, Sergeant-at-Arms, for the efficient and satisfactory manner in which he has discharged his duties.

Mr. Johnson, of Smith, moved to insert the name of Wm. J. Brown, Doorkeeper—

Which being agreed to,

The question was taken on the resolution, as amended, and unanimously adopted.

Mr. Hudson, of Yazoo, offered the following resolution, which was unanimously adopted;

Resolved, That the thanks of this Convention are due, and are hereby tendered to the Chaplains of this Convention, who have so kindly, ably and acceptably discharged the duties thereof.

On motion of Mr. Watson, the Convention took a recess for twenty minutes.

The recess having expired, the Convention then resumed business.

Mr. Simonton, from Special Committee on Printing, made the following report:

Mr. President:—

The Committee to whom was referred the matter of printing the journals, debates and ordinances of this Convention, have had the same under consideration, and respectfully report the accompanying resolutions, and recommend that they do pass:

Resolved, That twenty-five hundred copies of the Constitution, as amended, ordinances, proceedings and debates of this Convention, are hereby authorized to be published in pamphlet form, in the style and manner of the pamphlet laws of the State, excepting marginal notes. Said proceedings, debates, ordinances and Constitution, when so published, shall be delivered to the Secretary of State, whose duty it shall be to distribute the same, in the same manner that the pamphlet laws and journals of the State are required to be distributed, except that one copy shall be sent to each member of this Convention. The public printer shall receive for his services the necessary cost of issuing said reports, and thirty-five per cent added thereto; and the Auditor of Public Accounts is hereby authorized and required to issue his warrant on the proper officer for the amount of the account for said printing; the same being first approved by the Secretary of State.

Resolved further, That said printer be allowed the same length of time to complete the pamphlet proceedings and debates, as allowed by law for printing the laws and journals of the State, in the year 1861, and his duties and responsibilities as printer of the Convention shall not cease until the work aforesaid is accomplished.

Resolved further, That a committee of three, to consist of Messsrs. Johnston, Yerger and Potter, of the county of Hinds, are hereby appointed to read the proof sheets, and see that the printed copy corresponds with the action of this Convention.

On motion of Mr. Simonton,

The report was agreed to; and—

On his further motion, the resolutions were adopted.

The President announced as the Committee, to confer with the United States, relative to the rebuilding of the levees on the Mississippi River, Messrs. Alcorn, of Coahoma, F. A. Owen, of Tunica, Wm. Hunt, of Washington, Wm. S. Langley, of Issaquena.

Mr. Johnson, of Marshall, from the Committee on Enrolled Ordinances and Constitutional Amendments, submitted the following report, which was received and agreed to:

Mr. President:—

The Committee on Enrolled Ordinances and Resolutions, &c., beg leave to report: That they have examined, and found correctly enrolled the following resolutions, to-wit:

1.—A Resolution, allowing official Reporters extra compensation; adopted to-day.

2.—A Resolution, allowing J. L. Power, Secretary of this Convention, five days extra time, to complete the duties assigned him, adopted to-day.

3.—A Resolution, to appoint Commissioners to confer with the authorities of the United States, in relation to levees on the Mississippi River; adopted to-day.

4.—A Resolution, that this Convention adjourn to-day, at 2 o'clock, P. M.; adopted to-day.

5.—A Resolution, to authorize the Legislature to pay Committee on revison of the statutes of the State: adopted to-day.

6.—A Resolution, appointing Hon. Wm. Yerger, A. R. Johnston and Geo. L. Potter, a Special Committee on enrollment of the Constitution and Ordinances, with duties annexed, to act after the adjournment of this Convention, adopted to-day.

The hour for adjournment having arrived, the President, Hon. J. S. Yerger, said:—

Gentlemen, Delegates of the Convention:—The hour which you have designated as the proper period for adjournment has arrived. I would be faithless, gentlemen, to the emotion of my heart, if, after the courtesy you have shown to me, I could permit a separation, without expressing to you, the gratification I feel for the kind resolution, thanking me, for what you are pleased to style, the able and impartial discharge of the duties, which in your generous confidence, you devolved upon me, by selecting me, to preside over your deliberations.

I thank you, gentlemen, that acting under the impulse of that generosity and forbearance which has marked your intercourse with each other, on this floor, you have spread the mantle of your charity over the many faults and mistakes, that my inexperience caused me to commit. That I have been impartial and fair to all, I believe to be true—at least, such I intended to be; and I am gratified that you express the conviction of your minds, that such was the result of my conduct, as presiding officer. Should it be my lot, in the future, to again be called to preside over the deliberations of a public assembly; sustained by your expressed encouragement, I will struggle to merit the high estimation, which your partiality has placed upon me.

There has been no assemblage in the State of Mississippi, more distinguished for its urbanity, for its intelligence, for its patriotism, and for its singleness of purpose, to act for the public good, and prosperity of the State, than this Convention. No heated partizan feeling has been exhibited; no unbecoming recurrence to past differences of opinion, has been permitted to enter into the discussions and deliberations of this body; but we have met together in a spirit of harmony and forbearance—as I believe and trust in God, this great people will again come together, and all together, as brothers of a common land, and children of our common inheritance; with a determined purpose to cherish to the last day of our generation, and hand down to our children, to protect and cherish, forever and forever, this great form of public liberty—the Constitution and Union of these States.

It has been my fortune, gentlemen, to occupy a seat on this floor, in strange times, and during startling history in Mississippi. I was here when Mississippi was covered with desolatory consequences of commercial disaster, and of commercial ruin; such as this country had not before, and has not since witnessed. I beheld the people of Mississippi, with manly courage, and upright fortitude, bear themselves firmly and erect against the losses and destruction of that great commercial disaster. In the whole history of it; in the midst of the wreck of their fortunes and their hopes—in the view of those horrors, and the destitution to which many of their families were brought, I have seen that spirit of acquiescence to the supremacy of the law; that spirit, which every man competent to perform the duties of a freeman, always feels, to bow in submission to the judgments and mandates of the law, exhibited by a whole people, that no instance of resistance in the whole history of that desolated, pecuniary scourge, ever marked or stained the page of Mississippi history.

I feel and believe from the tone and bearing of the delegates in this Convention, coming as they do directly representing and reflecting the feelings and views of their constituency, that the people of Mississippi; with the same manly courage; with the same fortitude that enabled them, with becoming patience to meet the pecuniary disaster of that day, will meet and repair the ruins and desolation that has swept over their land in the track of war, blighting their homes, and devastating their fields.

It is by the encouragement of this feeling—and upon your return home, by stimulating your people to emulate the feeling of kindness, courtesy and harmony, that have been exhibited here, towards their brethren of the other States of this Union; and by the persuasive argument that it is a manly duty to bow to the necessity of the situation, and to meet every fall of our fortunes with courage and confidence; that the restoration of this State to its rightful position in the Union; to its former prosperity; and our homes to the comforts and enjoyments, we have lost in the past, may be hoped for in the future.

I was here, gentlemen, to witness the State of Mississippi, in the hour of delusion of her people, lay her hand to the destruction of the fabric of the Constitution and the Union of these States. I was a member of that Convention; I raised my voice against what I believe to be sacriligious wrong. It was in vain; I bowed my head in sorrow; in anguish, I beheld the purpose declared by my State, to destroy the inheritance that I had received from my father; and that I had endeavored to cherish, and transmit to the hands of my children. I could but bow my head and weep over the appaling ruin that was spread before me, threatening to overwhelm the State.

I have again met the representatives of the sovereignty of the people of Mississippi, in this Convention; come together, that they may, if possible, restore Mississippi to her proper and constitutional relations with the United States, and aid in the restoration of that beautiful form of government that they had imperilled—that great government, whose protecting influence was as a shield over this whole land, and under whose kindly rule we had been protected in peace, prosperity, and happiness. God grant, gentlemen, that your deliberations and example may aid in the consummation of this result.

In my conscience, I do believe that such will be their influence, and that you may return to your constituency with the comforting conviction and consciousness, that you have done much, to restore not only peace, but peace with harmony and prosperity, as extended as this republic.

Again, gentlemen, allow me to thank you for your kindness and forbearance, and assure you, that when we separate, if we should not meet again, my spirit will always go forth in anxious interest to meet every one of you in your desire, and exertion everywhere, in every place, that you may be upholding the Union of these States, and maintaining our rights, under the Constitution, founded on, and secured by that Union.

I thank you. I may forget your faces—I may not meet you again—but go where I may, there will always be with me the recollection of this day.

We now stand adjourned, to meet again under the order of the President of the Convention, if, in his opinion, a necessity should arise for re-convening you.

I trust, that it may never become necessary that I should issue that order.

This Convention stands adjourned.

(Signed) J. S. YERGER, President.

J. L. POWER, Secretary.

[NOTE.]—Wherever in the foregoing proceedings the names of Messrs. Owens and Owen occur, it should be Owen of Tunica, and Owens of Scott.]

TABULAR VIEW OF THE CONVENTION,

COMPILED BY J. L. POWER.

NAME.	AGE.	POST OFFICE.	COUNTY.	NATIVITY.	OCCUPATION.	POLITICS IN 1860.
J. S. Yerger, President*	55	Greenville	Washington	Pennsylvania.	Lawyer	Whig
Barr, Hugh A	48	Oxford	Lafayette	Sou. Carolina	Lawyer	"
Bailey, James S	46	Charleston	Tallahatchie	Tennessee	Lawyer and Plant.	Whig and Union
Binford, John A	64	Duck Hill	Carroll	Virginia	Planter.	Inveterate Whig
Billups, Thomas C	61	Columbus	Lowndes	Georgia	Planter.	Whig
Blackwell, Nicholas	27	New Albany	Pontotoc	Tennessee	Physician	"
Bond, Chas. T	48	New Albany	Pontotoc	Georgia	Merchant & farm'r	"
Brandon, William L	60	Fort Adams	Wilkinson	Mississippi	Planter.	Old Line Whig
Brown, Robert M	35	Coffeeville	Yalobusha	Virginia	Farmer.	Co-oper'n O. Line W
Byars, Eli J	55	Pittsboro'	Calhoun	N. Carolina	Farmer	Jackson Democrat
Cason, Braxton	55	Shannon	Itawamba	S. Carolina.	Farmer.	Whig
Carter, J. Prentiss	25	Augusta	Perry	Mississippi	Student	Co-operationist
Compton, William M	32	Holly Springs	Marshall	Kentucky	Physician & Plant.	Old Line Whig
Cooper, Richard	47	Brandon	Rankin	Georgia	Lawyer	Whig and Union
Cooper, Lunsford P	35	Panola	Panola	Tennessee	Lawyer	Whig
Crawford, Thomas G	39	Ellisville	Jones	Alabama	Farmer	"
Crum, William A	27	Hickory Flat.	Tippah	Tennessee	Farmer	State Rights Demo't

Cummings, M. C.*	54	Fulton	Itawamba	Alabama	Farmer	Democrat
Davis, L. L	35	Miss. City	Harrison	New York	Clerk of Court	Whig
Dorris, James H	59	Huntsville	Choctaw	Tennessee	Farmer	"
Dowd, Cornelicus	63	Smithville	Monroe	N. Carolina	Farmer	"
Duncan, William L	65	Corinth	Tishomingo	S. Carolina	Farmer	"
Farley, George P	54	Fayette	Jefferson	Mississippi	Planter	Old Line Whig
Franklin, Lucius C	36	Philadelphia	Neshoba	Georgia	Farmer	Secession Democrat
Gaither, Wiley W.	56	Woodlawn	Itawamba	N. Carolina	Lawyer	Whig
Goode, Edmund J.	42	Monticello	Lawrence	Virginia	Lawyer	Conservative
Gowan, Thomas R	30	Westville	Simpson	Mississippi	Lawyer	Union
Griffin, William	65	Pascagoula	Jackson	Georgia	Farmer	Whig and Union
Gulley, Henry J	35	De Kalb	Kemper	Alabama	Farmer	Whig–ops'd to Sec'n
Hall, Alex. H	50	Mt. Carmel	Covington	N. Carolina	Physician	Union Whig
Hamm, James S	44	De Kalb	Kemper	Virginia	Lawyer	Democrat
Harrison, James T	53	Columbus	Lowndes	S. Carolina	Lawyer	Old Line Whig
Hemingway, William	55	Carrollton	Carroll	Georgia	Farmer	Douglas Democrat
Heard, James A	44	Shubuta	Clarke	Georgia	Minister	Conservative
Hill, Robert A	54	Jacinto	Tishomingo	N. Carolina	Lawyer	Whig
Horne, James A	46	Winchester	Wayne	Mississippi	Banker	"
Houston, Lock E	48	Aberdeen	Monroe	Tennessee	Lawyer	Union Democrat
Hudson, Robert S.	45	Yazoo City	Yazoo	S. Carolina	Lawyer	Whig
Hurst, David W	46	Liberty	Amite	Mississippi	Lawyer	Oppos'd to uni'l suff.
Jarnagin, Hampton L.	53	Macon	Noxubee	Tennessee	Lawyer	Whig
Johnston, Amos R	55	Jackson	Hinds	Tennessee	Lawyer	Steadfast Whig
Johnson, Lawrence	38	Holly Springs	Marshall	S. Carolina	Lawyer	Co-operat'n Dem'cr't
Johnson, Robert C	53	Lodi	Choctaw	Virginia	Farmer	Old Line Whig
Johnson, Harvey F	34	Raleigh	Smith	N. Carolina	Minister	Conservative

TABULAR VIEW—[Continued.]

NAME.	AGE.	POST OFFICE.	COUNTY.	NATIVITY.	OCCUPATION.	POLITICS IN 1860.
Jones, Layfayette	55	Rosedale	Bolivar	Virginia	Planter	Democrat
Kennedy, James H	52	Lebanon	Tippah	S. Carolina	Farmer	Old Line Whig
King, Peyton	70	Enterprise	Lauderdale	Virginia	Farmer	Whig
Lambdin, Samuel H	53	Natchez	Adams	Pennsylvania	Planter	Whig–opp. to Sec'n
Lewis, John B	56	Steen's Creek	Rankin	Virginia	Farmer	Clay Whig
Lewers, Charles A	39	Pittsboro'	Calhoun	S. Carolina	Lawyer and plant.	" "
Lindsey, Caleb	58	Paulding	Jasper	S. Carolina	Physician	Whig
Lipford,		Salem	Tippah		Minister	Not reported
Loper, Joseph M	64	Chunkey	Newton	S. Carolina	Planter	Union Whig
Marshall, Thomas A*	52	Vicksburg	Warren	Kentucky	Lawyer	Whig
Martin, William T.	42	Natchez	Adams	Kentucky	Lawyer	Old Line Whig
Martin, William McD.	55	Greenwood	Sunflower	Georgia	Planter	" "
Maury, James H.	69	Port Gibson	Claiborne	Kentucky	Lawyer	Whig and Union
Malone, Franklin J	46	Horn Lake	De Soto	Alabama	Physician	Democrat
Matthews, Samuel	60	Pleasant Mt	Panola	Tennessee	Planter	"
Mayson, Hamilton*	33	Columbia	Marion	Tennessee	Lawyer	Conservative
McBride, William	55	Canton	Madison	Kentucky	Lawyer and plant.	Whig
Montgomery, Robert H	47	Durant	Holmes	Tennessee	Physician	Old Line Whig
Morphis, Joseph L	33	Pontotoc	Pontotoc	Tennessee	Farmer	" "
Niles, Jason	48	Kosciusko	Attala	Vermont	Lawyer	" "
Owens, Francis A	61	Austin	Tunica	Virginia	Minister	" "

Owen, John G	55	Hillsboro	Scott	Georgia	Farmer	“ “
Peyton, Epram G	62	Gallatin	Copiah	Kentucky	Lawyer.	Whig
Phipps, Richard W.	31	Oxford	Lafayette	Mississippi	Lawyer	Democrat
Potter, George L	52	Jackson	Hinds.	Connecticut	Lawyer	Whig and Union
Pressley, David.	45	Starkville	Oktibbeha	S. Carolina	Minister	Conservative
Quinn, James B	55	Summit	Pike	S. Carolina	Farmer and plant.	Whig
Reed, Absalom	37	Fearn Spri'gs.	Winston	Mississippi	Merchant	Secession Democrat
Reynolds, Arthur E*	45	Jacinto.	Tishomingo	Tennessee	Lawyer	Whig
Rives, Banjamin C	49	Jacinto.	Tishomingo	Tennessee	Lawyer	Old Line Whig
Rushing, Charles E	46	Marion	Lauderdale	N. Carolina	Merchant	Democrat
Sanders, Elijah H*	53	Kosciusko	Attala	Kentucky	Planter.	Old Line W. & Union
Sanders, Reuben T	58	Hernando	De Soto	N. Carolina	Farmer.	Whig
Sessions, Joseph F	28	Lexington	Holmes	Mississippi	Physician.	Old Line Whig
Simonton, John M	35	Shannon	Itawamba	Tennessee	Planter.	“ “
Slover, Abraham	65	Jonesboro	Tippah	E. Tennessee	Merchant	“ “
Sparkman, Dempsey.	64	Good Hope	Leake	N. Carolina	Minister	Opposed to the War
Stricklin, Walter L	25	Friar's Point.	Coahoma	Mississippi	Lawyer.	
Stanley, Daniel C	49	Gainesville	Hancock	N. Carolina	Merchant	Union Whig
Stone, William A	52	Hazlehurst	Copiah	Maine	Lawyer	Democrat
Swett, Charles	37	Vicksburg	Warren	Dis. Columbi	Planter	Whig
Tate, Thomas S	49	Senatobia	DeSoto	Tennessee	Merchant & farm'r	“
Trotter, James F	62	Holly Springs	Marshall	Virginia	Lawyer	Jeffersonian Democ't
Wallace, James M	51	Buena Vista.	Chickasaw	Virginia	Farmer	Old Line Whig
Wade, Lawrence T	46	Skipwith L'd.	Issaquena	Tennessee	Planter	Democrat
Wall, William	50	Holly Springs	Marshall	N. Carolina	Farmer.	Whig—opp. to Sec'n
Watson, John W. C	57	Holly Springs	Marshall	Virginia	Lawyer	Whig
Webb, K. R	50	McCall's Cr'k.	Frankin	Mississippi	Farmer	Old Line Whig

TABULAR VIEW—[Continued.]

NAME.	AGE.	POST OFFICE.	COUNTY.	NATIVITY.	OCCUPATION.	POLITICS IN 1860.
White, Allen	42	Houston.	Chickasaw	Tennessee	Lawyer.	" "
Wilson, James H	32	Yazoo City	Yazoo	Tennessee	Physician.	Co-operation Whig
Wier, James	62	Graysport	Yallobusha	Ireland	Planter.	Old Line Whig
Wooley, Robert B.	37	Huntsville	Choctaw	Kentucky	Physician.	" "
Woodward, George Y	35	Louisville	Winston.	S. Carolina	Physician.	Whig—opp. to Sec'n
Wylie, James M.	50	Chesterville	Pontotoc	S. Carolina	Farmer	Union Democrat
Yerger, William	49	Jackson	Hinds	Tennessee	Lawyer	Whig
Green county not represented.						
J. L. Power, Secretary	31	Jackson	Hinds	Ireland	Printer	Whig
Robt. C. Miller, Reading Clerk	43	Enterprise	Clarke	Tennessee	Printer	Democrat
F. S. Garner, Engrossing C'lk.	24	Clinton	Hinds	Maryland	Student	"
T. C. McMakin, Sergt-at-Arms	67	Jackson	"	S. Carolina.	Hotel keeper	"
Wm. J. Brown, Doorkeeper	50	"	"	Georgia	Printer	Whig
George Donnell, Page	14	"	"	Mississippi	Student	Potter Whig
Louis Fite, "	15	"	"	"	"	Whig
Leo. Phillips, "	13	"	"	"	"	Breckinridge Demo't
Chas. E. Tolbert, "	17	"	"	"	"	Secession Democrat

RECATITULATION:—The Convention consists of one hundred delegates—ninety-eight of whom were duly qualified. Green county not represented—no election having taken place in that county. Of the ninety-seven members, 51 are old line Whigs; 9 Whig and Union; 1 inveterate Whig; 2 Co-operation Whigs; 3 "Whig, and opposed to Secession; 1 steadfast Whig; 2 Clay Whigs; 1 "Whig, and death against the war." Total Whigs, 70. There are eighteen Democrats, of various shades, as follows: Unqualified, 9; Douglas, 2; Jackson, 1; State Rights, 1; Secession, 1; Union, 2; Co-operation, 1; Jeffersonian, 1. We find 5 Conservatives; 1 Co-operationist; 1 opposed to Universal Suffrage; 1 Union, and 1 opposed to the war. The Convention of 1861 was composed of 84 Democrats, and 25 Whigs.

PROFESSION.—There are in the Convention 35 lawyers; 38 planters and lawyers; 9 physicians; 6 merchants; 6 ministers; 1 student; 1 banker and clerk of court.

NATIVITY.—21 are natives of Tennessee; 14 of South Carolina; 12 of Virginia; 11 of Mississippi; 10 of North Carolina; 9 of Georgia; Kentucky, 8; Alabama, 3; Pennsylvania, 2; New York, 1; Vermont, 1; Connecticut, 1; Maine, 1; District of Columbia, 1; Ireland, 1.

RELIGIOUS PREFERENCE.—Medodists, 25; Baptist, 15; Presbyterian, 14; Episcopalian 4; Christian Church, 3; Christian Religion, 1; Catholic, 2; Bible, 1; 5 no choice; 28 friendly to all denominations.

MARRIED OR SINGLE.—82 married; 8 widowers; 9 single.

AGE.—The oldest delegates are Jas. H. Maury, of Claborne, who 69; and Peyton King, of Lauderdale who is 70. The youngest are J. Prentiss Carter, of Perry, and Walter L. Stricklin, of Coahoma—each being 25. The average age of 98 delegates is 45.

Seven members of this Convention were members of the Convention of 1861, viz: M. C. Cummings, D. W. Hurst, T. A. Marshall, Mamilton Mayson, Arthur E. Reynolds, E. H. Sanders, and J. S. Yerger. They are marked thus *. Six of these gentlemen voted against the ordinance of secession, and one for it.

INDEX.

APPENDIX.

Mississippi Constitutional Convention.

HON. J. S. YERGER, of Washington....President.
J. L. POWER, of Hinds..................Secretary.
T. C. MCMAKIN........................Sergeant-at-Arms.
WM. J. BROWN........................Doorkeeper.

Legislature, 1865.

HON. J. M. SIMONTON, of Itawamba.,President of Senate.
D. P. PORTER, of Hinds..............Secretary.
D. M. WILKINSON, of Hinds...........Doorkeeper.
HON. S. J. GHOLSON, of Monroe.....Speaker of House.
ROBT. C. MILLER, of Clarke...........Clerk."
HENRY MOODE........................Doorkeeper.
T. C. MCMAKIN.......................Sergeant-at-Arms.

State Officers.

BENJ. G. HUMPHREYS, of Sunflower...Governor.
C. A. BROUGHER, of Tippah............Secretary of State.
T. T. SWANN, of Hinds................Audi'r of Pub. Ac'ts.
JOHN H. ECHOLS, of Hinds.............State Treasurer.
C. E. HOOKER, of Hinds...............Attorney General.
JAMES M. KENNARD, of Claiborne.......Adjutant General.
JAMES F. MAURY, of Claiborne..........Private Secretary.
MARION SMITH, of Hinds...............Keeper of Capitol.

United States Senators.

WM. L. SHARKEY, of Hinds........Senator, (short term.)
JAS. L. ALCORN, of Coahoma....... " (long term.)

Representatives.

First District........................A. E. REYNOLDS.
Second District......................R. A. PINSON.
Third District........................J. T. HARRISON.
Fourth District......................A. M. WEST.
Fifth District........................E. G. PEYTON.

HIGH COURT OF ERRORS AND APPEALS.

First District......................H. T. ELLET.
Second District......................A. H. HANDY.
Third District......................W. L. HARRIS.

DISTRICT JUDGES AND ATTORNEYS.

First District......................JUDGE J. M. SMYLIE.
J. B. PATTON..............Attorney.
Second District......................JUDGE J. E. MCNAIR.
G. S. MCMILLAN..............Attorney.
Third District......................JUDGE J. S. YERGER.
F. VALLIANT..............Attorney.
Fourth District......................JUDGE JOHN WATTS.
A. Y. HARPER..............Attorney.
Fifth District......................JUDGE J. A. P. CAMPBELL.
S. S. CALHOUN..............Attorney.
Sixth District......................JUDGE H. W. FOOTE.
T. H. WOODS..............Attorney.
Seventh District......................JUDGE J. F. TROTTER.
G E. HARRIS..............Attorney.
Eighth District......................JUDGE W. M. HANCOCK.
C A. SMITH..............Attorney.
Ninth District......................JUDGE W. H. KILPATRICK.
J. A. BLAIR..............Attorney.
Tenth District......................JUDGE WM. COTHRAN.
W. R. BARKSDALE..............Attorney.

www.ingramcontent.com/pod-product-compliance
Lightning Source LLC
LaVergne TN
LVHW010213110826
845151LV00004B/1069